The Bible and its Rewritings

THE BIBLE AND ITS REWRITINGS

PIERO BOITANI

Translated by
ANITA WESTON

OXFORD
UNIVERSITY PRESS

OXFORD
UNIVERSITY PRESS

Great Clarendon Street, Oxford OX2 6DP
Oxford University Press is a department of the University of Oxford.
It furthers the University's objective of excellence in research, scholarship,
and education by publishing worldwide in

Oxford New York

Athens Auckland Bangkok Bogotá Buenos Aires Calcutta
Cape Town Chennai Dar es Salaam Delhi Florence Hong Kong Istanbul
Karachi Kuala Lumpur Madrid Melbourne Mexico City Mumbai
Nairobi Paris São Paulo Singapore Taipei Tokyo Toronto Warsaw

and associated companies in Berlin Ibadan

Oxford is a registered trade mark of Oxford University Press
in the UK and certain other countries

Published in the United States
by Oxford University Press Inc., New York

British Library Cataloguing in Publication Data

Data available

Library of Congress Cataloging in Publication Data

Data available
ISBN 0–19–818487–5

1 3 5 7 9 10 8 6 4 2

Typeset by J&L Composition Ltd, Filey, North Yorkshire
Printed in Great Britain
on acid-free paper by
Biddles Ltd, Guildford and King's Lynn

For Jonathan Steinberg
and Harold Fisch.
This English edition also
for Frank Kermode
and Robert Alter

Preface

'RI-SCRITTURE', the original Italian title of this volume—literally, 'Re-Scriptures', a word I use every now and then in the following pages—means rewritings of the Scriptures, and involves two textual focuses: the Bible and the work recreating it. This is no small matter, of course, as the present writer is uncomfortably aware. To rush into the Book not as a Bible scholar but as a critic, after thousands of years of exegesis, commentary, and, most recently, literary analysis, also means not fearing to tread where Erich Auerbach, Northrop Frye, Harold Bloom, Meir Sternberg, Robert Alter, Frank Kermode, Harold Fisch, and Gabriel Josipovici have gone before, to give simply an indispensable list of eight names which is by no means exhaustive. It is equally a challenge to the intellect and general sensitivity, since the Bible, Hebrew and Christian alike, is provocative as no other text can be. What it claims to do, whether we believe it or not, is to speak of the one true God, and 'to justify the ways of God to man' as one of its rewriters *par excellence* has it. The Book, it claims, speaks as a result of direct divine inspiration, but does so through the words of humankind.

I was aware, then, how heavy the gauntlet I had thrown down for myself was, and it came as an unlooked-for bonus to find myself actually enjoying it. Unwilling to risk more than my skin (given that eternal damnation may also be in question), I prudently accompanied the Scriptures with their rewritings, attempting a critical cross-fertilization, and made sure I kept to a strictly literary plane, although I have inevitably touched on philosophical and theological implications, in that neither God nor human beings speak idly, and re-Scripting is necessarily preordained by Scripture itself.

I deliberately avoided an organic construction (à la Frye, for example), believing in neither the Bible's absolute, monolithic quality (for these are *books* making up a Book), nor the total cohesion of Re-Scriptures. It is the rewritings themselves I propose to discuss, without offering a theory or even analysis of rewriting as such, if only because it would be next to impossible. Rewriting takes place within the Bible itself: Genesis rewrites Genesis, John rewrites Genesis, and the whole of the New Testament rewrites the Old, with the intention of 'fulfilling' it. Hundreds of Apocrypha exist of both, and interminable rewritings in all languages and mediums in Western culture alone, from painting and sculpture to music, theatre, and cinema: catacombs and Sistine Chapels, church portals, Christmas cribs, Bach *Passions*, Handel and Haydn Oratorios, medieval mystery cycles, Pasolini's *Gospel According to St Matthew*, and any number of Hollywood and television 'Bibles'. In literature, where after the *Iliad* rewriting is all, the rewritings, in all their direct and indirect forms, cannot even be reviewed. A random selection from the first names to come to mind include Dante's *Comedy*, Racine's *Athalie*, Alfieri's *Saul*, Klopstock's *Messias*, Du Bartas's *La Sepmaine*, Tournier's *Gaspard, Melchior & Balthazar*, Kazantzakis's *Christ Recrucified*, José Saramago's *Gospel According to Jesus*, Norman Mailer's *Gospel According to the Son*, Joseph Heller's *God Knows*, Mario Brelich's *Il navigatore solitario*, Timothy Findley's *Not Wanted on the Voyage*, Dostoevsky's *The Idiot*, and Tasso's and Franco Ferrucci's *Mondo Creato*.

I have taken a limited number of direct or oblique re-Scriptures, separated across time and space, to which the first and last chapters provide a frame. Every Author or author sees his task as that of rewriting God and humanity. The line stretches, continual but not continuous, from the Yahwistic document of Genesis (known as J) to Mann's *Joseph and his Brothers* (henceforth M), across thousands of years of rewriting, commentaries, *midrash*, and exegesis, M simply 'fulfilling' or 'filling in' J (the title of my first chapter is a jocose paraphrase of one of Harold Bloom's most famous essays). Far from 'ruining the sacred truths', however, M re-enacts all their mystery, humanizing it, discussing it, and creating a metaphysics, a theology, and a mystique of narrative right in the middle of the twentieth century. At the centre of this new narrative—as at the centre of the Book it is rewriting—lies the problem of recognizing God, Abraham's 'open text' which is then never closed. God cannot be known, cannot be the product of cognition but only, if at all, of re-cognition, and all Scripture is therefore a re-scripting, a re-Writing.

The second chapter, the story of Susanna, takes the first oblique track through centuries which I have made sure lead only to Rome. What interests me is how and why an episode from the Bible (apocryphal in the Hebrew and Protestant Bibles), part-detective story, part-exercise in voyeurism, has been translated into liturgy and the visual arts and interpreted by exegetes, and how, in its turn, exegesis responds to the events of history by creating, in stone and painting, further re-Scriptures which retranslate into art. Rewriting means building history and cities, and fixing time in a double legend, a fresco, a church.

I have always believed that the serious reader and the subtle rereader deserved to be entertained, and hope the third chapter, where my medieval priest has a cock rewrite Genesis with wonderful comic verve and devastatingly deconstructive results for interpretation, will fit the bill. Here, too, the rewriting is oblique, if not deliberately per-verse, as is the rereading through time with all the inter-pretative contorsions no agile critic should avoid. Let me also say here that if at the beginning and the end of the book I have planted two mysteries at the core of which there may shine a light—the light of expectation—here, in the middle of the book, 'doubt springs up like a shoot', as Dante would say, 'at the foot of truth'. And if the story in the second chapter seems to rise implacably *ad excelsa*, that of the fourth goes down, with Moses, towards a question which is a prelude to the expectation in the last, but sounds much more impatient than mere waiting.

The New World has often been considered, and has often considered itself, as the place where Scripture could finally be fulfilled, and the European colonizers rewrote it as the Promised Land. But what happens when chain-gangs of black slaves, or wretched Jews from Central and Eastern Europe, are introduced into this new Canaan? Who is to rewrite one or the other Exodus? How? In the fourth chapter I take the version of a white man from the American South who joins and deconstructs the first two books of the Bible with sleight of treacherous hand, again throwing back at us the problem of how we can—must—read history and the Scriptures. In this English version I also contrast Faulkner's with a more recent, French rewriting of Exodus, that of Michel Tournier, to highlight the crucial differences between them and prepare the way for the book's conclusion. Finally, the last part of the fifth chapter examines an Eastern European, Jewish rewriting of Job which superimposes Genesis, Exodus, Psalms, the Prophets, and even, in part, the shadow of the Christian Gospels.

In the fifth chapter I return to subjects and scenes in the first, above all to the divine mystery which lies in recognition (among humans too), and in the recognition of God and of the man-God. I examine very disparate works, all— two excepted—linked only obliquely by situation, connotation, or intertextual allusion. The central problem is articulated by a pagan, classical author, imbued with the philosophy of his time. It is then revisited in one of the most extraordinary of the New Testament texts, after which it passes into the Western imagination, Christian and otherwise. Even if I had wanted to, then, I could not have avoided a final Jewish rewriting.

I offer no conclusions other than the partial hypotheses posited within the single chapters, and would very much like my readers to deduce their own, from what I have written and, above all, from the re-Scriptures I present.

For this reason I have drawn directly on the texts themselves, quoting from them, summarizing them, and rewriting their plots (re-writing is of course the first, and perhaps the last stage of criticism). I want the book, in psychologist-speak, to be 'part of the problem, not part of the solution'. A representative example: Scripture is presented to us as divinely inspired story and history, while the rewritings examined are all 'fictions'—one of them, Shakespeare's *Pericles*, a self-aware theatrical fiction at two removes from its putative referent. All of them, however, examine or take upon themselves 'the mystery of things' *as if* they were God's spies—as Lear explains to Cordelia imagining their future life in prison, and prefiguring all Shakespeare's romances. Where exactly is the dividing line between biblical 'history' and human 'fiction'? Is there some irreducible nucleus of revelation in the former, and some changing entity which pursues that nucleus without ever reaching it in the latter? Perhaps we should be looking for the answer in re-cognition rather than cognition; perhaps—as we shall see—we should simply wait.

In one of the most resonant essays of *Poetry with a Purpose*, 'What Is Beautiful?', Harold Fisch examines the definition of the 'beautiful' as given in Isaiah 52: 7: 'How beautiful upon the mountains are the feet of him that brings good tidings, that announces peace; that brings good tidings of good, that announces victory; that says to Zion, Thy God reigns!' What is important, Fisch comments, is not static, balanced beauty, but 'the message that the herald is yet to deliver and which, in fact, he will deliver only when his feet have stopped running. In the meantime, that undelivered message sheds beauty on his moving feet—the beauty of an annunciation'. 'If we can think of this scene in terms of the art of painting, then the figure of the messenger will have to be striving for something outside the painting, some yet-to-be-disclosed image of glad tidings'. Such is the aesthetic-beyond-aesthetics of the Hebrew Bible, and of every rewriting, whether comic or serious. Even the New

Testament, where the 'good tidings' have been announced, awaits the final return of the Messiah, the coming of the Kingdom. In the new testament which every re-Scripture proclaims or foreshadows, the beauty of the 'foot' is still there, and the foot is still running, bringing its tidings. Hence my choice of cover, a pre-sacral, non-static scene, a threshold, from the stories of Joseph: Lorenzo Ghiberti's panel from the 'Door of Paradise' of the Baptistry in Florence, which seems to me the perfect visual representation of the dynamics of the present study.

It is now fifteen years since I began to think about these themes. In such a long period of time, everything happens by chance or by some unforeseeable preordination of things. I could not know that, by meeting Jonathan Steinberg over a quarter of a century ago, I would not only find a friend for life, but also the person who in a hundred different ways, at times without knowing it, would open up to me the boundless, fascinating horizons of Hebrew culture, and a faithful, enthusiastic reader to boot. To him in the first place this book is therefore dedicated. Nor could I know, fifteen years ago, that I would make the acquaintance of Harold Fisch, a figure I had always much admired from a distance (and behind whom there looms in my memory the image of Morton Bloomfield). Somewhat unexpectedly, he has become to me a father and a maestro: our friendship has become ever deeper, and his qualities as a man and as a critic, his knowledge of the Bible, our discussions, have been essential for my writing of this book. It is therefore dedicated to him, too.

Likewise, my reading of the works of Frank Kermode and Robert Alter, and my knowledge of them as people, have been fundamental. The former read the whole book and even discussed it in public, but I owe him more than just gratitude for that, for there is a way in which one becomes someone's pupil without ever having been one, and this is precisely my case. Intellectual and human conversation with

Frank have helped me become what I am. Robert Alter listened, a long time ago, to the germ of the third chapter and later patiently went through the first, prompting the uncertain author, with a letter that arrived on New Year's eve, to release it finally for publication. Their names are therefore added to the dedication of this English edition. My gratitude to Douglas Gray for his enthusiasm in reading this work should be, and is here, recorded in print.

I also owe a lot, in a completely different way, to Northrop Frye, Harold Bloom, and George Steiner: without having read and, as well as met, reread them, I would not have been able to focus my thought on these matters. Likewise, studying Gabriel Josipovici's *The Book of God* and finally conversing with the author have been great pleasures. Michael Paul Gallagher, SJ, has examined the last chapter with the friendly wisdom of the theologian and the literary critic, making important suggestions.

Among readers of preceding versions of some of these chapters I cannot forget Richard Ambrosini, Barbara Calvo, and, for the entire volume, my wife, Joan FitzGerald. I am grateful to the publishers and the editors of the volumes where earlier versions of Chapters 2, 3, and 4 appeared— Ellen Spolsky, Richard Newhauser and John Alford, Agostino Lombardo—for allowing me to use here some of that material. The friends of Il Mulino, in particular Carla Carloni and Ugo Berti, deserve special 'riconoscimento' and special 'riconoscenza', as does one of the reviewers of the Italian edition, Gianfranco Ravasi, who made me see a few things which I did not know were in the book and a few which I had failed to see were not there. I would like to thank Anita Weston for having spent several months in the Purgatory of translators, possibly deserving quick translation to the highest; and Jason Freeman, Kim Scott Walwyn, Sophie Goldsworthy ought, for their kindness and friendly dealing with the English publication, to receive truly Roman gratitude.

I could not have completed the book without two visits

to Israel and Palestine. The places I saw and visited again, the friends who welcomed me with great warmth (I would like to mention here Joyce and Harold Fisch, Ellen and Dov Spolsky, Ahuva and Jon Whitman, Judith and Larry Besserman, Monique Jutrin, Jerome Mandel, and Michael Finkenthal), the conversations and discussions I had with Jews, Christians, Muslims, and Pagans make me write down this Preface in Rome (and rewrite it on the Sabine hills) after having thought about, and first sketched it, in Jerusalem.

P.B.

23 December 1996–23 January 1997–15 August 1998

Contents

CHAPTER ONE

From J to M

Recognizing and Rewriting God

Behold now, I have taken upon me to speak unto the Lord,
which am but dust and ashes

A S Abraham is sitting in the plains at Mamre, at the
entrance to his tent, in the heat of the day, God appears.
This is not the first time it has happened to him: God has
always appeared directly on the scene, from the very beginning of his vicissitudes, when he was commanded to leave
his home in Ur of the Chaldees for an unknown land, and
his words later come to him 'in a vision' to confirm his
promise, covenant, and blessing. Nor will it be the last time:
the most terrible moment is still to come, when, in a few
years' time, the Voice will call 'Abraham!' to order the
sacrifice of his beloved son Isaac. This, however, is the first
time the Lord has appeared to Abraham in the flesh, in
human semblance, and in the flesh, to boot, of *three* people.
'And Yahweh appeared unto him in the plains of Mamre:
and he sat in the tent door in the heat of the day; And he lift
up his eyes and looked, and, lo, *three men* stood by him'; or
as Robert Alter translates the scene, 'And the Lord appeared
to him in the Terebinths of Mamre when he was sitting by
the tent flap in the heat of the day. And he raised his eyes
and saw, and look, three men were standing before him'.
The verses are from the beginning of chapter 18 of the Book
of Genesis, the whole of which is included in the seminal
document Bible scholars call J—the Yahwist—because it
attributes to God his 'proper' name, represented by the tetra-
grammaton YHWH. The meeting between God and man
is totally normalized, if not actually understated, with none

of the divine special effects—pillars of clouds or burning bushes—which accompany, for example, that between God and Moses. Yahweh indulges in none of the disguises the Homeric gods assumed when appearing to their protected; nor do we get the sensation, which Erich Auerbach described so well in the first chapter of *Mimesis*, that God is arriving unannounced from unknown heights or depths. Abraham is having his siesta in what the Bible defines 'the heat of the day', the intense, midday heat which produces mirages and blurs outlines. When the three appear, however, the old man does not rub his eyes or make any move of surprise, irritation, or of simple courtesy. He merely moves towards them, throws himself on the ground, and greets *him*: 'My Lord, if I have now found favour in *thy* sight, pass not away, I pray *thee*, from *thy* servant', adding, as a good host, 'bathe *your* feet, and rest *yourselves* under a tree, and I will fetch a morsel of bread, and refresh *yourselves*; after that *you* may go on: for have *you* not come by your servant?', to which the three reply, 'Do as you have spoken.'

There follows one of the most extraordinary scenes of recognition in literature. Subtle, sophisticated, enigmatic, and breathtaking in speed and intensity, it constitutes a wholly new type of agnition with respect to those which are so frequent in Greek literature, and which Aristotle catalogues and analyses in some of the most important sections of the *Poetics*. With the exception of two characteristics which are so general as to form part of any detailed description—which Aristotle summarizes in his definition of 'anagnorisis' as the 'passage from ignorance to knowledge' and an element of the 'complex' plot—Genesis 18 has nothing in common with Greek artistic practice nor, consequently, with the philosophy which analyses it (the order Aristotle gives to the different types of anagnorisis corresponds to the movement he describes in knowledge, from that of the senses to memory, intellect, and 'intuition'). Here there are no 'signs' like the famous scar by which Odysseus is recognized by his nurse Euriclea, no 'memory' like that by which, according to Aristotle, Odysseus recognizes and is recognized when he weeps at Demodocus' song of the events at Troy; no 'reasoning', the *syllogismos* which tells Electra that Orestes has arrived when Aeschylus, in *The Libation Bearers*, has her find a lock of hair and footprints similar to her own at their father's grave; no perfect coming together of details due to chance, destiny, and the 'detective' enquiry which makes the agnition explode as if regulated by a timer in Sophocles' *Oedipus Rex*. The recognition scene in Genesis 18 is 'constructed by the poet', thereby fulfilling one of Aristotle's conditions for his second type of anagnorisis, but not the other, that it should be 'without art'. Lastly, it will hinge on 'false deduction'—a subspecies Aristotle attributes to the public—but in a totally unpredictable manner.

What Genesis 18 unfolds is a silent, mysterious, dual process of recognition: that whereby Abraham sees three men and understands that one of them is the Lord; and that whereby the readers, who are told from the start that 'Yahweh' appears to Abraham, will recognize the truth of this through Abraham himself and J's narration. The two agnitions are based on elements extraneous, strictly speaking, to the agnition proper: Sarah's laughter, the words and thoughts of Yahweh in person, the conversation between Yahweh and Abraham, and the readers' powers of interpretation and linguistics.

The point is this: when the three men appear, Abraham addresses them as 'my lord'. The Hebrew text uses the expression *'dny*, which, according to the vowels added (the original, of course, was written only in consonants) can mean *'adōnī* ('my lord'), *'adōnay* ('my lords'), or *'adōnāy* ('my Lord'), the form used exclusively for God. In principle, then, the choice is the reader's, who should consider first grammar and context, and secondly exegetical tradition. The latter, both in its Jewish and Christian versions, favours a divine being who manifests himself as messengers or angels. Rabbinic interpretation, however, presents significant variations, in some cases indicating the Holy Presence (*Schechinah*) and simultaneously 'angels' (front-ranking angels to boot: Michael, Raphael, and Gabriel who appear disguised as a Saracen, a Nabatean, and an Arab respectively, or as a baker, sailor, and Bedouin), in one case 'the greatest of them, namely Michael'. Christian exegesis basically concurs. Nicholas of Lyra, working from the Hebrew tradition, summarizes his position as follows: 'Catholic elucidators state that the apparition was one alone, because the Lord appeared neither as himself nor in any image representing him, but in the form of angels which he made to appear, of which one then spoke in the person of God himself.'

At all events, we shall, for the moment, take it that Abraham was aware that it was *the* Lord (in Mario Brelich's fine rewriting in *Il sacro amplesso*, the patriarch is scared witless at 'being able to harbour no doubts as to their identity'). In the rest of his greetings to them, Abraham uses three singulars: 'My Lord, if I have now found favour in *thy* sight, pass not away, I pray *thee*, from *thy* servant.' Immediately afterwards he uses the plural: 'bathe *your* feet, and rest *yourselves*', and all three together, *they*, reply: 'Do as you have spoken.' Shortly afterwards, he tells Sarah to make three bread loaves, orders his servant to dress a calf, and fetches curds and milk which he then 'sets before *them*'. He stands under the tree while they eat, afterwards asking him where his wife Sarah is, receiving the reply 'There, in the tent.'

In the next verse the pattern changes again when one of the three suddenly addresses Abraham with familiarity, using the first person singular: 'I will surely return to you at this very season and, look, a son shall Sarah your wife have.' At this point we—and Abraham with us—can be in no doubt that these are far from normal human visitors, and that one of them has a particular prominence.

Abraham and Sarah, the narrator reminds us, are 'old, advanced in years', adding that Sarah 'no longer had her woman's flow': i.e. she was post-menopausal. Sarah, who must have been all agog during this conversation, now chuckles to herself, 'After being shriveled, shall I have pleasure, and my husband is old?' Abraham and his readers now divide. The readers receive from J a direct confirmation that one of the three is God in person: 'Yahweh said to Abraham.' Abraham himself has to be content with an oblique sign, an indirect self-revelation: 'Why is it that Sarah laughed, saying, "Shall I really give birth, old as I am?" Is anything beyond Yahweh? In due time I will return to you, at this very season, and Sarah shall have a son.' Only a superior being could divine her secret words, and if that being asks 'Is anything beyond Yahweh?', the hearer should presume that this is indeed Yahweh himself, or a messenger sent by him: an angel, or angels, as the *midrashim* have it. Abraham, however, infers nothing, no *syllogismos*, and J fails to show us the old man's reaction at this juncture. In actual fact Abraham remains strangely unmoved throughout, giving no sign of surprise, fear, or enthusiasm. His duties as host seem to be his only preoccupation, and the words of his guests are accepted with great simplicity (the text as it stands invites us to speculate but fails to clarify whether Abraham remembers the events of the previous chapter— part of the Priestly document—where he himself laughed at God's promise to give him a son by Sarah, and said 'in his heart': 'To a hundred-year-old will a child be born, will ninety-year-old Sarah give birth?'). He seems in no hurry to establish who his interlocutor is, to recognize him or them, and the first part of Genesis 18 ends with the exchange between Sarah and Yahweh, when Sarah nervously denies laughing, and Yahweh quickly rejoins, 'Yes, you did laugh.' The section ends, in other words, with the shadow of Isaac, the son to be born to them, the Hebrew for 'he laughed', *way-yishak*, punning on the name of the future patriarch.

Until this point, then, Abraham has seen three men, and addressed first one, then all three; one of them then speaks to him. The readers have been listening in, knowing all this while that one of the three was Yahweh, and waiting with some anxiety for Abraham to reach the same conclusion.

The second part of the episode opens with the three men getting up and going to contemplate Sodom, Abraham going with them to see them on their way. J then makes a sudden qualitative leap. For five verses J concentrates on Yahweh alone, revealing his thoughts and quoting his direct words. Sodom and Gomorrah's fate is being prepared:

And Yahweh had thought, 'Shall I conceal from Abraham what I am about to do? For Abraham will surely be a great and mighty nation, and all the nations of the earth will be blessed through him. For I have chosen him, and he will command his children, and his household after him, to keep the way of Yahweh, to do righteousness and justice, that Yahweh may bring upon Abraham all that he spoke of him.' And Yahweh said, 'The outcry of Sodom and Gomorrah, how great! Their offense is very grave. Let me go down now and see whether they have done altogether as the outcry that has come to me, and if not, I shall know'.

What happens in this passage is anomalous and unexpected, the knowledge revealed in it emerging as both abysmal and singularly inverted. In the first place, the narrator of J claims to know God's actual thoughts, and expounds them briskly and factually. In the second place, J speaks not of Abraham's recognizing the Lord, but of God's recognizing Abraham: 'for I know him', 'for I have chosen him' is based on the Hebrew root *yd'*, which means 'to know' in the sense of *savoir*. Yahweh, in sum, remembers 'recognizing' Abraham as his instrument. Philo, the Alexandrine Jew who produced one of the most splendid of Old Testament commentaries, glosses the episode as God's recognizing Abraham's wisdom.

God's agnition is a total understanding of the human being, but equally the memory of a past choice which translates into God's present self-awareness: how can Yahweh keep hidden from Abraham what he is about to do if he has 'recognized' him, and found in him his 'way' and the aim of all his promises; when, in other words, he has realized that Abraham is his indispensable interlocutor, his earthly *alter ego*, a part of himself? What dizzying inversion is this, God recognizing that he is recognizing a man! I shall come back to this later. We should note in passing that Yahweh's thoughts and words mysteriously set off the anagnorisis mechanism in Abraham. No sooner has he finished speaking than the other two 'men' move towards Sodom, while Yahweh and Abraham stand before each other. Abraham turns to the Lord with the utmost respect, but most direct familiarity:

And Abraham stepped forward and said, 'Will you really wipe out the innocent with the guilty? Perhaps there may be fifty innocent within the city. Will you wipe out the place and not spare it for the sake of the fifty innocent within it? Far be it from you to do such a thing, to put to death the innocent with the wicked: and that the righteous should be as the guilty, making innocent and guilty the same. Far be it from you! Will not the Judge of all the earth do justice?'. And Yahweh said, 'Should I find in Sodom fifty innocent within the city, I will forgive the whole place for their sake'. And Abraham spoke up and said, 'Here, pray, I have presumed to speak to my Lord when I am but dust and ashes. Perhaps the fifty innocent will lack five. Would you destroy the whole city for the five?'. And he said, 'I will not destroy if I find there forty-five'.

Abraham, we know, drives a hard bargain, finally bringing God down to ten. Yahweh then disappears, J states, and Abraham returns home, while the other two men (now at the beginning of chapter 19 identified as 'angels') reach Sodom. How does Abraham know what God intends to do, particularly since God himself is in doubt about revealing it to him? Perhaps when Yahweh states, 'the outcry of Sodom and Gomorrah, how great! [. . .] Let me go down and see', Abraham spots the divine avenger-fixation and realizes that the bringer of the Flood is now about to raze the two cities to the ground. Or perhaps Abraham, like J, is a party to God's thoughts. Or again, the narrator may simply be skipping a logical link which is not strictly relevant to the story, the purpose of which is to show that man can intercede with God and be listened to, and that God is infinitely merciful in his absolute justice. No hypothesis can be ruled out, and there exists a series of *midrashim* which take Psalm 25 (14) to gloss the passage, and proclaim that 'the *secret* of the Lord is with them that fear him'.

The reader, however, remains swallowed up in this whirl-pool of awareness, announced without even the most muffled of fanfares. The agnition is implicit—almost in-visible—with Abraham's 'Far be it from you' and 'Judge of all the earth', and reaches its peak when he addresses his interlocutor as 'the Lord' (here clearly *'Adonai*), in contrast with his own being of 'dust and ashes'. In other words, when Abraham's recognition of God is finally explicit, it is presented accidentally, as part of a considerably more impor-tant narration of how he speaks to God and bargains with him. This silent anagnorisis, however, has deafening rever-berations. It forges, in an instant, Abraham's whole self-knowledge: in the *captatio benevolentiae* he deploys in his negotiations with God, he understands his own frailty as a man. He also understands, however, as Yahweh had, that this fragile mortal is the Lord's *alter ego*, which thus gives him the courage to negotiate with God. Lastly, this is also Yahweh's self-recognition: by appealing to his justice, Abraham creates it and creates the awareness of it. Having proclaimed his omnipotence ('Is anything beyond Yahweh?'), Yahweh now *discovers* justice, and accepts Abraham's logic: fifty, forty-five, forty, thirty-five, thirty, twenty-five, twenty, ten—*one measure* of innocence would suffice to save Sodom and Gomorrah: it would be unjust to destroy the innocent and the guilty alike.

This Yahweh is a very different one from that who repented of his creation and decided to wash from the earth man and beast, bird and reptile; or from the one who confounds language and scatters men abroad after Babel (both episodes, Genesis 6–8 and 11: 1–9 are attributed to J, the first with Priestly interpolations), even if Noah, as the only 'just' man, who had 'found grace with the Lord', was spared along with his family and 'two of every sort' of animal. Divine justice is a reality, then, at the time of the Flood (while it seems to play no central role in the Babel episode), but it takes Abraham's logic to fulfil it completely. Recognizing Abraham, for Yahweh, means recognizing himself in his image, and progressing along the 'way' he himself had pointed out to Abraham and his descendants; while for Abraham, recognizing God means recognizing himself and offering his own image up to God: it means confessing the vast distance between them, and still entering into a dialogue with him, sounding his unfathomable depths and, by exercising his own maieutics, acting, as it were, as God's midwife.

Readers, in the meantime, need only to set this episode against those of the Flood and Babel to see that the Bible is *rewriting* the Bible, that J composes by swift superimposition of images, stories, and sudden intuitions, through trains of thought offered and withheld, and using all the devices of language and narrative. J plays with suspense and readerly uncertainty, while presenting himself as so omniscient a narrator as to know God's own thoughts. J informs the readers from the beginning that it was Yahweh who appeared to Abraham, but then leaves them to work out how the three become *one*, and then three again, and then Yahweh with two angels, all the time remaining at some level 'the Lord' (and even if these variations derive from successive editors, they are there, in the text we read, and thus valid even for the post-structuralist world). J plays with our readerly capacities, offering Sarah's laughter and God's recognition of it as keys, but then confuses us with grammar games of singular, plural, name, and noun, drawing us into the trap behind the slow, silent process of agnition between Abraham and God.

What is the reader to do? Accept the version of the Hebrew—and most of the Christian—exegetical tradition, that the three are angels, manifestations of the Divine, but not God in person? Or, as the medieval Christian tradition predictably has it, that the three-in-one is a prefiguration of the Trinity? Should we see it as a throwback to an anthropomorphic God, a Yahweh made man for the first time, like the Jesus of the New Testament? In his *Questions on Genesis*, Philo of Alexandria proposes a solution which is both intellectually elegant and astute. God, he argues, appeared to the eyes of Abraham's soul in his essence, but with his first powers, creative and regal, and thus a triad in one person. The apparition was in any case double, Abraham seeing three strangers, perfect in body and in holiness. Struck by both apparitions, he 'was unable to decide which was the true one', so addressed both—the one out of piety, the other out of love for his fellow men, i.e. he addresses the strangers, as the text proves, speaking of 'one' and of 'God', but also of 'three' and of 'men'. After all, Philo concludes, even Homer, in his cunning wisdom, maintains that the divinity manifests itself in astoundingly beautiful human form, and has Ulysses say that the gods often appear as 'strangers from far-off lands'. Philo repeatedly brings us back to the text; and the text, with equal insistence, repeats five times over that at least one of the three is Yahweh, God's *proper* name, in one, *a posteriori*, case clarifying that one was Yahweh (the one who departs at the end of chapter 18) and two angels (the ones who reach Sodom towards evening at the beginning of chapter 19). Now uncertain in our certainty, the act of recognition becomes for us an exercise in narrative interpretation, an interrogative which increases as we read on. In a formula, our anagnorisis becomes a form of *anagnosis*—the Greek word which means 'reading' and is so cognate with the word for recognition.

No formula, though, could summarize the encounter between man and God. Think for a moment. Whether believers or not—Jew, Christian, Muslim, agnostic, or atheist—we still have to recognize that Genesis 18 intends—claims—to set the Divinity before us, centre-stage. This, of course, it can only do by using human instruments (whether inspired by God or not): and it is these instruments which pitch us into the interpretative abyss we have contemplated. Nor can we simply shrug it off: the claims of the text (whether read as history, myth, or fable) will not allow it. The reader's task is to understand, whatever the cost.

The reader's position faced with Genesis 18 is that of Dante at the end of his journey through Paradise, when, within the blazing divine light, he sees three circles of three colours and one magnitude, the Trinity; then, within the second circle, sees the appearance of our image, of a human face: Christ incarnate. Dante here feels like the geometer who 'fixes all his thought' to measure the circle but, thinking, does not find again the principle he needs. The readers of Genesis 18, as human readers, will equally want to know *how* the image fits the circle, and 'come vi s'indova', *how* it finds its place there. Like Dante, they will however recognize that their 'wings are not up to it', and, saving some unlooked-for grace, will at this point go their separate ways, leaving Dante to his 'fulgore', the flash—undoubtedly divine in origin—which illuminates his desire and his understanding. We, as mere readers, receive no such sudden road-to-Damascus flash from Genesis 18: just a series of quiet gleams often received indirectly, reflected in Abraham's eyes.

And we, as readers, must then become like Abraham. Abraham recognizes his God, and makes him recognize himself, because ready to receive God within that clod of earth he recognizes as himself. Like every human, Abraham is very little, but very far from being nothing: nothing more, but not a grain of dust less. Like Yahweh, Abraham *is*: the One incommensurable and omnipotent, Judge of all the earth; the other, infinitely less, but resilient, a clod of that earth. Even dust and ashes, the lowest measure of being, are able to conceive of, quantify, and maximize divine justice, *because* able to receive the guest even without initially recognizing him.

Abraham recognizes God because he is ready to accept him. One of the Bible's central themes, from Genesis to

Exodus, and, in the Christian Bible, beyond, as far as the first words of John's Gospel, is precisely that of God who wants to be recognized by Israel, and who fails, unless through exceptional means, or individuals, like Abraham, Jacob, Joseph, Moses, Job, the Prophets, and, later, the Apostles. In Exodus 10: 1–2, God tells Moses to:

Go in to Pharaoh: for I have hardened his heart, and the heart of his servants, that I might show these my signs before him: and that thou mayest tell in the ears of thy son, and of thy son's son, what things I have done in Egypt, and my signs which I have done among them; that you may *know* that I am the Lord.

Throughout the Old Testament (more than seventy times in Ezekiel alone) there runs the 'formula of recognition', whereby God proclaims: 'they may know that I am the Lord' (the human response to this is the expression of faith and adoration as exemplified in Sirach 36: 5: 'Let all nations know thee, as we also have known thee, that there is no God beside thee, O Lord'). The Bible dwells almost obsessively on two aspects of this theme: in the first place, that the recognition process is begun by God himself—he who, by definition, *is he that is*, but needs human awareness to exist in history; in the second, that in order to know God, man must be ready within himself, and must know himself as a human being (and human becoming), and be able to look within and be open towards the 'other', whether it be from earth or heaven. Translating this concept into Greek allegory, Philo considers Abraham as the self-awareness which proceeds towards knowledge of God. In Hebrew, *hakēr* ('to recognize' in the strict sense of the word) plays an essential role, as we shall shortly see, but one which is still less important than *jadāʿ*, 'to know' in the sense of both *connaître* and *savoir*. When *jadāʿ* is applied to humanity's knowledge of God, however, it always implies recognition, confession, acknowledgement, and gratitude—or, to give it the precision and patterning open to German commentators, *Erkenntnis*, *Anerkenntnis*, *Bekenntnis*, and *Erkenntlichkeit*. Job is the most extraordinary exponent of this when, having heard the voice of God thundering from the whirlwind, exclaims, 'confessing Him': 'I recognize that thou canst do everything, . . . I knew of thee by the hearing of the ear: but now my eye sees thee. Wherefore I abhor myself, and repent in dust and ashes'.

Genesis' message, then, would seem to be that we must become like Abraham if we are to recognize God. Is this, though, a feasible position? From the oblique re-Scripting given us by the first of our Ms, Milton, the answer has to be in the negative. In Book V of *Paradise Lost*, Milton tells how the archangel Raphael is sent to Adam and Eve to put them on their guard against the serpent's temptation. There are overt references to the Mamre scene in Genesis, with Adam seated 'in the door' of his 'cool bower', as the 'mounted sun | Shot down direct his fervent rays to warm | Earth's inmost womb' while Eve, fulfilling her allocated gender role, is in the kitchen preparing 'savory fruits'.

At God's command, Raphael had hurled himself in flight towards Earth, through a sky clear of the smallest cloud 'as when by night the glass | Of Galileo, less assured, observes | Imagined lands and regions in the moon', or like the pilot perceiving the Cyclades:

> Down hither prone in flight
> He speeds, and through the vast ethereal sky
> Sails between worlds and worlds, with steady wing
> Now on the polar winds, then with quick fan
> Winnows the buxom air; till within soar
> Of towering eagles, to all the fowls he seems
> A phoenix, gazed by all, as that sole bird,
> When to enshrine his relics in the sun's
> Bright temple, to Egyptian Thebes he flies.

If the archangel's sight is like Galileo's, his actual flight more closely resembles that of Hermes in the *Odyssey*, Mercury in the *Aeneid*, Michael in Tasso's *Gerusalemme*

Liberata, or the phoenix in Ovid's *Metamorphoses*. Once at the 'eastern cliff' of the garden, however, Raphael reassumes his natural, six-winged Seraph shape and stands, 'like Maia's son', shaking his plumes and perfuming the air. The angels on guard duty recognize him immediately; Adam, seated in his bower, like Abraham by his tent, immediately 'discerns' that a 'glorious shape' is approaching, which 'seems another morn | Risen on mid-noon', and asks Eve to bring food worthy of their 'heavenly stranger'. Eve, after an unexpected excursus into her housekeeping principles, goes off to pick their lunch from 'bough and brake', and crush 'inoffensive must' from the grape by way of drink, while her husband 'walks forth' in dignified simplicity to meet their 'godlike guest', 'without more train | Accompanied than with his own complete | Perfections'. He then addresses Raphael reverently, 'though not awed', bowing low, 'As to a superior nature', and invites the 'native of heaven' to 'rest, sit, and taste'.

The encounter is in various ways similar to that between Abraham and God. Unlike Abraham, Milton's Adam immediately realizes that his guest is from heaven; even more than Abraham, however, he behaves extremely naturally with him, aware both of the difference between them, and of his own dignity. There is an equality of being between them, one might say, as confirmed by their conversation and by the fact that the archangel actually eats the food Eve has prepared (Milton underlines the point that he considers the angels *corporeal* spirits, because created). For Adam too, as for J's Abraham, there is no problem of recognition, and Raphael is able to appear before him in all his six-winged, seraphic splendour. More to the point, there is no problem for the reader either: from the start, we are told that the central character is Raphael (as Bible readers are told it is Yahweh), and are faced, not with three figures, but one, and one whom we are able to recognize from classical and Renaissance similes: Homer, Virgil, Tasso, Ovid. Raphael is not 'disturbing' because prefigured by Mercury and the phoenix.

The episode, however, has an exact parallel in Book XI of *Paradise Lost*, when Adam and Eve have committed original sin and Michael is sent to announce the dismissal from Eden. This time Adam perceives 'mute signs' which bode no good. He asks himself 'why in the east | Darkness ere day's mid-course, and morning light | More orient in yon western cloud that draws | O'er the blue firmament a radiant white, | And slow descends, with something heavenly fraught?', and his misgivings are quickly confirmed ('he erred not') by the narrator: at that moment 'the heavenly bands' alight, 'from a sky of jasper', on a nearby hill, 'a glorious apparition' 'had not doubt | And carnal fear that day dimmed Adam's eye'.

The eye of the flesh, of the flesh that has sinned and is frightened, can no longer recognize the divine messenger at first glance. The reader, too, seems to have fallen with Adam, as Milton abandons classical comparisons for biblical: the angels that appear to Jacob at Mahanaim, where 'God's host' are assembled (Genesis 32: 1–2), the horses and chariots of fire that fill the mountain, around besieged Elisha, in Dothan (2 Kings 6: 13–17). Michael now emerges from the angelic 'maniple' and walks, slowly and 'not unperceived', towards Adam. Adam now finally understands that it is one of the Potentates or Thrones approaching, and feels its majesty, 'not terrible, | That I should fear, nor sociably mild, | As Raphael', but 'solemn and sublime'. The archangel manifests himself not in his 'shape celestial' but 'as man | Clad to meet man', a warrior in purple, died by Iris herself, with 'starry helm' and sword hanging 'as in a glistering zodiac'.

His sight dimmed by sin and the shadow of death, man learns to recognize what is sent from God: painstakingly, as something no longer familiar, but still sublime, and able to span, by human semblance and the images of war, the abyss which has now opened between them. The readers of this re-Scripting are allowed no comfortable escape into myth and poetry: if they want to recognize the divine, they have to look the uncompromising, incomprehensible original Scriptures full in the face.

To become an Abraham is not, then, a choice open to us. 'Nor for us the ultimate vision', then? Genesis offers a further model for recognizing God, which is less direct but also less disturbing: a more 'human' and therefore gratifying model: the story of Joseph, his brothers, and his father Jacob. This episode occupies the entire second section of the book, which subsumes the J document, the E (the Elohist, calling God 'Elohim'), and, to a considerably lesser extent, the Priestly one.

In the story of Joseph God only makes one direct appearance, when, towards the end, in a nocturnal vision, he exhorts Jacob to go down into Egypt, although he is at several points presented to the readers as Agent. When Joseph has been sold into Egypt and is prospering in Potiphar's household, J assures us that 'God was with him' and on his account 'blessed the Egyptian's house'. And God continues to stand by him, and act for him, in prison, after the attempted seduction by Potiphar's wife. Both Potiphar himself and Pharaoh are well aware of this special protection, the king throwing at his ministers the rhetorical question as to whether they would ever again find a man like Joseph, 'in whom is the spirit of God'. It is Joseph himself, amid his many crises, who recognizes in God the agent not so much of his personal fortunes (this will occur explicitly when he reveals himself to his brothers) as of the whole interweaving of earthly events and their exegesis. When he explains Pharaoh's dreams (actually the same dream repeated twice), he states openly that it is God, not himself, who is decoding ('do not interpretations belong to God?') and that they indicate 'what God is about to do', adding that 'the repeating of the dream to Pharaoh twice, this means that the thing has been fixed by God and God is hastening to do it'.

The recognition of God, then, is far from absent in the story, as it constitutes an important theme and the very *telos* or aim of the narrative. What is missing at first reading is human agnition. Joseph's story begins when, as his father's favourite, 'because he was the son of his old age' (Benjamin, younger than himself and equally the son of Rachel, appears on the scene later), he is cordially detested by his brothers. The dreams Joseph reveals to the ten of them, first their sheaves of corn, then the sun, moon, and eleven stars 'bowing to [his] sheaf', can only increase their hatred, appearing as pure solipsism and vanity. Jacob, too, puts the same gloss on it, 'rebuking' him but at the same time pondering over it ('his father kept the thing in mind'). With this singular opening towards the future, which narrative reticence immediately closes, although the reader continues to 'keep the thing in mind', there begins the game of ignorance and recognition which is so splendidly analysed by Robert Alter in his *The Art of Biblical Narrative*. It almost seems as if Jacob ponders over the second dream (which involves him too, as the sun) because it might contain elements of the truth, and reveal some awareness of events to come (the *midrash* does indeed state that Jacob foresaw that the dreams would come to pass).

The opening out quickly becomes closure again in the following scene. When, sent by his father, Joseph joins his brothers feeding their flocks in Dothan, they begin to plot his murder. The eldest, Reuben, objects, and at his insistence Joseph is stripped of his famous 'coat of many colours' (actually, just an 'ornamented tunic') and thrown into an empty pit, whence Reuben plans to rescue him later; Judah, to stop them from spilling their own brother's blood, suggests more practically that they sell him to some Ishmaelites going to Egypt. Meanwhile, some passing Midianite merchants pull the boy out of the pit and sell him, for twenty pieces of silver, to the Ishmaelites. Thus (either by hand of the Midianites or the Ishmaelites, or both), Joseph ends up in Egypt.

Ignoring Reuben's anguish on finding the pit empty, Joseph's brothers decide to manufacture the proof of their innocence, dipping his coat in the blood of a kid and taking it to their father with the words: 'This we have found: recognize (*haker-na*), pray, is it your son's tunic or not?' And Jacob 'recognizes' (the verb used is the perfect of *haker*) the evidence his sons have fabricated, and cries that 'a vicious beast has devoured him, Joseph has been torn to shreds!'. In other words, Jacob believes the sign, dumb to logic, but to the emotions devastatingly eloquent, which the ten brothers allow to speak for itself. Here Jacob no longer ponders, but, without the slightest rational deduction— with no attempt at a *syllogismos*—leaps to the conclusion that his sons had projected when, on the point of killing Joseph, they had decided to tell their father (although, significantly, they fail to do so) that 'a vicious beast has devoured him'. Upon his act of recognition, Jacob is plunged into pain and ignorance: into Sheol, as he says in his funeral lament over Joseph: 'For I will go down to my son in Sheol mourning.'

'Signs', then, the reader will conclude, are meaningless: misinterpretation can lead to false recognition, *méconnaissance*, although the following chapter's account of the story of Judah and Tamar forces us to think again. Judah, Jacob's fourth son, has three sons: Er, Onan, and Shelah. Tamar is given in marriage to Er, but, 'wicked in the sight of the Lord', he is put to death by God. Tamar is then given to Onan, who, asked to 'raise up seed for his brother', and knowing it would not be considered his, 'when he would come to bed with his brother's wife, he would waste his seed on the ground', thereby incurring the Lord's displeasure: 'wherefore He put him as well to death.' To save his third son's life, Judah decides to return her to her father. When she discovers that Judah is nearby, shearing his sheep, the girl covers her face with a veil, and waits for him 'in an open place'. Not realizing (*jadá*) that it is his daughter-in-law, Judah takes her 'for a whore because she had covered her face', and asks her to lie with him. As pledge of his promise to send a kid in payment, he gives her his seal-and-cord and

staff, but when, later, Judah tries to keep his word, the men
of the place fail to recognize his description of her: '"Where
is the harlot, the one at Enaim by the road?". And they said,
"There has been no harlot here".' Three months later,
Tamar is pregnant, and Judah orders her to be burnt. But
she sends him his seal-and-cord and staff with the message,
'Recognize (haker-na), pray, whose are these?', which Judah
'recognizes' (the same verb, in the perfect), declaring that
she has been 'more in the right' than he (because he did not
offer her his son Shelah); after which 'he knew (jadāʿ) her
again no more'.

'True' signs, then, far from being meaningless, turn out to
be watertight proof leading from ignorance to knowledge,
from error to a recognition of guilt, and from carnal knowledge to quiescence. They speak eloquently because they
speak to the conscience, and have an ethical impulse which
finds almost a physical 'objective correlative': Judah is the
first of the brothers to experience recognition 'in the flesh',
while Tamar's deceit, unlike that of Joseph's brothers (and
the inversion is re-enacted in the agnition's verbal formula)
is aimed at continuing the family line, and life itself (her
twins join Israel's line of descent).

We have not yet done with signs. When, in the following
chapter, Joseph is sold to Potiphar and made his attendant
and overseer, Potiphar's wife is not slow to 'cast her eyes'
(and soon hands) on the youth 'comely in features and
comely to look at'. This time the Judah–Tamar model is
inverted, and it is the woman who asks Joseph to lie with
her. His conscience needing no signs to rouse it, he refuses,
arguing his earthly and heavenly master's trust. She continues to harass him, until one day, finding him alone, she
seizes him by his garment, saying, 'Lie with me'. When
Joseph indignantly tears himself free, his garment remains
'in her hand'. Potiphar's wife, then, calls out to her servants, accusing 'this Hebrew man' of having tried to rape
her and showing as proof the garment which, she says, he
left 'by' her. When her husband returns, she repeats the

whole story, and he has no choice but to throw Joseph into prison.

Once more, like Joseph's coat, a 'garment' becomes a sign, mute and therefore manipulable in the inversion of truth. Fragile proof in itself, it only needed to be moved a few inches from her hands to 'by her', for it to assume a far more decisive nature: her hands could have grasped the garment while Joseph was escaping; on the contrary, it could have fallen 'by' her when Joseph removed it to attempt to rape her. It is interesting that in the Koran's re-Scripting of the episode, in the twelfth Sura, the sign is rightly questioned. Here, Joseph escapes with his garment ripped down the back, meets his master on the threshold, and, at the woman's accusations, retorts that the violence was hers. One canny bystander offers the correct sign-deduction detective solution: if the garment is ripped down the front, then the woman is right and he is lying; if down the back, then the opposite is true. Despite the evidence, Joseph is thrown into prison anyway.

The sign in itself, then, is neutral: this much at least is clear to the reader of Genesis. It can lead equally to ignorance or knowledge, death or life; it only leads to recognition, and thus true knowledge, if accompanied by self-awareness. Aristotle's scientifico-philosophical criterion is here replaced by a moral one, introspection. Sophocles' Oedipus recognizes that he is guilty of parricide and incest not because the clues he gathers make him feel guilty, but because they reveal the truth of the facts committed unwittingly. J's Judah, on the other hand, acknowledges his blame as regards Tamar. Oedipus' responsibility belongs to general human fallibility, while Judah's is purely personal. The former, necessarily, has tragic consequences; the latter can announce a renewal of life.

Indeed, signs are not only neutral, but can be downright ambiguous. They can be created to disturb or alarm, raise anxious questions, and promote the *stirrings* of conscience. To take a proleptic leap: once in prison Joseph, we know,

prospers on account of God's blessing. He interprets correctly the butler's and baker's dreams, then, when Pharaoh
dreams of the seven fat cows and the seven lean cows, and
the seven good and seven thin ears of corn, the butler, re-
instated in the palace, has the young Jew called to give his
explanation: seven years of plenty, and seven of famine. The
king raises Joseph to general overseer, second only to himself in power (this is Joseph's third 'rebirth' after the three
'falls' or deaths: into the pit, into slavery, and into prison,
and the third time Joseph has been involved with dreams).
Under the new name of Zaphenath-paneah (in Egyptian,
'God says: he lives', but which the *midrash* interprets more
significantly as 'with his knowledge he reveals hidden
things'), happily married to Asenath, the daughter of an
Egyptian high priest, Joseph travels the length and breadth
of Egypt amassing grain during the years of plenty, and is
then ready to trade with the whole world when the famine
starts.

Then, when Joseph is almost a naturalized Egyptian (he
calls his firstborn Manasseh 'for God hath made me forget
all my father's house'), his brothers appear before him to buy
grain (the youngest, Benjamin, remaining at home because
Jacob is afraid 'lest mischief befall him'), and it is at this point
that the anagnorisis begins, tortuous and ludic, among
delayed and anticipated effects. Joseph being the regent of
Egypt, the ten bow down before him, thereby fulfilling his
original dream; he recognizes them, but plays the stranger to
them (in the original this is a play on the root of the same
verb); Joseph recognizes his brothers, but they do not recognize him: the repetition underlines the contrast between his
knowledge and their ignorance (the *midrash*, always hungry
for concrete signs, maintains that Joseph recognizes them
because they are bearded, as when he last saw them, while
they fail to recognize him precisely because he is bearded
now but was not at the time of his being sold). He immediately remembers his dreams of them, and accuses them:
'You are spies.' Joseph's memories and agnition immediately

start up a mechanism to test the ten, punish them, and fulfil his dreams. Above all, however, as Meir Sternberg has brilliantly demonstrated in *The Poetics of Biblical Narrative*, the past is recreated at a dramatic, psychological, and interpretative level, along two basic axes: role duplication and reversal.

The process is now taken over by the ambiguity of signs— or, more correctly, everything becomes an ambiguous sign. Joseph throws them into prison, asking as proof of their sincerity ('No, my lord, for your servants have come to buy food. We are all the sons of one man . . . twelve brothers; . . . the youngest is now with our father, and one is no more') that one of them return to fetch Benjamin. Role reversal: it is the ten of them now who prove helpless before power, and are falsely accused and imprisoned. He keeps them in prison for three days, afterwards changing his mind ostensibly because he 'fears God'. One of them, Simeon, is now to remain in prison, and chained before their eyes, while they return to Canaan, taking provisions to stave off the famine in their homes; in exchange for which they are to return to Egypt with their brother Benjamin. Role duplication: Simeon's arrest is not only a reversal (Simeon for Joseph): it also jump-starts them into reliving their past crime (how to behave with this brother, who now faces the same treatment they meted out to the one who 'is no more'?). The interrelating sign, silent and secretive, is the prison.

The ten immediately grasp the implications without understanding the facts. Even before Joseph picks out Simeon, they tell each other: 'Alas, we are verily guilty for our brother, whose mortal distress we saw when he pleaded with us and we did not listen. That is why this distress has overcome us.' Reuben is unable to resist a 'told-you-so', concluding, 'And now, look, his blood is requited'. Surrounded by the ambiguity of the signs, then, they *recognize* the past and for the first time confess their own responsibility: in other words, they begin to know themselves. At the same time they remain totally in the dark concerning external circumstances, because—the E text adds with a super-sleuth semiotic touch rarely equalled in Western literature—'they did not know that Joseph heard/understood; for there was an interpreter between them'. A whole series of Chinese boxes of knowledge suddenly opens before the reader: a sudden flash—the presence of the interpreter—illuminating the preceding scene, the present, and all those to come. Joseph's knowledge, which has no need of a translator, is revealed as total, like God's; while the ten brothers, just as they begin to know themselves, fall into the most complete *agnoia*, an ignorance which, beginning with the linguistic barrier, implies total emptiness. Joseph's knowledge, on the other hand, is 'filled' by his recognition and their ignorance, and overflows—and this is the sign that behind the mask of omnipotence there is a man—in tears: understanding their words, Joseph turns away from them and weeps. He recognized his brothers immediately, but his anagnorisis is only now emotionally complete.

The game of signs goes on. The nine depart with the corn, leaving Simeon as hostage; in each sack is 'every man's money' (they had, years before, received twenty silver pieces from the sale of their brother, as the reader and no doubt Joseph remember). This is a further, incomprehensible sign, meaning everything and nothing, but which fills them with surprising dread ('their heart failed them') and uncertainty. 'What is this that God has done to us?', they ask each other when, on the road, one of them finds the money. Later, when at home all the others discover the same in their sacks, both they and their father are 'afraid'.

Jacob is aghast at their story: 'Joseph is no more, and Simeon is no more, and Benjamin you would take away!', and refuses to let Benjamin 'go down' with them, even when Reuben offers the life of his own sons in hostage. But the famine continues 'sore in the land', and their father is obliged to ask them to search for more corn. Finally, Judah sets himself as a pledge for Benjamin, telling his father that if he fails to bring the youngest back he will bear the blame 'for ever' (thus now accepting full responsibility for a brother, a son of Rachel, and a favourite). And Jacob consents, sending gifts for 'the man' and 'double the silver' (for the new purchase of corn, and as a refund). With Benjamin, the brothers once more go down to Egypt and stand in Joseph's presence. Seeing his blood brother, Joseph orders a meal to be prepared in his house, at which ambivalent sign the brothers are terrified (together with the readers of King James's stark translation: 'Bring these men home, and slay, and make ready; for these men shall dine with me at noon'), convinced that they are to be punished for the 'theft' of the money. They earnestly assure the steward that they had no idea how it came to be in their sacks, but that they have 'brought it back in [their] hand', with further money for corn; he, with a significant but enigmatic 'Fear not: your God, and the God of your father, has placed treasure for you in your bags. Your silver has come to me', brings Simeon out to them, and leads all eleven in to Joseph. Again they bow down before him (the old dream being re-enacted once more), while he questions them with a repetition that betrays his anxiety and obsession ('Is all well with your aged father of whom you spoke? Is he still alive?'), his eyes fixed on his youngest brother, for whom 'his bowels did yearn'. A silent anagnorisis again takes place: at the sight of Benjamin, at the knowledge that his father is alive, perhaps at the recognition of his brothers' honesty, and his satisfaction that the old dream is again fulfilled (the open text gives no clue, but, having been explicit in the parallel scene, it invites the reader to fill the silence). The anagnorisis then explodes at the very moment it is deferred: without waiting for them to confirm Benjamin's identity, but invoking God's grace on him, Joseph resists no longer. He hurries out and, overwhelmed, goes into his chamber and weeps, unseen of all, for the second time. Then, restraining himself, he comes out and orders the meal to be served. The 'bread' is 'set' at separate places: for himself, for the Egyptians, and for his brothers, each placed in order of seniority, from the oldest to the youngest. At this further sign of almost divine knowledge, the brothers are understandably amazed, even more so when they see that Benjamin's portion is five times as much as any of theirs. Gulping down amazement and food, however, they drink and are merry with him.

Ambiguous signs—both devoid and full of meaning—have been heating up and overcharging: in the following sequence they short-circuit and explode. Before the eleven set off, Joseph orders the steward to put every man's money in their bags and his own goblet (silver, like the twenty pieces) in the sack of the youngest. Then, when the eleven leave, he is ordered to go after them, search them, and accuse them of stealing the goblet 'from which my lord drinks, and in which he always divines'. Naturally, it is finally found in Benjamin's sack (the text infinitely delays, painstakingly passing from eldest down to the youngest)—another sign, further false proof of a false accusation. In mortification, while protesting their innocence with near watertight logic, they return to Joseph and fall before him on the ground. Seemingly enraged, he plays painfully and perfidiously with his omniscience and their ignorance: 'What is this deed that you have done? Did you not *know* that a man like me would surely *divine*?' Again Judah acts as mouthpiece. With no attempt to deny the particular evidence of the sign, he interprets it as a vaster proof of older, more general crimes finally lived as if present and ongoing: 'What shall we speak and how shall we prove ourselves right? God has found out your servants' crime', suggesting that they make expiation, all eleven, through slavery. Joseph borrows from the idea of justice that had emerged from the dialogue between Abraham and Yahweh: 'Far be it from me to do this!': only the culprit will be made a slave; the others are to return to their father.

Judah's first, brief confession then becomes an oration: not strictly defensive, given that the sign is seemingly irre-futable, but, paradoxically, an act of self-accusation, in that he now recognizes, once and for all, the higher law of their father's incomprehensible love for Rachel's two sons. He recalls in the first place, now adding details hitherto omitted as to the special love linking Jacob, Joseph, and Benjamin, their answer to Joseph on the occasion of their first meeting: 'We have an aged father and a young child of his old age, and his brother being dead, he alone is left of his mother, and his father loves him.' He then tells of Jacob's reaction before their second journey into Egypt, again underlining the special love for the two youngest, and, with irony, the foolish ignorance of the others: 'You *know* that my wife bore me two sons. And one went from me and I thought, Surely he is torn in pieces; and I have not seen him since. And should you take this one, too, from my presence and harm befall him, you would bring down my gray head in evil to Sheol.' 'His life is bound to the lad's', Judah now fully recognizes. Unwittingly, and for the readers significantly, his oration now moves imperceptibly towards Jacob: 'And so, should I come to your servant, my father, and the lad be not with us, he would die.' To this father Judah made himself pledge for the boy, he explains, and he will 'bear the blame for ever' if he fails to return him, and so offers himself in exchange, ending, again, with the image of his father's despair: 'For how shall I go up to my father, if the lad be not with us? Let me see not the evil that shall come on my father.'

The sign—the goblet—has vanished. Jacob's shadow now darkens both scene and consciences, and subsumes the whole affair, with its near-unbearable charge of hatred, love, pain, death, and rebirth. This third time, faced with Judah's repeated evocation of his father and his total recognition of their collective duty as sons and brothers, Joseph can hold back no longer; 'Cause every man to go from me', he orders, 'And there stood no man with him, while Joseph made himself known unto his brethren', weeping so loudly that he was heard in Pharaoh's house. The anagnorisis expected for over twenty years, prepared and deferred through many a page, now comes about, from revelation through words and gestures to agnition. 'I am Joseph: is my father still alive?', Joseph cries out, while his brothers are too stunned and 'dismayed before him' to make any response. He makes them come closer, and repeats, offering as proof of his statement the most disturbing sign of the whole story and of their guilt: 'I am Joseph your brother, *whom you sold into Egypt*' (the *midrash* adds a second sign, when Joseph shows them he is circumcised). Then, to relieve them of their fear and displaying his omniscience, he informs them of what he has known for years: that it is God guiding the history of the world, of their particular family and people, towards life:

And now, do not be pained and not be incensed with yourselves, that you sold me down here, because God did send me before you to preserve life. Two years now there has been famine in the heart of the land, and there are yet five years without plowing and harvest. And God has sent me before you to preserve you a posterity in the earth, and to save your lives by a great deliverance. And so, it was not you that sent me here, but God, and he has made me a father to Pharaoh and lord to all his house and a ruler over all the land of Egypt. Hurry and go up to my father and say unto him, 'Thus says your son Joseph, God has made me lord to all Egypt. Come down to me, do not delay. And you shall dwell in the land of Goshen and shall be close to me, you, and your sons, and the sons of your sons and your flocks and your cattle, and all that is yours. And I will nourish you there, for yet five years of famine remain—lest you lose all, you and your household and all that is yours'.

After this near theophany, recalling God's apparition and words to Jacob in Bethel ('I am El Shaddai. Be fruitful and multiply. A nation, an assembly of nations shall stem from you, and kings shall come forth from your loins. And the land that I gave to Abraham and to Isaac, to you I will give it, and to your seed after you I will give the land'), there follows the recognition which works through human means. 'And, look, your own eyes can see, and the eyes of my brother Benjamin, that it is my very mouth that speaks to you', Joseph assures them ('in Hebrew', the *midrash* adds, providing a further material sign), again inviting them to bring their father into Egypt. He then gives his final sign, and definitive proof: his affection. He falls, weeping, upon the neck of Benjamin, who weeps on his; then he kisses all his brothers and weeps over them. At which point they feel able to speak to him.

The process of recognition does not, however, end with this scene of anagnorisis, the only Western literary parallels of which are the encounter between Penelope and Odysseus and those between Jesus and Mary Magdalene and Pericles and Marina that I shall examine in the last chapter. As in the *Odyssey*, there remains the agnition between father and son, prefigured in the text in its insistence on the paternal image, the repetition of the noun. When his brothers return to Canaan, with twenty ass-loads of food and goods (and three hundred significant pieces of silver for Benjamin), and inform their father that Joseph is still alive and governor of the whole of Egypt, Jacob's heart stops, because he does not believe them. Signs are needed: Joseph's exact words, and the wagons sent to transport him to Egypt, at which point he revives, and can conclude: 'Enough! Joseph my son is still alive. I will go and see him before I die.' Convinced by the words of God himself, appearing in his 'visions of the night', that he will make of him a great nation in Egypt, Jacob descends to the Nile delta while Joseph goes up towards Goshen to meet him. As soon as the long-lost son appears before him, Jacob falls on his neck and weeps long, while finally exclaiming, 'Now I may die, since I have seen your face, for you are still alive'.

And indeed the events of Genesis end shortly afterwards, with the death and funeral of Jacob (his body, embalmed in Egypt, is transported into Canaan and buried in the ancestral tomb, 'in the cave of the field of Machpelah, before Mamre'), although only after a long final blessing, recognizing Judah's supremacy and the place of Joseph's sons in the 'twelve tribes of Israel'. When Joseph's turn comes to die, aged 110, he extracts from his brothers the promise that they shall carry away his bones when God leads them out of Egypt into the Promised Land. But between the two epi-sodes, a curious scene opens the old wounds for a moment. After Jacob's death the brothers fear that blood may prove thicker than water, that Joseph may bear resentment against them and finally extract his revenge. They consequently send him a message (which Joseph again weeps on receiv-ing), afterwards going in person to prostrate themselves before him and offer to be his servants. Joseph's answer closes the wound in a double act of recognition: of himself and of divine providence: 'Fear not, for am I in the place of God? While you meant evil towards me, God meant it for good, so as to bring about at this very time the survival of many people.'

It should now be very clear that the whole story of Joseph and his brothers constitutes a process of anagnorisis, the passing from ignorance to knowledge (in Aristotle's defini-tion), based on three basic, complementary, and intercon-nected devices: sign, recognition, and revelation. Totally human, they at the same time project a divine shadow over events. Signs, for example: this part of Genesis organ-izes its signs to construct a discourse, not in analytical but in *narrative* philosophy, which constantly adumbrates the meeting-point between human and divine. It explores the material, evidential value of signs (i.e. the value Aristotle would attribute them in the process of sensory knowledge) intentionally created by human individuals, and foregrounds the importance for their correct reading of the context of the events embedding them (Joseph's coat for Jacob; seal-and-cord and staff for Judah; Joseph's garment for Potiphar; Joseph's words and the wagons for Jacob). It also underscores the psychological resonance generating and being generated by them (Joseph's coat; the brothers' imprisonment; the money and goblet in the sacks; the seating arrangements at Joseph's table). This resonance originates in the memory

(Aristotle's third phase of knowledge) and the feelings—
pain, amazement, fear, terror—and awakens in the addressee
self-knowledge, moral awareness, gratitude, and confession
(Judah at Tamar's evidence, and again when the goblet is
found in his brother's sack; the brothers when accused of
spying and when asked to fetch Benjamin). Without the
paradigm created here, the *Comedy* as it stands would have
been impossible for Dante, and Dostoevsky could not have
written *The Brothers Karamazov*. Here everything becomes
sign: objects, words, gestures, actions, and even knowledge
itself (for example Joseph's in arranging his brothers according to age). Then, through doubt and wonder, the human
sign provokes the crucial question, and *allows us to glimpse
God*: 'What is this that God has done to us?', the brothers
ask on finding the money in the sacks.

   There can be no agnition without signs: Judah needs all
the objects given to Tamar; Joseph's brothers need his sentence, 'I am Joseph your brother, whom you sold into
Egypt', his weeping, and his embrace. However, while later
midrash gives a decisive weight to this, as we saw above,
Genesis considers it necessary but insufficient: here agnition
is not possible without a recognition of personal responsibility, without which the sign is open to misinterpretation
and the agnition becomes *méconnaissance* and ultimately
ruin. This recognition once again involves God: 'God has
found out the crime of your servants', Judah proclaims in his
great speech. Lastly—and this is the real key to the narrative's anagnorisis—agnition is impossible without revelation,
and vice versa. The brothers cannot recognize Joseph until
he is ready to reveal himself; when he does decide, he must
do it through signs, however oblique. 'I am Joseph your
brother, whom you sold into Egypt' is an emblematic fusion
of the two procedures. Neither agnition nor revelation
occurs by chance: they are born, as Aristotle rightly states
for those of *Oedipus Rex*, 'out of the events themselves': but
those events are orchestrated by man, and willed by God.

   This kind of anagnorisis ultimately points, of course, to

the revelation-recognition process of God himself. Not only does the opening formula—'I am Joseph'—recall that through which God reveals himself to the patriarchs, but Joseph's next statement points explicitly, for a full three times, to a recognition of the divine plan: 'God has sent me before you to preserve life.' Neither Joseph nor his brothers can know God through direct revelation, be it encounter, vision, or summons. What happens between Joseph's generation and those of his ancestors is not the Fall, but the definitive entrance into the world and into history: significantly, God will remain the God of Abraham, Isaac, and Jacob, and will never become the God of Joseph. Joseph's own destiny within Jewish tradition will be double-edged: considered wise and righteous, he will however belong both to good and evil, Israel and Egypt. But within history, humanity's only way of knowing God is the way indicated here, in the story of Joseph, his brothers, and his father, and in this sense Genesis now rewrites Genesis. For life to be preserved and multiplied ('Joseph' means 'may God give increase') it was necessary to go down into Egypt, into the world. In the Hebrew Bible this is acknowledged in the powerful Psalm 105:

> When they were but a few men in number;
> of little account and strangers there [in Canaan];
> When they went from one nation to another,
> from one kingdom to another people;
> he suffered no man to do them wrong: . . .
> Moreover he called for a famine upon the land:
> he brake every staff of bread.
> He sent a man before them:
> Joseph was sold for a servant:
> whose foot they hurt with fetters:
> he was laid in iron:
> until the time that his word came to pass:
> the word of the Lord had tested him.
> The king sent and loosed him:
> and the ruler of the people let him go free.

He made him lord of his house,
and ruler of all his substance
to bind his princes at his pleasure;
and teach his senators wisdom.
So Israel also came into Egypt;
and Jacob sojourned in the land of Ham.
And he increased his people greatly . . .

This is confirmed for the Christian Bible in Stephen's important speech in chapter 7 of the Acts of the Apostles; it is repeated, with some fascinating touches, in the twelfth Sura of the Koran. The story of Joseph, his brothers, and the elderly Jacob reveals exactly how the anagnorisis becomes a further stage in the discovery of God, theo-centric discourse, *theo-logy* as the history of salvation, *Heilsgeschichte*, in which the individual recognizes his or her true role, that of other individuals, and that of the Lord: 'God has found out the crime of your servants', Judah admits, applying the manifestation of God to the sphere of personal responsibility. 'Am I in the place of God? While you meant evil towards me, God meant it for good, for the survival of many people', Joseph chides and comforts his dismayed brothers, extending the question from personal sins to the ways God uses them to act in the world.

It is most certainly true, as Gabriel Josipovici maintains in his admirable analysis of the episode in *The Book of God*, that within the perspective of the Hebrew Bible, where no definitive revelation exists, the anagnorisis of Joseph and his brothers fails to constitute the point of arrival it would represent in classical drama. It is equally true, however, that this 'closure' is not offered us by the *Odyssey* either: after the recognition scene between husband and wife we are not only presented, as in Genesis, with that between father and son, but with the opening towards infinity of Ulysses' destiny through the repetition of Tiresias' prophecy that the hero set sail once more for a country which does not know the sea. And the long process of *méconnaissance* and recognition leads to a scene of anagnorisis which represents the

acme—albeit temporary and bristling with future interro-
gatives—of one definite stage in the relation between God
and man represented by the Bible. Henceforth this phase
will be a given in terms of human awareness: the phase in
which, through human conflict and recognition, man will
glimpse God's definitive passing from the world of being and
promise to that of becoming and fulfilment. It is for this
reason that the recognition scene between Joseph and his
brothers, and then his father, is so disturbing but so satisfying
for the humans which are its real addressees. To possess this
knowledge, however many times it will be called into question in the Bible and in history, down to our own awesome,
terrible century, it is worth paying the price of so many
crimes, so many confessions; it is right and inevitable, for
this supreme intuition of the Plot, to shed so many tears. For
its sake it might even be possible, for one moment only, to
forget Abraham and become like Joseph—or, more prob-
able for us as common mortals, like his brothers.

Re-writings of Joseph and his brothers, in whole or in part,
are common in literature: from Flavius Josephus' *Jewish
Antiquities*, the Greek *History of the Most Handsome Joseph
and his Bride Aseneth*, the Koran and *Joseph and Sulaika*, to
the Persian Djami and Grimmelshausen's *Edifying Description
of the Life of the Chaste and Excellent Joseph in Egypt*. The
figure of Joseph has attracted writers such as Goethe, who in
Poetry and Truth tells how he virtually rewrote the whole
story in his youth, developing it and giving it closure, only
to destroy it some time later; and Tolstoy, who in *What is
Art?* considers it the exemplary masterpiece, a paradigm for
all works of art. And of course down to Pascal at least, the
Christian tradition has read Joseph as a prefiguration of
Christ himself.

When Thomas Mann—this chapter's second M—follows
the young Goethe's example (explicitly) and undertakes the
monumental rewriting of Genesis in his tetralogy *Joseph and
his Brothers* (published between 1933 and 1943), the whole

of preceding literature, from the *midrash* to Christian exegesis and Arab adaptations, is absorbed and amalgamated in a
palimpsest including history, mythology, ancient compara-
tive religion, archaeology, and psychology: a *summa*, in other
words, a 'text-world' which Mann himself compares to the
pyramids.

The theme and problem of recognition pervades Mann's
gigantic amplification of the Bible story both because it
comprises, in itself, the ultimate point of the story, and
because the story offers itself as rewriting. Mann immediately underlines that recognition begins in Genesis long
before the story of Joseph, when, at his mother Rebecca's
instigation, Jacob tricks his father Isaac into giving him the
blessing of his brother Esau. While in Genesis Isaac fails,
falteringly, to 'recognize' Jacob because his arms are hairy
like Esau's, in Mann's *The Tales of Jacob*, the first of his four
volumes, Isaac is both more uncertain and at the same time
convinced by the evidence of the material sign offered him.
His 'sighted blindness' is played on more openly, and Jacob's
reply, which glances at Christ's words to Pilate, 'Thou sayest', foregrounds it even more. '"Yea", said he, "these are thy
hairy limbs and Esau's red fleeces, I see them with my seeing
hands and must be convinced. The voice is the voice of
Jacob, but the hands are the hands of Esau. Art thou then
my very son Esau?"' Upon which Jacob answers, '"Thou
seest and sayest it"'.

The theme later resurfaces in the retaliatory deception
Jacob undergoes when Laban tricks him into spending his
wedding-night with Leah instead of Rachel. Mann's
reworking of the briefest of scenes in Genesis is a virtuoso,
lyrico-erotico-ironic triumph. The girl is introduced,
veiled, in the dark, into the room where Jacob is eagerly
waiting, and at his question 'Is it thou, Rachel?', pronounced only to let her hear his voice, she replies with a
coy nod of the head. Jacob then begins his paean to love,
tenderly tracing the history of his love-story with Rachel,
finally asking her if she, too, is 'enraptured by the greatness

of this hour'. At her reply, 'I am thine in bliss, dear Lord', Jacob muses out loud that the voice could be Leah's, immediately reassuring himself with the idea that similarities do, indeed, exist between the voices of two sisters. He then hazards a proclamation which for the reader ironically recalls both his brother and his father's 'seeing hands', and directly involves God himself:

Let us be glad of the distinction [*Unterscheidung*] that thou art Rachel and I Jacob, and not, for instance, Esau my red brother! My forefathers and I, at night beside the flocks, have pondered much upon the person of God, who He is, and our children's children will follow us in our musings. But I at this hour will say and make clear my words, that the darkness may roll back away from them: 'God is the distinction [*Unterscheidung*]!' And therefore now I lift thy veil, beloved, that I may see with seeing hands . . .

It is no surprise then when he wakes up and is aghast to see, in the clear light of day, that the woman in his bed is Leah. J's terse 'when the morning came, look, it was Leah' will not do for M. For his Jacob recognition is a more complex business. Stammeringly he asks the girl 'since when is it thou?' and only when she replies, 'Always it was I', does he understand his night-long 'misconception'. His arm leaning on the wall, and his head on his arm, he weeps 'bitterly' like Peter at the crowing of the cock: tears which are to put the seal on the last scene of agnition in the novel, that between Jacob and Joseph.

Lastly, two recognition scenes form the frame to Joseph's own story. Mann counterbalances the canonical scene at the end of the novel with another, at the beginning. The merchants pull Joseph from the pit and take him with them while the brothers are deciding to sell him. When the Midianites pass by the nine brothers (Reuben has gone to the pit to save Joseph), their leader asks whether they by chance know a boy is missing. When they say no, he reveals Joseph under a mantle, the brothers naturally recognizing him immediately. For a moment they are nonplussed, but then immediately talk their way out of the situation and begin to negotiate the sale. The basic price is fixed by Judah at thirty pieces of silver, and at one sticky point in the haggling, behaving as though he were quite infatuated 'with the article of sale', he kisses the mute and blinking Joseph on the cheek. From this moment of deliberate denial until the revelation in Egypt, the anagnorisis is suspended, playing with and drawing on all our expectations as readers of the Bible and insinuating itself around the entire tetralogy.

We saw above how, in the story of Joseph, Genesis develops an articulate but strictly narrative logic when dealing with the signs and the issue of recognition. This holds for Mann's novel too, as for example in Jacob's deceit when the sheepskin he is wearing is read by Isaac as definitive proof of the identity of his son. In Mann's extended version signs are inevitably diluted, particularly in the first stages, where three hundred pages separate the Isaac and Jacob scene from that of Jacob and Joseph's coat, and three hundred more are to pass before we meet Potiphar's wife and Joseph's garment. While the theme is mimetically foregrounded within the narrative cohesion as the novel accelerates (very relatively speaking, of course) towards the end, here at the beginning more diegetic comment prevails. When, for example, the ten brothers take Jacob the bloody coat of many colours, so that he may 'interpret' it for himself, the narrator stops and asks if the sign really is more 'merciful' than words, as Judah maintains. In the two pages dedicated to the question, the narrator adopts the point of view of the addressee and not, like Judah, that of the sender. So viewed, there can be no doubt, he writes, that the sign is considerably crueller. The word can initially be laid aside, a 'rearguard action against the forces of truth', and only gradually work its way into an unwitting consciousness: whereas the starkness of the sign, here the 'blood-stiffened rags', admits no illusion or 'temporizing fiction'. The sign is real, tangible, allows no ambiguity, but forces us to recognize as our own, as born in our own brains, a thought which, if expressed in words, would be rejected as madness. 'Mute' the sign certainly is—'not out of gentleness, however, but only because it needs not to speak to be understood, being the thing itself'. The sign is irrreducible by virtue of its *Wirklichkeit*, its being a material entity. In Genesis Jacob would have been obliged to recognize Joseph's coat, but could, in theory, have avoided jumping to the conclusion it indicates (Joseph has been torn to shreds). Mann's Jacob is not allowed even this theoretical possibility: for him there is no let-out, neither psychological nor epistemological. 'Without and within it lays you low', M writes of the sign.

M here seems to adopt a conception of knowledge which goes way beyond Aristotelian rationalism towards the certainties of empiricism and positivism. This is later confirmed in the scene in which Potiphar's wife (in the novel Mut-em-enet, wife of Peteprê) shows her husband Joseph's garment, the 'sign' or 'proof' that speaks 'the incorruptible language of things'. The effect on the reader is naturally the opposite, doubly sure as she or he is, thanks first to Genesis, and now to Mann, that these proofs are false, and it is precisely because M underlines the irrefutable reality of the sign that the reader will conclude, with stronger conviction than after going through Genesis, that the language of things, far from being incorruptible, is rotten to the core, and no empirical certainty can be adduced from it in our groping towards knowledge.

Against such a conclusion, in *Joseph and His Brothers* there stands no story of Judah and Tamar. While in Genesis this occurs between Jacob's receiving the bloody coat and Joseph's first success in Egypt, in Mann it is deferred until after his elevation by Pharaoh, just before the arrival of his brothers. By so doing, the sign's reversal from negative to positive, and its significance in Judah's inner recognition become an immediate announcement of what Mann calls the 'sacred game', the whole re-enacting of the process of anagnorisis which takes up all the final section of the tetralogy.

I intend now to have a detailed look at this, to see quite how Mann rewrites Genesis. For years Joseph reads the reports sent him from the frontier posts in expectation of the one which will tell him his brothers are on their way. It finally arrives, and Joseph is beside himself with excitement. He has always known, he reveals to his phlegmatic steward Mai-Sachme, that they would come, and that God would turn evil into good. The 'story' he already knows: the problem is how to fulfil it, enact it to perfection, and recognize and reinvent all the details, not least the agnitive plot itself:

What a history, Mai, is this we are in! One of the very best. And now it depends on us, it is our affair to give it a fine form and make something perfectly beautiful of it, putting all our wits at the service of God. How shall we begin, in order to do justice to such a story? That is what excites me so much . . . Do you think they will recognize me?

Joseph's anxious, excited questions obviously have no precedent in Genesis, but they reveal one of the main directions in which the novel will develop the recognition process, perforating the aspect of mystery through the psychology of the brothers. Mai-Sachme's answer is significant: no, he is sure they will fail to recognize him after so many years; they will have not the slightest suspicion. And then, 'to recognize and to know that you recognize are two very different things'. What is about to take place is no simple agnition, but its lunging into the gap between awareness and non-awareness: its searching for itself within the recognition of recognition.

Joseph's re-enactment has to match this. Nervous that they will recognize him, but at the same time desirous that they should, he decides against revealing himself immediately: 'the thing should first draw itself out before I speak the words and say I am I.' He first wants to do his own detective work, and 'shape and adorn the tale', not to ruin a good story before 'act' and 'result' tally and transform into 'a

feast of no common sort', something the world can laugh
and cry over for the next three thousand years. When
Mai-Sachme raises the point of what language to use, Joseph
hits on the idea of an interpreter, while together they think
up the idea of pretending to believe them spies, 'of course,
because it is the only right one and as good as written down
already'—indeed, 'this whole story is written down already
in God's book'.

The second direction for M's agnition will then be this:
rewriting is recognizing, fulfilling, and reincarnating the
prefiguration in the book of God. The book of God is
not, however, only Genesis, the first of the Pentateuch,
but the entire Bible (including, for M, the Christian one)
and, in the exegetical tradition, Isaiah's Heavenly scroll, the
book written within and without of Ezekiel, Revelation's
book sealed with seven seals: divine Wisdom and the earthly
world; omniscience, the universe, its happenings, and
human destiny. Here, then, on the subtle threshold between
the Book of Genesis and the 'book of life', between past,
eternity, and present, lie the re-Scripturing, the rewriting of
Scripture and recognition: 'It will run off as though it were
already written down and was being played according to
script'—Joseph informs his steward before meeting the ten
and Benjamin, 'There are no surprises, only the thrill of
seeing the familiar of long ago become the present.'

Some very surprising special effects are, however, produced in the Joseph of M's re-enacting of his biblical prefiguration. When the ten appear in front of him for the first
time we do indeed wonder whether, in his words to his
steward, he 'can make even God Himself, the great
Unanswering, to laugh':

'So many?' he asked in a muffled voice which, oddly enough, he
had pitched almost in a growl. 'Ten all at once? Why not eleven?
Interpreter, ask them why there are not eleven of them or even
twelve—or do you men understand Egyptian?' . . . While the
interpreter rapidly and monotonously translated Naphtali's words,
Joseph devoured with his eyes the men standing before him. He

knew them every one and had no trouble in marking in each the work the hand of time had done upon them too . . . Good God, how old they had got! It was very moving—as all life is moving. But he shrank back at the sight of them, for with them so old it was unbelievable that the father was still alive.

With his heart full of laughing and weeping and dismay he looked at them, recognizing every single one despite the beards, which some of them in his time had not yet worn. But they, looking at him in their turn, had no such thoughts; for their seeing eyes were wrapped in blindness against the possibility that it could be he.

The audience continues in the form of a stringent questions-and-answers for some ten pages, the omission points in the quotation above standing for at least fifteen lines each time. Mann's lines of development of the Genesis story are clear, however, even from this abridged version: his intention is to further increase Joseph's knowledge, and his use of it as provocation ('why not eleven or even twelve?'), at the same time as he transforms it into explicit emotion and awareness of the passing of time; and to herd the brothers' ignorance, psychologically, into the minimal but essential gap between recognizing and knowing that you recognize, and, epistemologically and morally, into the blindness of those who, seeing, fail to see, like those who hear the prophecies of Isaiah and the parables of Christ 'from outside'.

Joseph continues with his game of cat and mouse, in the process discovering that his father is still alive and that Benjamin has eight children; he then closes in on them, launching his accusation of spying, his third-degree questioning as to the twelfth brother ('What! So now all of a sudden you are twelve men?'), and finally their imprisonment. Here Scripture is rescripted in three different ways. The first, extra-biblical, belonging to fiction, centres on two touches of narrative genius: when Judah confirms that his father is still alive, adding that theirs is a particularly long-lived family and that their 'ancestor was a hundred years old when he begot the true and right son, their father's father', Joseph, 'his voice breaking', exclaims: 'How uncivilized!' Then when he learns that his small brother is himself a father, without waiting for the translation and thereby earning himself 'a private nudge in the back' from his steward, he blurts out, 'Impossible!'.

Mann's second and third methods reveal that he was familiar with the art of biblical narrative long before modern critics. His second, a Wagnerian, but ironical and profoundly biblical resurfacing of the recognition *Leitmotif*, is shown when Reuben first answers to the charge of spying: 'we recognize you in your greatness, but you recognize us not in our good faith.' The third is a double example of intra-textual, ultra-biblical allusion. In clear contraposition to the episode of Potiphar's wife, Dan reminds Joseph that it is up to him to prove his accusation; at Reuben's defence, Joseph replies with a further suspicion: two or three of them, he insists, evoking the Genesis episode in which Simeon and Levi avenge the violation of their sister Dinah with the Sichem slaughter, would be more than capable of entering the city and slitting the throats of men and beasts.

The theme of agnition is never, however, abandoned. When the ten brothers find themselves in the very pleasant, 'flower-twined' chambers in which they are 'imprisoned', their minds immediately run on the strange events and stranger character, cruel and attractive at the same time, which had brought them to their present state. And then comes the moment when they put together the 'unreasonable suspicion' of espionage 'with another most reasonable one', namely, that there is some link between the haughty foreigner's suspicion and that which hangs over them constantly at home; 'in short, that this visitation was a punishment for long past guilt.' The narrator instantly doubles up as commentator, foregrounding the theme of recognition and turning himself into not merely the only rereader but the ultimate re-Writer too:

It would be a mistake to conclude, or to gather from the text, that they first mentioned the suspicion in front of Joseph, at their second confrontation with him. No, it had occurred to them before that. Here in the place of their first arrest it mounted to their lips and they spoke of Joseph. That was strange. They were capable of not even the faintest mental association between this lord of the corn and their sold and buried brother, yet—they spoke of him. It was not a merely moral association; they did not at first come on to it by such a route, one suspicion leaping back to the other. At first it was not a matter of guilt and punishment, it was a matter of contact [*Berührung*].

Mai-Sachme had been right when he had remarked in his imperturbable way that it was a far cry between knowing and knowing that you knew. A man cannot come into contact with his blood-brother without knowing it, especially if he has once spilled that blood. But confessing it to oneself is a different pair of shoes. To assert that the sons had at this point in the story recognized the keeper of the market as their brother would be a clumsy way to put it and could only be denied forthwith; for why then their boundless amazement when he revealed himself? No, they had not the faintest idea. And quite specifically they had no idea either why Joseph's image and their ancient guilt came to their minds after or even during their first contact with this attractive and alarming potentate.

In an analysis focused on the acts of discerning and distinguishing (the *Unterscheidung* Jacob claims for his race and for God), M transforms the *Erkennen* into mystery, 'contact' between blood, images of blood and the reflection of blood, and into an inexplicable *Berührung* suspended between recognition and awareness of recognition. The enigma remains at a psychological level, and the narrator can continue to play on the theme of external recognition; as they are about to leave Simeon as hostage, Reuben recalls how he had tried to talk them out of laying hands on Joseph, and 'now God is asking us: "Where is your brother Abel?"' (Joseph's nose here starts to prickle, and he turns away, his eyes full of tears). But then at their second meeting, when Joseph adds to the indecipherable signs of the money and the seating arrangements the fact that he knows their names in order of age, and that Benjamin's mother is dead, with the vision of a silver cup inside her tomb and that of an adolescent in a many-coloured coat, the mystery moves from the psychological to the ontological.

The first mechanism to be released is of the Proustian *madeleine* variety, but inverted and complicated. Benjamin stares at the mighty Egyptian who treats him with such embarrassing fulsomeness: he looks, searches, loses, and suddenly dredges up an image buried deep within him, and is 'pervaded by an old, familiar, childhood air: pungent, sun-warmed, spicy, the essential aroma of all the love and trust, security and adoration, all the childlike bewildered sympathy, intuition, and half-knowledge' he had ever known. It is the scent of myrtle, the 'spicy scent of child-hood' and the child Joseph. At the same time Benjamin feels in himself the need to establish an identity, and guess how and why 'the jolly, friendly present' should be connected with 'something far higher, something of the divine'. The recognition process which began as an instinctive retrieval of lost time now grows as the inner enquiry, the 'bewitching riddle' of a numen which is both known and seemingly irretrievably remote. Shortly afterwards, during the night following the banquet, it collides with the barrier of the sheer incomprehensibility of the theophany and the impos-sibility of the very knowledge acquired. Benjamin, M writes, 'had seen a man in whom was Joseph': how could that possibly be described? Men have frequently encoun-tered a God who chose to manifest himself in human form, and behave as a known, familiar figure. But here 'it was the other way round: the humanly familiar was not semi-transparent for the divine, but the high and divine semi-transparent for the long-familiar childhood.' Joseph is God, man, and memory at one and the same time, and to identify him, and guess the 'how and why' will be constitutionally impossible for a human being. In *Time Regained*, Proust writes:

For to 'recognize' someone, and, *a fortiori*, to learn someone's identity after having failed to recognize him, is to predicate two contradictory things of a single subject, it is to admit that what was here, the person whom one remembers, no longer exists, and also that what is now here is a person one did not know to exist; and to do this we have to apprehend a mystery almost as disturbing as that of death, of which it is, indeed, as it were the preface and the harbinger.

Mann proclaims exactly the same mystery in which, however, the term of comparison is not death but the forbidden threshold between divine appearance and human essence. This is the continuation of the passage on Benjamin's tormented night:

Yet the disguised is not that behind which he disguises himself and from behind which he looks. They remain two. To recognize the one in the other does not mean to make one out of two, to relieve one's breast with the cry: 'It is he!' It is impossible to produce the one out of the other, however desperately the mind struggles to do it. The cry was dammed back in Benjamin's breast though his heart nearly burst to contain it. Or rather it is not quite right to say it was dammed back, for it was not yet there, it had no voice or body—and therein precisely lay the indescribable thing.

This is as far as the game of agnition can go: from this point the reader simply waits for Joseph to reveal himself, for theophany and human epiphany unfathomably to meet. And when it occurs, in the strangest of close third encounters, after Judah's powerful speech (in which, in M's version, the crime against their eleventh brother is explicitly confessed), the revelation takes place in a sacred formula rewritten in familiar human terms. Hundreds of pages earlier, at the beginning of the last volume of the tetralogy, *Joseph the Provider*, Mai-Sachme, then Joseph's jailer, had asked him if he was Peteprê's ex-steward. The prisoner had answered, 'in all simplicity', 'I am he' (*Ich bin's*; literally, 'I am it'): a deceptive simplicity, however, M immediately remarks; in the first place, the register was wrong to a superior, and in

the second, the 'he' (the *es*) exceeds the question, inviting a
further one: '*What* are you?' or even '*Who* are you?' over
and above that. Joseph's answer, the narrator tells us, 'was a
formula' of considerably wider resonance, 'from ages past. It
was the time-honoured revelation of identity, a ritual statement beloved in song and story and play in which the gods
had parts. In such a play it is used in order to string together
a whole gamut of effects and plot sequences, from mere
casting down of the eyes to being thundered at and flung on
one's knees'. It is, in other words, the formula of theophany.
Now, *Ich bin's* is also the title of the chapter in which Joseph
finally makes himself known to his brothers, and the sentence he pronounces is a colloquial translation: *Kinder, ich
bin's ja. Ich bin ja euer Bruder Joseph* ('Children, here I am, I
am your brother Joseph!'). The novel has fulfilled the
shadow of the theophany of Joseph implied in Genesis.

The human and divine come together, the 'it', the *es*, of
the formula containing the essence of the mystery; and it is
more than clear that, in M's rewriting, the mystery is allud-
ing to its figural fulfilment in the New Testament. *Kinder* is
the word Jesus uses, in the Lutheran Bible, in addressing the
disciples when he appears to them, after the Resurrection,
on Lake Tiberiad, and *es* is the pronoun with which his
beloved disciple recognizes him immediately afterwards, as
we shall see below, in chapter 21 of John's Gospel: *Es ist der
Herr*, 'It is the Lord'. *Ich bin's selber* is the sentence Jesus uses
with the disciples, in Luther's translation of Luke, when they
see him for the first time after the Resurrection and believe
him a ghost. Joseph also echoes Christ's 'come unto me'; he
returns the kiss on the cheek which *Judah* had given him
before the Midianite merchants while selling him for *thirty*
pieces of silver; and, lastly, again paraphrasing Luke's Jesus,
he invites the brothers to touch him with their own hands
to verify the truth of his words. It seems almost inevitable,
then, that in the concluding agnition of Mann's tetralogy
Jacob should weep bitterly, like Peter after the cock had
crowed, when recognizing and embracing Joseph.

We reach this final threshold by delicate degrees. While Benjamin immediately grasps Joseph's true identity, and has his premonitions confirmed ('Of course he is, of course he is! I knew it, I knew it!'), the other ten brothers stand with 'bursting brains' as they try to reconcile Joseph's two faces: the brother, betrayed and sold, and the Lord of the Corn, now elevated to worldly glory; they have to recognize the one in the other and, in M's words, 'to work to hold the two together'. The revelation must be followed by the steady, painstaking adjustment of the mind to the realities of present and past which is called, precisely, 'recognition': the mystery which, as Proust has it, means 'to predicate two contradictory things of a single subject'.

At the same time Joseph has to voice full public knowledge of himself, as it were, and openly proclaim in front of his brothers that he is no 'god-hero, no harbinger of spiritual salvation' but only he who provides for the nourishment of his people, 'a farmer and manager'. Then, as penultimate fulfilment, Jacob must receive the news (M calls it 'annunciation') of the recognition, with delicate, ludic indirectness, through the song of the 'little maid' Serah, Asher's daughter.

Only then can the old patriarch go down into Egypt, and the final scene of anagnorisis take place. Everything is prepared with cinematographic care, through a rereading of the Septuagint translation of a single sentence in Genesis: '[Jacob] sent Judah before him to Joseph, so that he may appear in Goshen.' After the long journey from Canaan, Jacob's litter is set down on a wide plain, in the shade of three palm trees, 'growing, it seemed, from *one* root' (M's italics). Judah is sent ahead to inform Joseph, who advances in a cavalcade of chariots and horses. As soon as he can make out distinct figures, Jacob asks Judah who might be 'the fairly thickset man, arrayed in all the splendour of this world'; at Judah's reply, 'that is your son Joseph', he gets up and 'in laboured stateliness, limping from the hip more than ever', moves towards him, Joseph in his turn hurrying 'to shorten the distance between them'. M's Joseph, however, unlike that of Genesis, does not fling his arms round his father's neck: M's Jacob does not allow it. When 'the man' mouths the word 'father', Jacob stretches out his arms, 'like a blind man groping', moving his hands 'as though beckoning, yet partly too as though to protect himself'. He holds his son at this distance, while his tired eyes peer 'with love and sorrow into the Egyptian's face', and *do not recognize him*. But something Scripturally unexpected, yet completely natural, happens:

But it came to pass that Joseph's eyes slowly filled with tears under Jacob's gaze. Their blackness swam in moisture, they overflowed; and lo, they were Rachel's eyes, Rachel's dewy cheeks where Jacob in life's dreamy long-ago had kissed away the tears. Now he knew his son. He let his head fall on the stranger's shoulder and wept bitter tears.

In order to recognize his son, Jacob must relive his 'life's dreamy long-ago': he must become blind like Isaac, remember Rachel, and weep bitterly as when he discovered Leah in his bed. To recognize his son, he must read the one true sign the stranger can offer him: his eyes full of tears and the shadow of his dead mother. This is hardly a full-blooded, biblical anagnorisis, but it may be the only one the Bible was able to produce, moving for two thousand years in another culture. In classical literature no recognition is produced by a glance between two pairs of eyes. Only the inner space that the Scriptural text leaves open to readerly speculation in its silences and sudden, extreme flashes of emotion could, after centuries of re-elaboration, inspire such a purely fictional, romantic re-Scripture, where all the mystery of recognition remains intact. Above all, this final gesture 'fulfills' the work, but raises in the reader a question destined to generate further questions: why is Jacob weeping 'bitter tears'? Is his a recognition of guilt, like Peter's at the crowing of the cock? What is Jacob's 'betrayal'? Perhaps, as he considers shortly afterwards, he had perverted the divine plan by conferring primogeniture on Joseph in his gift of the coat of many colours, and now recognizes that God has punished both of them. Or are they purely human tears at the sight of a son who is now such a 'stranger', found and lost in the same moment? Perhaps the betrayal Jacob weeps for was Joseph's, who, as his father tells him in their next conversation, has become god of the world, and of corn, but not of salvation. Or again Jacob may be weeping because God has dictated events according to his plans without taking into account human doings and desires. And surely Jacob is weeping for his whole life, passing now before his drowning eyes: for the whole awesome, miraculous plot of the tetralogy which his recognition re-evokes. To paraphrase the work's opening sentence, very deep is the well of rewriting and recognizing.

It is so deep, in fact, as to shroud the very foundations of the work in mystery. When M the commentator wonders, in the third volume, *Joseph in Egypt,* how many years Joseph actually spent in Potiphar's house and how many in the 'pit'—i.e. the Egyptian prison—because, he writes, the commonly ascribed tradition leaves us in doubt, he immediately adds that the question may appear inept. 'Do we know our story or do we not?', he asks with every sign of impatience. Is it 'proper and suitable to the nature of story-telling that the narrator should openly reckon dates and facts?' Should he be present in the story as the anonymous source of what is told, or rather, which 'tells itself as it goes'? No, the narrator, he insists, should be inside the story, not outside: 'But how is it with God', he asks, 'Whom Abram thought into being and recognized?' (*Wie aber ist es mit Gott, den Abram hervordachte und erkannte?*). God 'is in the fire but He is not the fire. Thus He is at once in it and outside it', M writes, borrowing the image with which 1 Kings 19 describes Elijah's theophany on Oreb. Being a thing is rationally and ontologically very different from observing it. Yet 'there are places and spheres where both happen at once: the narrator is in the story, yet he is not the story; he is

its scene but it is not his, since he is also outside it and by a
turn of his nature puts himself in the position of dealing
with it.'

What M is sketching here is a true narrative theology,
with all the gnoseological problems every theology implies.
The narrator is like God (and isn't a divine Author exactly
what the Bible claims for itself?): he is in the fire but is not
the fire: is at once in it and outside it. M reaches this
conclusion in recalling Abraham's recognition of God, the
subject in Genesis which was our starting-point in this
chapter, and to which we shall shortly return. What, exactly,
does this being-in-but-not-being, which affects both God
and the narrator, mean? In 1 Kings 19, after the wind, the
earthquake, and the fire, God manifests himself as a 'voice of
still silence', or, in Luther's translation, *ein still, sanftes
Sausen*: a silent, soft murmur. And to this murmuring
M's voice is also reduced: because he has never wanted
to create the illusion of being the source of Joseph's story:
'before it could be told, it happened, it sprang from the
source from which all history springs, and tells itself as it
goes.' Word and becoming, both springing from a mysterious being, touch and mingle in this mystique of myth.
The narrator's task, his silent murmuring, is to bring the
plot to self-knowledge. The story has been in the world
since it happpened, and has told itself. 'Everybody knows
it or thinks he does' because the knowledge is as often as
not 'casual', of little consequence, almost a dream soaring
and floating on high for no good reason. Joseph's story has
been told hundreds of times, in a hundred different mediums: 'And now it is passing through another, wherein as it
were it becomes conscious of itself [*Selbstbesinnung*] and
remembers how things actually were with it in the long-
ago, so that it now both pours forth and speaks of itself as
it pours.' The impersonality of the approach increases the
affinity with Genesis, almost as if M were positing himself
as simply another 'documentary hypothesis' like P, E,
and J.

Abraham's recognition of God and recognition of the story: these are the central points of the theology and gnoseology of the rewriting M proposes. The first is a recurring theme in the tetralogy, but is foregrounded in the chapter in the third volume, *Young Joseph*, called 'How Abraham Found God'. The discovery, the elderly Eliezer tells Joseph, was arrived at through tortuous ways. Abraham had been moved to undertake his search by a question regarding man: who or what he 'serves'; to which the *Urvater*'s strange reply had been: 'the Highest alone'. In the beginning, then, there was human self-awareness: with considerable audacity, and robustly despising the easy way out, Abraham had refused to worship any second-rate god. He, Abraham, *as human being*, could only serve the highest. He had then sought to identify this 'highest' in 'mother earth', as sustainer of life, then in the sun, 'with all its powers of blessing and cursing', and lastly in the moon and the stars, all divinities of his Chaldaean land. But none of these was the highest: the earth needs rain to produce its fruits, while the sun, the moon, and the stars all set—all are subject to becoming: all are powers, none is the prime cause. What was wanted was a Ruler, a Lord, who commanded those same powers. He had 'to lay hold upon the manifold and the anguishingly uncertain and convert it into the single, the definite, and the reassuring, of whom everything came, both good and evil'. Gathering all the powers into one power, then, Abraham 'exclusively, once for all called them the Lord'.

He had, of course, 'invented' monotheism, and had become what, according to M, *Abiram* means: 'Father of the exalted'. 'Father' indeed, since, if the qualities of God's which Abraham had discovered were God's alone, he, man, had *recognized* them, predicated them, and 'by thinking made them real'. This is the 'psychological theology', connected to oriental initiation, which Mann speaks of in his lecture on 'Freud and the Future', published in the collection *Essays of Three Decades*:

But on the whole a psychological conception of God, an idea of the godhead which is not pure condition, absolute reality, but one with the soul and bound up with it, must be intolerable to Occidental religious sense—it would be equivalent to abandoning the idea of God. Yet religion—perhaps even etymologically—essentially implies a bond. In Genesis we have talk of the bond (covenant) between God and man, the psychological basis of which I have attempted to give in the mythological novel *Joseph and His Brothers* . . . God's mighty qualities—and thus God himself—are indeed something objective, exterior to Abram; but at the same time they are in him and of him as well; the power of his own soul is at moments scarcely to be distinguished from them, it consciously interpenetrates and fuses with them—and such is the origin of the bond which then the Lord strikes with Abram, as the explicit confirmation of an inward fact.

It is perfectly clear that recognition is the central nexus in this bond, this *religio* (and appears, significantly, in a lecture on Freud). In the novel, moreover, it is represented by the recognition scene between Abraham and Yahweh with which the present chapter opened. God's greatness, M there elaborates, was most definitely fearsomely real and living, something that existed outside Abraham; it also coincided, however, with the greatness of his soul. And the fear of God—the *timor Dei*—was not just (Kierkegaard's) 'fear and trembling', but also 'the existence of a bond, a familiarity and friendship'. Faced with Sodom and Gomorrah, Abraham had rapped God gently over the knuckles in a way 'which was not far from insolence', Mann's Abraham admits. 'Hearken, O Lord', M has him say, reproducing the *midrash* word for word: 'it must be one way or the other, but not both. If thou wilt have a world, then thou canst not demand justice, but if thou settest store by justice, then it is all over with the world. Thou wouldst hold the cord by both ends: wouldst have a world and in it justice. But if thou dost not mitigate thy demands, the world cannot exist.' On that occasion, M opines, Abraham also reminded God of the promise he himself had made, never again to send a Flood.

Abraham understood—he writes—that 'the contradiction of a world which should be living and at the same time just resided in God's greatness itself'. It was impossible for the living God to be only good: he had to include evil, 'and was therewith sacrosanct; was sanctity itself'. And he, Abraham, stood before God, 'an I before a Thou'. 'God remained a powerful Thou, saying "I" independent of Abraham and independent of the world. *He was in the fire but was not the fire.*' But God was also in Abraham, 'who *recognized* Him— by virtue of his own power', thereby reinforcing his I, extending his sense of self. Abraham had no desire to lose himself to God, but to remain Abraham, 'stoutly upright in face of Him at a great distance, certainly, for Abraham was but a man, and made of *clay*—but bound up with Him through *knowledge* and consecrated by the high essence and presence [*Du- und Da-Sein*, literally, the 'being-Thou' and the 'being-there'] of the Deity'. M's rewriting, in a word, is figural and agnitive: M fulfils J, through Abraham's recognition between Mamre and Sodom.

The day will come, he goes on, when the full reality of God will be universally recognized: this will be the advent of his kingdom. For the moment, there is only Abraham's 'secret' knowledge, a promise, and—here M glances at the conclusion of the present work—'a time of waiting', and the pain of waiting, 'that brought lines of suffering into the countenance of the God of today'. Between this and his fulfilment, however, the recognizing of God will go on apace, as in Genesis and the whole Bible (the Hebrew and then the Christian one). It is no chance that, at the end of the tetralogy, the Mamre episode again surfaces, and is interpreted by Jacob only a few pages before the recognition scene with Joseph. The ancient patriarch now decides to teach his people, sitting them down 'under the tree' (a 'giant tamarisk') and giving an out and out lecture to all the seventy who are to go down with him into Egypt (the promise to multiply has clearly found ways and means and casts allusive shadows of further rewriting: Abraham had

gone down with only his wife Sarah; it is in Egypt that
Jacob's seventy will become the Septuagint, the Greek translators of the Hebrew Bible), and his subject is the difference
between polytheism and monotheism, the 'difference
between the many-namedness of Baal and that of their
Father the highest and only'.

The God of Jacob subsumes all the separate qualities of
the other various gods, because everything flows from him.
His 'I' embraces every thing, 'the Being of all being [*das
Sein alles Seins*], *Elohim*, the many as one'. He is no longer,
then, simply *Du-* and *Da-Sein*, existence, and existence as
'other', but *summa* of being (*Sein*, not *Dasein*). Jacob is not,
here, on the point of converting to Aristotelianism or
Heideggerism. What interests him is *Elohim*, the name,
which, obviously, also 'means' the nature of God, and the
main question concerning that name: singular or plural? He
seems to decide in favour of singular, since the plural of *El*,
God, would be *Elim*. *Elohim* is 'an honorific expansion,
nothing else—as *Abraham* is of *Abram*. God is One, not
many.' Yet three men came to Abraham in the grove of
Mamre, as he sat at the door of his house in the heat of
the day. And these three men were, as Abraham 'soon saw,
God the Lord'. He had addressed them as 'Lord' and 'thou',
but also 'now and then "Lords" and "you"'. And when they
had eaten they told him, 'I will come to you in a year'. 'That
was God', Jacob comments. 'He was One, but He was
explicitly threefold. He practised polytheism, but always
and on principle said "I", whereas Abraham had addressed
him by turns in the singular and the plural.'

In our end, then, is our beginning. The Jacob of M interprets J, as I attempted to do at the beginning of the present
chapter. He, of course, has the advantage of being inside the
story while not being the story, while I am most definitely
outside it. Hence the two basic differences between his
interpretation and mine. Jacob, in the first place, maintains
that Abraham immediately recognizes the three as the Lord,

and that 'his experience of God, like Abram's, had been threefold, and had comprised three men' in one. He speaks of a 'Father-God' (or of 'God the Father'), and of a Good Shepherd who feeds his flock, and of one whom he calls the 'Angel' who to the seventy seems to 'overshadow them as with the wings of doves'. These, according to him, comprise the Elohim, 'the threefold unity', shadow of the future Trinity, of the symbolic dove (Jacob will shortly rest beneath three palms born of a single root, will recognize his Son, and, like Peter, weep bitter tears).

Yet there is something which links me with the Jacob of M. I maintained that to understand the mystery of the recognition of God between Mamre and Sodom, it is necessary to become as Abraham; Jacob interprets it through his own experience, which, he insists, is not unlike that of Abraham. Both of us set out to solve the enigma: both of us reach the conclusion that to do so we must take as departure point our being as humans. Like Abraham, Jacob, too, wants to recognize God by thinking him.

The reader of *Joseph and His Brothers* has, however, one advantage over Jacob: outside the story, she or he is able to see that the recognition is, for M, also a metaphysics, a psychology, and an aesthetics. Like Joseph, but more so, the reader, we saw above, recognizes the whole story. And in the first place he or she understands—because M never tires of repeating it—that every individual follows in the footsteps of another, and each one is the 'type' of a mythical character whose origins are lost in the origins of time. The Eliezer who explains to Joseph how Abraham discovered God abolishes time, and identifies, writes Mann in his essay on Freud, with 'all the Eliezers of the past [who] gather to shape the Eliezer of the present, so that he speaks in the first person of that Eliezer who was Abram's servant, though he was far from being the same man'. This is in fact the life of myth, and 'one may as well say "lived myth" as "lived life"'. Life which affirms itself by claiming the authority of a mere quotation: like Cleopatra's, the incarnation of Ishtar-Astarte and Aphrodite; or Caesar's, who took Alexander the Great as his prototype; or Jesus's, who, in crying out on the cross, 'Eli, Eli, lamma sabachthani' is repeating the opening of the twenty-second Psalm on the Messiah.

The tetralogy treats this subject with supremely light irony, and M's smile is an integral part of his 'voice' as narrator-God. At the same time the fundamental seriousness is never in doubt: retracing the past leads back ultimately to its 'infinity' where all origins are revealed as imaginary bases and non-definitive ends, and all discourse becomes 'mystery'. The mysterious nature of origin, M writes in *The Tales of Jacob*, attempting to explain how Esau can be both Esau and Edom the Red, lies in the fact that 'its essence is not the line, but the sphere'. It is the sphere which constitutes the mystery. It consists in 'correspondence and reintegration', in the two halves which come together in a whole; in the two hemispheres, celestial and terrestrial, which rotate and alternate. And so we find ourselves faced with the (almost mystical) metaphysics to which the re-enacting of myth inevitably returns. A twofold manifestation of mystery emerges—of *mutual recognition* and *mutual change*:

The sphere rolls—that lies in the nature of spheres. Bottom is soon top and top bottom, in so far as one can speak of top and bottom in such a connection. Not only do the heavenly and earthly recognize themselves in each other [*sich in einander wiedererkennen*], but, thanks to the revolution of the sphere, the heavenly can turn into the earthly, the earthly into the heavenly, from which it is clear that gods can become men and on the other hand men can become gods again.

Recognition thus becomes one of the two fundamental laws of the universe: of myth, of time, and of the relationship between the human and the divine. This recognition, readers will however have noticed, is now called not *Erkennen*, but *Wiedererkennen*: re-cognition, a word that mirrors a whole ontology and aesthetics. When, in *Joseph in Egypt*, M wondered whether he knew his story or not, his reply, as we saw above, lay in the mystery of Abraham's recognition of God. The same mystery, however, holds for the story, the characters, and not least the narrator himself. Shortly before, in the same chapter, M had stated:

I feel indeed as though I had once already reached this point in my story and told it once before; the special feeling of recognition [*des Wiedererkennens*], of having been here before and seen it all [*des Schongesehen*] and dreamed the same dream [*des Schongeträumt*], moves me and challenges me to dwell upon it—and such precisely were the feelings, such the experience of my hero.

The bond between Joseph and his father is also his bond with God, in that the event he now experiences is 'imitation' and 'repetition', such as Jacob had already experienced. In them, the personal and the voluntary mix with the element that 'leads us and guides us', so much so that it is no longer possible to distinguish who really is imitating and willing to imitate the past, whether the human being or destiny. In brief, if, previously, the recognition and mutual interchange was between the human and the divine, it is now between the 'inward' and the 'outward', between what lies inside, and what outside the individual. These 'play into each other' and are made concrete in the event which is unique (*eins*) and 'always' (*schon immer*). From the foggy mystery of 'origins' we have reached, then, the equally mysterious shores of history and story; in a word, of life: 'For we move in the footsteps of others, and all life is but the outpouring of the present into the forms of the myth.'

The *Wiedererkennen* is inseparable from this way of being, since it is the awareness of forming part of the process of imitation. The only recognition is a re-cognitive process. But this *déjà vu*, this *Schongeträumt*, this re-cognition, are the feelings of the narrator, too; he has already 'told it once before', he tells us. And it is here that the process of recognition joins life with narrative. In 'Freud and the Future' Mann writes that if older schools of biography seek self-endorsement and verisimilitude through the fact of narrating 'as it always was' and 'as it has been written', it is precisely because 'man sets store by recognition [*dem Menschen ist am Wiedererkennen gelegen*]'. In the new, we seek the old; in the individual, the type. It is from that recognition that man draws 'a sense of the familiar in life'. Mann, clearly here in sympathy with the Freud who, in *Jokes and their Relation to the Unconscious*, posits the 'joy of recognition' (*Freude am Wiedererkennen*) as one of the central impulses of the human being, would seem to share this comfort, and does everything in his power—and how could he not, given the nature of rewriting?—to involve us in the same emotion. For, if M is the rewriter, we are rereaders. We too, then, are the addressees of the answer given by Aristotle (or one of his close followers) to the question, in the *Problems*, as to why we enjoy familiar music so much more than a new piece: 'because in the one instance we simply acquire knowledge; in the other we use it in a form of *recognition* [*anagnorizein*].' And with this, we shall have recognized, if not God, at least man.

CHAPTER TWO

Susanna in Excelsis

the basses of their beings throb in witching chords

THE story of Susanna and the elders is in every sense the most 'suggestive' in the Bible. A short story, taking up just one chapter in the Book of Daniel, it is extant not in Hebrew but in two different Greek versions, that of the Septuagint and that of Theodotion, and thus apocryphal. Right up until the Reformation, however, Christians considered it inspired, despite the polemics as to its authenticity among the Fathers themselves, and despite its shifting collocation: at the beginning of Daniel in the Greek Bible, and as an appendix in Jerome's Latin text.

Susanna, it will be remembered (the Hebrew *shoshanah* means 'lily', and the whole episode could be read as a *midrash* on the verses in the Song of Songs, 'I am the tulip of the Sharon, the lily of the valleys. Like the lily among thorns, so is my love among the daughters') is the beautiful young wife of Joakim, a rich Babylonian Jew. Adjoining his house is a wondrous garden where Susanna walks daily. Here she is observed by two elders, elected judges of the people, who fall passionately in love with her. This goes on for some time, each carefully keeping his shameful passion from the other, until one day they pretend to go their separate ways, only to end up shortly afterwards back at their bower of bliss. They confess to each other their lustful thoughts, and work out a plan of action. At this point Susanna enters the garden accompanied only by her two handmaids, whom she orders to prepare oils and perfumes for her bath. (In neither version, be it noted, does Susanna actually manage to have her bath: all the pictorial representations of the scene are therefore the pure projection of painterly voyeurism.) The moment the maids' backs are turned, the two old men declare their burning passion, and proceed to prove it by blackmail: lie with us, or we will swear you dismissed the maids because you had some lusty youth with you. Susanna cries out in desperation, knowing the alternatives are death in the eyes of the Lord or at the hands of human justice. The two men add their voices, informing the maids that their mistress is an adulteress.

The following day, the people are called together at Joakim's house, and the two elders force Susanna publicly to remove her veil ('that they might feast upon her beauty': a voyeur's rape, vile and violent) and accuse her of adultery. The people inevitably believe the elders, but as Susanna is led away to be stoned, protesting her innocence to God, the latter moves a young man present, Daniel, to cry out, 'I am innocent of the blood of this woman!'. Questioned by other Israelites, Daniel urges them to re-examine the case and ascertain the truth, as he is convinced the men are lying. Sitting in judgment, he questions the two separately, asking them under which tree exactly they had seen Susanna and the youth together. Each producing a different tree, and thereby proving their perjury, they are condemned by Mosaic law to the same sentence they had passed on Susanna.

The episode is a powerful one, symmetrical and sophis- ticated: strong in its extremes of passion, eros, and the fear of God; refined in its particulars—the garden, bathing prepara- tions, the trap, and visual rape, and geometrical in the plot and its *dénouement*: false and real proofs, human and divine justice, and the two death sentences. It must be one of the first examples of a juridical erotico-detective story in which the guilty end up by being the judges themselves (and their own judges at that). It is hardly surprising that it has so seized the imagination, at least in the West, and—given its fable quality—from childhood onwards.

Let us return to childhood then, taking an oblique approach to Susanna's story on the trail of further stories it

might have spawned: further rewritings. When I was a child
the Catholic Mass was in Latin, and the *Sanctus* was
solemnly intoned as follows: 'Sanctus, Sanctus, Sanctus
Dominus Deus Sabaoth . . . Hosanna in excelsis' ('Holy,
holy, holy the Lord God of hosts . . . Hosanna in the highest'). At times—this was witnessed by the present writer in
Rome—out of ignorance of Latin and an attempt to make
some sort of sense out of the words, part of the congrega-
tion would chant 'Sanctus, Sanctus, Sanctus Dominus Deus
sabato [Saturday] . . . *Susanna* in excelsis'. The all-powerful
Lord God of Hosts was transformed into the peaceable God
of the Sabbath, the day which was generally considered even
then, long before the weekend of the leisure society, 'the
most welcome', as Leopardi puts it, 'of the seven'. And
Hosanna, the cry of prayer and welcome, greeting Christ
on his triumphal entrance into Jerusalem on Palm Sunday,
became a woman's name—sister, girlfriend, neighbour—
and at the same time the name of a saint, Susanna, virgin
and martyr, who has her own marvellous basilica in Rome.

The ways of literature and the imagination are almost as
infinite as those of the Lord. This transformation of *Hosanna
in excelsis* into *Susanna in excelsis* clearly meant something: in
the Scriptures, 'without him was not anything made that
was made', as John has it, and no mistake in translation or
interpretation is ever completely wrong. Everything can be
turned to good account. And the Hosanna–Susanna super-
imposers can claim illustrious precedents. In the *Man of
Law's Tale*, Chaucer has his heroine Constance (who at
one point finds herself in something like Susanna's position)
send up the following, significant prayer:

> Immortal God, that savedest Susanne
> Fro false blame, and thou, merciful mayde,
> Marie I meene, doghter to Seint Anne,
> Bifor whos child angeles synge Osanne,
> If I be guiltlees of this felonye,
> My sucour be, for ellis shal I dye!

Some seven centuries later we find Wallace Stevens exploit-
ing the same rhyme and Bible story to denote, in 'Peter
Quince at the Clavier', the synaesthesia of his desire-cum-
music-cum-lasting beauty of the flesh:

> Music is feeling, then, not sound;
> And thus it is that what I feel,
> Here in this room, desiring you,
>
> Thinking of your blue-shadowed silk,
> Is music. It is like the strain
> Waked in the elders by Susanna.
>
> Of a green evening, clear and warm,
> She bathed in her still garden, while
> The red-eyed elders watching, felt
>
> The basses of their beings throb
> In witching chords, and their thin blood
> Pulse pizzicati of Hosanna.

Susanna in excelsis indeed, in that the rewriting here is the
account of the progressive elevation of Susanna in the city of
Rome, as prefigured by the felicitous mutation of *hosanna*
into *Susanna*. Whenever and wherever the Susanna story
originates, one thing is certain—that by the beginning of
the third century of our era it reached the capital of the
empire and acquired considerable popularity there among
Christians. This, as far as we know, is the first time the tale
of Susanna became a subject of Western art—painting and
sculpture—and an important topic of theological, exegetical, and political debate. It is this meeting-point between
myth, representation, and history, between interpretation,
liturgy, and art—its meanings, and the various ways this
comes about—which now becomes our act of rewriting.

Appropriately enough, this story of a *gradus ad excelsa*
begins underground. It is here, in those endless mazes of
tunnels later known as catacombs, and excavated by
Christians in the tufa—the soft yellowish-brownish clay
which makes up the soil of Rome—that Susanna enters

the Western *imaginaire*. The début is quite impressive, since paintings of the third and fourth centuries portraying her figure and her story are still extant in all the catacombs which, outside the walls and along the main roads, surround the city from north-east to south as in a series of extensive webs.

The oldest surviving instance, from the second half of the third century, is the left-hand side of the *arcosolium* vault in the St Eusebius crypt at the catacombs of Callistus on the Appian Way, the Roman catacombs *par excellence*. In this scene, which earlier interpreters read—significantly, as we shall see—as the 'judgement of a martyr', we have only one episode of the Susanna story. An adolescent standing on a stool is addressing three figures, two men and a woman. The latter wears a long tunic which will become *de rigueur* in these representations, and has been identified as Susanna. The former is young Daniel. One of the two elders seems to be leaving, a somewhat chastened look on his face; the other is receiving his sentence on the spot. Clearly, what is essential here is the moral message of the story: virtue rewarded, vice punished, human justice exposed, divine Justice firmly established.

The second surviving instance of the Susanna story in Rome, from about a century later, is much more articulate, and is a piece of actual *narrative* found in the so-called Greek Chapel, in the catacombs of Priscilla on the Via Salaria. Here, the two walls of the nave are decorated with four episodes of the Susanna story. On the right-hand side, two separate moments: the seduction attempt, and Daniel getting ready to defend Susanna from the accusation. Susanna stands at the centre, taller than any other figure, wearing a long sleeveless tunic and, over it, a mantle which forms a hood on her head. Her arms are stretched out and up to eye level as if in prayer. To her left, Daniel lifts the hem of his cloak with his left hand, keeping the right underneath it. The two elders enter from the other side, side by side, illustrating verses 19–20 in Theodotion: 'When the maids had gone out, the two elders rose and ran to her, and said: "Look, the garden doors are shut, no one sees us, and we are in love with you; so give your consent, and lie with us".' In the fresco, each keeps his right hand stretched out before him, rushing towards Susanna, each seemingly trying to outrun the other. One is marginally ahead and turns to his companion. The latter has his eyes fixed on the woman.

The story continues on the opposite wall with two more episodes. The first illustrates verses 34–5 of Theodotion: 'Then the two elders stood up in the midst of the people, and laid their hands upon her head. And she, weeping, looked up towards heaven, for her heart trusted in the Lord.' In the fresco, they stand to the left and right of Susanna, laying one hand each on her hooded head while with the other each seizes one of her arms. Separated from this group by a small tree, a man and a woman, the latter veiled, are praying with their arms stretched out as if to thank God for delivering Susanna from the false accusation. Although, following Theodotion 63, these could represent Hilkiah and his wife (Susanna's father and mother), or even Joakim and Susanna, they are almost certainly Daniel and Susanna.

Clearly, what interests the painter here is to organize the narrative not in chronological sequence, but by pairing and contrasting different moments. On each wall we have an early and a late stage of the story, and on each wall the main opposition is between a static and a dynamic scene. In the latter, movement conveys passion and violence; in the former, stillness indicates dignity and conformity to God's will. Ultimately, the opposition is summed up in the contrasting movements of the characters' arms: those of Susanna and Daniel are always stretched and lifted in the typical position of prayer, those of the elders seek to touch the woman and consecrate dominion on her by laying hands on her head. By grabbing and pinning down Susanna's arms, the two elders effectively bind her and break her prayer posture. This, however, is triumphantly resumed in the same picture, at the chronological end of the story. If I were to express the basic contrast of the two frescoes in one sentence, I would say that they represent the struggle of coercion against prayer.

Archaeologists and iconologists have identified at least four more Susanna paintings (all from the fourth century) in the Roman catacombs. Each represents only one scene of the story, thus neglecting the diachronic or narrative dimension which is so prominent in the catacombs of Priscilla and returning to the monothematic formulation we have seen in Callistus. I choose one for purposes that will become clear presently. This appears on the front wall of the Celerina *arcosolium* in the catacombs of Praetextatus, also just off the Appian Way. Here, mimesis itself (let alone narrative) has disappeared, to be replaced by symbolism. A lamb occupies the centre of the picture, surrounded on either side by a wolf. Above the wolf on the right-hand side, the word SENIORIS makes clear that this is one of the two elders, whilst the name, SVSANNA, is visible above the lamb. 'Violence and lust lay a trap for innocent purity' is clearly the primary message of the fresco—a simple, straightforward moral reading of the Susanna story.

For any Christian, however, the lamb is also, very directly, the figure of Christ, the paschal victim, and (Revelation 21: 9–10) the bridegroom of the heavenly Jerusalem, i.e. of the Church. In a more historico-political perspective, the wolves could then stand (Matthew 7: 15) for the false prophets against whom Jesus warns his disciples (the heretics threatening the integrity of the Church), or, following the traditional interpretation of Matthew 10: 15 and Luke 10: 3—'I send you forth as lambs among wolves'—the Jews and pagans let loose against the faithful. In other words, the Susanna story has left the realm of narrative to enter that of morality and interpretation. In less than two hundred years it has become a sign, suspended as it were between symbolism and allegory.

I shall soon return to this important metamorphosis. But

in order to understand it we must, I think, ask a preliminary question. Why are paintings of Susanna so frequent in the catacombs? Catacombs are burial grounds, and pictorial decoration, though not uncommon, is not exactly extensive in early Christian graveyards. It is normally to be found only in the chapels where the faithful would assemble to commemorate the departed and the martyrs, or around the most important tombs. The paintings are relatively limited in subject: apart from the symbolic peacock, dove, fish, and anchor, Old Testament scenes (which in the period before Constantine outnumber those from the New Testament) portray Adam and Eve, Noah's ark, the sacrifice of Isaac, Moses striking water from the rock, Jonah and the whale, the three young men in the burning furnace, and Daniel in the lions' den. Why, then, Susanna and the elders? Early Christians seem to be uninterested in the legal aspects that might fascinate readers of the Septuagint, or in the sexual prurience the story possesses for Renaissance observers, or in the juridico-detective plot that so appeals to us in the late twentieth century. Why do they find the story so relevant to their concerns as to have it painted and sculpted again and again on their sarcophagi—four times at least in Rome alone?

The answer concerns the idea of salvation or survival, personal on the one hand, political on the other. Susanna has to do with death, the single crucial event of human life—with death and resurrection. She is indeed condemned to death by the people, and cries out in a loud voice, in Theodotion's version (42), 'kai idou apothnesko': literally, 'and behold, I die'. She is, however, rescued from death by Daniel, or rather by God, 'who saves those who hope in him' (Theodotion 60), through Daniel. The Saviour vanquishes death, and Susanna is risen. In fact, Susanna's association with death is neither merely verbal nor purely metaphorical, but also liturgical. In the *Ordo commendationis animae quando infirmus est in extremis*—the Prayer ordained for the sick on the point of death which apparently goes

back to the period between the third and fourth centuries—
the example of Susanna was presented to the dying faithful
as one of the reasons for their trust in God's mercy. After a
long litany beginning with the iterated acclamation, 'Kyrie
eleison, Christe eleison' ('Lord, have mercy; Christ, have
mercy'), the celebrant would recite: 'Suscipe, Domine, ser-
vum tuum in locum sperandae sibi salvationis a misericordia
tua' ('Lord, receive your servant there where he hopes to
receive salvation through your mercy'). Then, within a list
which includes Enoch and Elijah, Noah, Abraham, Job,
Isaac, Lot, Moses, Daniel ('Lord, free his/her soul as you
freed Daniel from the lions' den'), David, the three Jews in
the fiery furnace, Peter and Paul, and the virgin Thecla, the
celebrant would say: 'Libera, Domine, animam ejus, sicut
liberasti Susannam de falso crimine' ('Lord, free his/her soul
as you freed Susanna from her false crime'). Thus Susanna
(like Daniel freed from the lions' den) typologically signifies
the soul of every Christian. By evoking her at the hour of
death, Christians voice their trust in the survival and salvation of the soul. One could hardly imagine a stronger reason
for the Christians' attachment to the story; and it immediately becomes clear why our heroine is so often portrayed in
those places where the bodies of the faithful rest and rot
awaiting resurrection: catacombs and sarcophagi.

Yet the destiny of Susanna is not just that of meeting and
overcoming individual death—a high enough elevation 'to
the highest'. By coming to Rome between the second and
third centuries she enters history and becomes the paradigm
of *Christianity*'s survival as an organized body of individuals,
in short as an *ecclesia*, a Church. It could, indeed, be said that
the fifty years which comprise the last two decades of the
second and the first three of the third century constitute to
all effects an 'age of Susanna'.

 Perhaps the best way of proving this assertion is to look at
the work of Hippolytus and the context in which it develops. Hippolytus was an important personality among the

SUSANNA IN EXCELSIS   67

Roman presbyters during the first decades of the third century: when Origen came to Rome around 212 he attended one of his sermons. Hippolytus refused to accept the teaching of the Bishop of Rome, Zephyrinus (198–217), and under his successor, Callistus (217–22), whom he rejected as a heretic, he seems to have set himself up as an 'anti-Pope'. However, he must have enjoyed a high reputation in the city, for a statue of him with a list of his writings was erected in a public place probably during his own lifetime. His works, all in Greek, include a *Philosophoumena* or *Refutation of all Heresies*, treatises on the nature of the universe against Noetus and Plato, on the *Apostolic Tradition*, on God and the resurrection of the flesh (addressed to Julia Mamaea, mother of the emperor Alexander Severus), a *Commentary on the Song of Songs*, and finally a *Commentary on Daniel*.

In this latter work Hippolytus takes a decisive political stance. Up until then, the Books of Revelation and of Daniel had been combined in exegetical interpretation. For instance, Irenaeus of Lyons, whose disciple Hippolytus is sometimes supposed to have been, had maintained that the last of the four beasts of Daniel was the image of the Roman Empire, which would be divided amongst ten kings. Its 'little horn' prefigured the Antichrist, which was also foreshadowed by the 'beast out of the sea' of Revelation. Yet Irenaeus, who lived in the period of the 'great waiting' for the end of time attested by the Muratorian Canon (which, significantly, aligns the oldest canon of the New Testament and the *finis temporum* of the present, which succeeds the age of the prophets and the apostles), still believed that the practical attitude Christians should have towards the Roman Empire ought to be that dictated by the Pauline *logion*, 'non est potestas nisi a Deo' ('the powers that be are ordained by God').

Hippolytus, on the other hand, goes much further. In Discourse IV, chapter ix of his *Commentary on Daniel* he writes that the Roman Empire 'kratei kat'energeian tou satana' ('rules through, or according to the power of Satan'). It is, he says, a counterfeit of Christianity because, unlike the Babylonian, Persian, and Greek empires, it represents not one nation but a sum of nations united for the sake of war. Hence, it is inevitably destined to die. Since the world was made to last six thousand years and Christ was born five thousand five hundred years after the Creation, Rome will die in the year 500 AD, its empire divided 'according to nations' by ten kings, then reunited by the Antichrist, and finally destroyed by the divine *parousia* in the Second Coming.

It is in the context of this prophecy—a singularly accurate one as to the date and manner of Rome's fall—that Hippolytus looks at past and present circumstances. When he comes to comment on the Susanna story (I. xii), he rearranges, first of all, the genealogy of Jesus constructed by Matthew (1: 1) so as to make the issue of Levi and that of Judah come together in Susanna and in Christ. He thus rather fancifully rewrites the past as follows: Susanna was the daughter of Hilkiah, the priest who found the book of the Law in the house of the Lord when King Josiah ordered the Holy of Holies to be purified (2 Kings 22: 10; 2 Chronicles 34: 14). She was the sister of the prophet Jeremiah (whose father's name was Hilkiah). Her husband Joakim (rather than Matthew's Jechonias) was one of King Josiah's five sons, and thus priesthood, prophecy, and monarchy are joined by the marriage of Joakim and Susanna; of them Jechonias was born, and from him Matthew's line of descent can start all over again and culminate in Jesus.

What interests Hippolytus here is not just the correcting of Matthew's notoriously problematic genealogy. He is aiming—indirectly perhaps—at a figural parallel between Susanna and Jesus, who share the same 'messianic' ancestry. This is confirmed later on, when Hippolytus draws the parallel between Daniel's words, 'I am innocent of the blood of this woman' (Thedotion 46), and those of Pilate in Matthew's Gospel (27: 24), 'I am innocent of the blood of this just person'. Susanna is indeed being elevated to the highest.

But concern for the past is never Hippolytus' main pre-occupation: for him, as for all Christian authors from the time of the evangelists, the past is instrumental—a means of speaking about the present. And the present is the cultural and political reality of Christianity. For example, Hippolytus prefaces his discussion of the Susanna story with two brief allusions to the question of its canonicity. He asks himself 'how people in captivity and servants to the Babylonians could meet in one place as free persons', and answers that, after deporting them, Nebuchadnezzar treated them humanely, allowing them to meet so that they could do whatever the Law demanded. He then adds that 'the chiefs of the Jews want to take this story out of Scripture, claiming that nothing of the sort ever took place in Babylon, because they are ashamed of what the elders did at that time'. 'They do not recognize in it', he concludes, 'the divine plan [oikonomia] of the Father.'

Question, answer, and explanation repeat (or anticipate) the argument between Julius Africanus and Origen as to the canonicity of the Susanna episode. Origen firmly believed that Susanna was a true part of the Book of Daniel, since it was contained in both the Septuagint and Theodotion. Moreover, the story showed the Jewish elders in a less than fortunate light, so that the Synagogue had obvious reasons for suppressing it. Origen's view, however, was challenged in a letter by Julius Africanus—a Palestinian who became chief librarian of the Roman emperor Alexander Severus. He maintained that the famous verbal pun in verses 54 ff. is possible only in Greek. When Daniel questions the elders separately, the first answers, 'Under a lentisk tree' (skhinon); the second 'under an ilex' (prinon); to the first Daniel replies, 'the angel of the Lord will cut [skhisei] you in two', and to the second, 'the angel of the Lord awaits you with his sword to saw [prisai] you in two'. It therefore follows, according to Julius Africanus, that the story of Susanna is an addition to the original Book of Daniel. Origen replied that the pun could have been introduced by the translators, but that did not prove that there was no Hebrew original.

Origen, Julius Africanus, Hippolytus: it is in Rome that Susanna becomes a hot cultural issue. The court of the Roman emperor works as a great catalyst. Alexander Severus' mother, Julia Mamaea, is pro-Christian, and summons Origen to Antioch for a discussion. Hippolytus' treatise on the resurrection of the flesh is dedicated to her. The emperor himself keeps statues of Apollonius of Tyana, Orpheus, Abraham, and Christ in his *lararium* or private chapel.

Hippolytus' *Commentary*, however, is there to testify that questions of philology and canon are never neutral, but always have a highly political significance. The chiefs of Israel, he writes, do not recognize in the Susanna story the *oikonomia* of the Father. For him, this 'economy' is neither literary nor merely moral. It is historical. 'Susanna', he continues, 'had to suffer from the elders what one still has to suffer from the princes of Babylon. She was the figure of the Church, her husband Joakim that of Christ. The garden adjoining his house figured the society of saints, planted like fruitful trees amidst the Church. Babylon is the world. The two elders represent the two peoples who conspire against the Church, that of the circumcised and that of the Gentiles.'

We thus return to the symbolic fresco in the catacombs of Praetextatus. In Hippolytus' *Commentary*, the allegory has both the swell of the great waves of history and the dramatic urgency of the present political situation. Susanna, he maintains, is a prefiguration in the sense Paul gives to the word (1 Corinthians 10: 11): 'Now all these things happened to them in figure: and they are written for our correction, upon whom the ends of the world are come.' Joakim's garden—that garden where Susanna bathes, representing the baptism of the Church, administered on Easter Sunday by the two maids, Faith and Charity, and accompanied by

the oil of the Spirit and the cosmetics, i.e. the commandments of the Word—is the earthly correlative of the Garden
of Eden. And this, in turn, is the figure or 'model' of the
true garden, the Church. The Church is 'the spiritual garden of God planted on Christ as if eastward, where one sees
all kinds of trees: the issue of the patriarchs who died in the
beginning, the works of the prophets accomplished after
the Law, the chorus of the Apostles who had their wisdom
from the Word, the chorus of the Martyrs saved by the
blood of Christ, the procession of the Virgins sanctified by
water, the chorus of the Doctors, the order of Bishops,
Priests and Levites'. In this grand vision, the *Ecclesia* is built
up in successive historical stages, in a liturgical procession,
a sequence, a litany, as if it were in a truly Roman concretion of different epochs and different orders. *This* is the
'economy' of the Father; *this* is Susanna. In purity, she is
the female equivalent of Jacob's son, Joseph. She stands at
the beginning of human time, prefigured by Eve, and at the
centre of time, as the 'spouse of Christ'.

But the enemy lies in wait for her *now*, as Hippolytus
writes in his *Commentary*. For him as for the painter of the
Susanna allegory in the catacombs of Praetextatus, the 'lying
seducers' are those who 'pervert by means of their heretical
teachings'. Alternatively, they represent external adversaries.
Daniel, Hippolytus writes, speaks to one of the elders as to a
man 'learned in the Law'; he calls the other 'offspring of
Canaan and not of Judah'. What he obviously means,
Hippolytus states confidently, is that the former stands for
the Jews and the latter for the pagans (but story and interpretation strike back: for Luther and the Protestant play-
wrights the youthful Susanna will become the new
reformed movement, and the old hypocrites the aged,
unbending Catholic Church!). 'The two people, prompted
by Satan who acts in them, never cease to meditate persecutions and tribulations against the Church', often misunder-
standing each other. But 'when they agree', then their
attack against the Church is subtle and sudden:

They spy for the opportune day and, penetrating as intruders into the house of the Lord, when all pray and sing hymns to God, they seize a few people and drag them outside and do violence to them, saying: 'Come on, have commerce with us and honour the gods. Otherwise, *we will testify against you.*' And as these do not consent, they bring them before the tribunal and accuse them of acting against Caesar's decree and have them condemned to death.

This has all the urgency of a contemporary scene. It 'happens today', Hippolytus writes. 'When the saints are arrested and dragged to court, the crowd assembles to see what is going on.' Their enemies start shouting: 'Dispatch them from the earth, people of this kind. They must not live.' 'Christianos ad leonem!', Christians to the lions, as Tertullian, an older contemporary of Hippolytus, reports. In 202 Septimius Severus had promulgated his edict against Jews and Christians. It was not always enforced, and in 212 Tertullian calls Septimius Severus 'Christianorum memor', friend to Christians, and says that his successor, Caracalla, was brought up 'lacte Christiano', on Christian milk. But it was always possible to accuse someone of being a Christian and denounce him or her to the authorities. If the judge was a traditionalist, a pagan, the Christian would be convicted on the basis of the edict and condemned.

Something similar had in fact happened before Septimius Severus' reign, to Callistus, whose story we have from his great opponent, Hippolytus himself. Callistus was a slave and a Christian. His master, Carpophorus, was a Christian freedman of Commodus' imperial household. Carpophorus appointed his slave head of his own private bank, a bank which made good profits by getting money from Christians and lending it to non-Christians at high interest rates. At some point, however, Callistus and his bank went bankrupt, probably because a number of Jews failed to refund a huge loan they had received. Carpophorus threw his manager into the *pistrinum*, the living hell where slaves were forced to turn the millstone. Freed from it shortly afterwards,

Callistus disturbed a Jewish religious ceremony on a Saturday. The Jews beat him up and accused him of being a
Christian before the tribunal of the city prefect. Although
the powerful Carpophorus denied it, Callistus confessed he
was indeed a Christian. The prefect, a 'schoolfellow' of the
emperor Marcus Aurelius, was a strict pagan. He condemned Callistus to the Sardinian mines. The two elders
had indeed conspired against Susanna.

The story's sequel is also fascinating. Marcia, the emperor
Commodus' concubine, was *theophiles*, God-fearing. She
succeeded in getting Callistus out of the Sardinian mines.
He returned to Rome, where the bishop, Victor, gave him a
monthly cheque and sent him to Anzio. Victor's successor,
Zephyrinus, called him back to the City and appointed him
'curator' of Rome's most famous Christian graveyard, which
was eventually named after him: the catacombs of Callistus
on the Appian Way. When Zephyrinus died, Callistus was,
to Hippolytus' great dismay, elected 'Pope'.

The oldest surviving pictorial representation of Susanna
and the elders, it will be remembered, appears in the crypt
of St Eusebius at the catacombs of Callistus. This, then, is
how a story becomes history and how history turns into
painting. In this double metamorphosis, exegesis works both
outside and inside. On the one hand, it acts as a *reagent*, a
substance employed in chemistry as a test to determine the
presence of some other substance by means of the reaction
which is produced: it allows us to observe the change from
our external point of view, prompting our own interpretation of the phenomenon—of words, pictures, and events.
On the other, as an *agent*, exegesis precipitates the transformation itself. It operates on events, shaping them into words
and pictures.

But this is not all it does. It also changes words and
pictures into new events, it makes stories happen. The
Roman Church has always possessed an extraordinary abil-
ity in this respect. When the elders force Susanna to decide
whether to lie with them or live with the accusation of

adultery, she sighs: 'I am hemmed in on every side. For if I
do this thing, it is death for me; and if I do not, I shall not
escape your hands.' Hippolytus interprets these words as
expressing the anguish of the Christian martyr. 'Those',
he writes, 'who are arrested because of Christ's name, if
they do what men command to them, die to God and live
for the world; if they do not do it, they cannot escape the
hands of the judges, but are condemned by them and die.'

It did not take long for the Roman Church to transform
this piece of exegesis into a story, a canon: history. Diocletian
became emperor in 284, fifty years after Alexander Severus'
death. He reigned until 305, having divided the empire into
East and West, with an Augustus and a Caesar to rule each
section, and having started in 303 the last great wave of
persecutions against the Church before Constantine made
the empire itself Christian in 313.

The Bishop of Rome between 283 and 296 was Caius.
His brother Gabinius, a presbyter, had a daughter renowned
both for her beauty and for her learning in 'sacred letters'.
Her name was . . . Susanna. Diocletian decided she should
become the wife of his partner in the empire, the Augustus
Maximian. He consequently sent Claudius to ask for her.
Susanna, 'fortified by the Holy Ghost', refused, declaring
before her father that she wanted to preserve her chastity.
Claudius, struck by her strength and instructed by Caius and
Gabinius, became a Christian with all his family. One
month and sixteen days later, Diocletian charged one of
his retainers, Maximus, to enquire what had become of
Claudius and Susanna. Maximus found Claudius 'praying
in a hairshirt'. Awed by what he had seen, and subsequently
instructed by Caius and Gabinius, Maximus, too, was
christened. Two weeks later, Diocletian learnt of these
events. He sent another man, Julius, to punish Claudius
and Maximus and imprison Susanna. The outcome is not
known, but fifty-five days later Diocletian ordered Susanna
to be brought to his wife Serena, 'who was secretly a
Christian'. The two women began to pray and sing Psalms.

When this was reported to Diocletian, he decided that Susanna should be led back to her father's house either—the sources are not clear on this point—by his son Maximin or his partner Maximian. The former was in any case instructed to rape Susanna. But Maximin found her praying, an extraordinary light shining upon her, and returned to the emperor. Diocletian then dispatched a fourth man, Macedonius, to force Susanna to sacrifice to the gods. She resisted. Macedonius stripped her naked and whipped her, while she repeated the words, 'Gloria tibi, Domine', until she was killed by his sword. Her body was collected by the empress Serena and buried near the Baths of Diocletian.

So goes the version printed in the *Acta Sanctorum* together with the critical emendations supplied by Cesare Baronius in his late sixteenth-century *Annales Ecclesiastici*. It seems obvious that, whether or not there actually was a Roman martyr named Susanna, her story was invented (in all likelihood, quite some time after the events it purported to relate), to create a Christian and Roman parallel to the old Susanna. The sexual innuendoes in the legend are clear enough, as is the multiple spying on the virgin. Nor would I be surprised if a functionalistically inclined critic were to maintain that in the Christian version Diocletian and Macedonius played a role somewhat akin to that of the two elders. Whatever the case, this is the way Susanna enters the Roman canon of saints—the manner, that is, in which she is 'translated' to the highest.

The Catholic Church, possibly because it opted for Rome as its headquarters, has always been rather thorough in its practices. In the Tridentine Mass for the Saturday after the third Quadragesima Sunday, in Lent, the first reading is the Susanna story from the Book of Daniel, the Gospel— with impeccable figural cogency—John's account of the woman taken in adultery. The station church, i.e. the church where the Pope would celebrate Mass on this particular day, is the church of St Susanna near the Baths of Diocletian. Thus, as if this really were the 'economy of the

Father', the story—a double one by now—returns to liturgy, and Susanna once more embodies the *Ecclesia*, a physical church of stone and marble.

The church was built as a basilica in the fourth century, rebuilt in 687, transformed in the ninth century (when Leo III apparently called a public Council there in Charlemagne's presence), restructured in the fifteenth century under Sixtus IV, and virtually rebuilt from 1595 to 1603 by Cardinal Girolamo Rusticucci in the context of Sixtus V's great new urban plan for that area of Rome—a true example of Roman historical and artistic concretion. The architects called to work on it were Domenico Fontana and Carlo Maderno. Maderno, who a few years later was to design the present façade of St Peter's, built for St Susanna's what art historians consider as the prototype of all baroque façades.

The programme for the interior decoration was almost certainly inspired by Cardinal Cesare Baronius. It began with the presbytery and the apse, where Cesare Nebbia and Tommaso Laureti painted the altarpiece, the spherical vault of the apse, and the side walls with scenes from the story of St Susanna. The opposite wall and counterfaçade were decorated by the Bolognese painter Baldassarre Croce with six great frescoes. The theme: Susanna and the elders.

Thus the stories of the two Susannas are definitively joined. Moving in history through the sediments of imagination, canonization, and liturgy, the double myth becomes architecture and painting. From the catacombs to a baroque basilica: the rewriting is completed, the ascent to the highest achieved. The apse of this church on the Quirinal hill in Rome shows us St Susanna 'in gloria'. 1603: *Susanna in excelsis*.

CHAPTER THREE

In the Begining Was a Cock
Animal Farms and the Plain Sense of Things

For al so siker as In Principio,
Mulier est hominis confusio.

ANIMAL farms, *pace* Orwell, are very ancient literary inventions. There may be none in the Hebrew Bible, which postulates man's likeness to God, but they abound in Greek and Latin literature, where the names of Aesop, Babrius, and Phaedrus, the greatest writers of animal fables, are enough to conjure up a whole world of lions, wolves, foxes, lambs, cocks, and asses.

Animal fables of the old kind rely on two basic assumptions. The first is the fundamental similarity and difference between human beings and animals summed up in the classic Aristotelian and Thomist definition of man: *homo est animal rationale*. The second is the belief that, however fictitious they may be, animal fables somehow represent truth. In his *Progymnasmata*, the second-century AD Alexandrian rhetor Theon states that a fable is a *logos pseudes eikonizon aletheian*, a false discourse, or story, giving semblance of the truth.

It seems obvious to me that the key words in these two assumptions are *est*—'is'—in the first, and *eikonizon*—giving semblance—in the second. How are we to take the precise meaning of 'man is a rational animal'? And what exactly do we understand by 'giving semblance'? How, in other words, are we to read the epistemological status and the plain sense of animal farms?

The question is further complicated in the modern kind of animal fable, because what have been called 'Darwin's Plots' alter the two basic assumptions of antiquity and replace them with a much stronger continuity between animals and men. If, post-Darwin, you inform your neighbour, in streetwise American, that he is a monkey son of a bitch, he should, before calling you a 'filthy pig' (or worse) and accompanying it with a suitable physical gesture, reflect patiently and seriously that your utterance may be theoretically true, there being by nature no guarantee as to the sexual mores of his animal Ur-mother, the evolutionary likelihood of it being that she was indeed an 'animal' of easy virtue who has gone forth and multiplied with the help of a good dose of promiscuity. Furthermore, if in reading stories of this kind one were to take into account Konrad Lorenz's ethology, the perspective would once more be turned upside down, for in Lorenz's work animals seem to be more admirable, normal, and fortunate creatures than the human species.

Modern (i.e. pre-Lorenzian) animal fables are thus based on the reversal of the old assumption: *animal est homo rationalis*, one would now, with Kafka's and Orwell's blessings, say—an animal is a rational human being. But even here, the problem is one of language and interpretation: what exactly is Gregor Samsa, the protagonist of Kafka's *Metamorphosis*? Of what truth is he the 'semblance'?

Hence, my concern in this chapter will be with the problems of interpretation, particularly those arising from the conflict between the literal sense on the one hand and the moral, allegorical, and anagogical on the other. These problems surface not only when we look at a specific text; they also, as we have just seen, possess a theoretical and historical dimension. Reading has always produced exegesis, and once it goes beyond the philological stage, exegesis cannot rest satisfied with the mere letter. At its extreme, literal interpretation runs the risk of restating the facts, the events recounted by a narrative text, or that of repeating a text word for word, as Borges's Pierre Menard does when he rewrites *Don Quixote*. How, for instance, can there be a purely literal reading of Orwell's *Animal Farm*? Or of the

Scriptures, of which it has been stated both that 'no verse shall ever lose its plain sense' (*peshat* in Hebrew) and that it is highly polyvalent, and that when two contradictory conclusions derive from one phrase, both are to be considered 'the word of the living God'?

To this theoretical problem I shall attempt to give an empirical answer by examining the several layers of a work of literature. The problem of literal interpretation is also historical, however, in the more specific sense that so many people have pondered it, and variously approached it, throughout the ages. Let me, then, provide some historical depth by taking other texts, from both theory and literature, from the medieval and the modern period. Here, too, we shall be dealing obliquely with the theme of rewriting the Scriptures—the regenerating of Genesis in particular—with the questions which require us to interpret this rescripting, and the equivalence between Bible and fable it seems to involve.

All these are issues which will emerge as we go on, and more forcefully in the second part of this chapter. But to begin with, we need a story. And, as the questions we shall ultimately have to face are serious ones, I shall choose the story of a cock. Readers will probably be familiar with it: it comes in Fragment VII of Chaucer's *Canterbury Tales*, as the *Nun's Priest's Tale*. If I now recount the tale, this in no way means I do not trust my readers as readers, and particularly as readers of Chaucer, but simply that I am aware of the fact that interpretation begins precisely with the way a story is told.

On a farm owned by a poor widow there lives a cock called Chauntecleer, whose voice, we are reliably informed, is better than the church's organ and whose crowing is more precise than a clock or 'an abbey orlogge' because by nature he knows 'ech ascencioun | Of the equynoxial in thilke toun' to the point that, when fifteen degrees have 'ascended', he unfailingly crows. Chauntecleer has a harem of seven hens at his disposal, but his favourite is 'damoysele Pertelote', with whom he sings in perfect, 'sweete accord', the popular tune, 'My love has departed to the country'. One morning our cock wakes up flustered and distressed by a nightmare he has just had in which he was about to be seized by some terrible beast. Pertelote accuses him of cowardice, advises him to follow the *sententia* in the *Distichs* of 'Cato', 'somnia ne cures' ('do not pay attention to dreams'), adds that his dream is clearly due to 'greete superfluytee of rede colera', and recommends taking a 'laxatyf' of various herbs which she herself will concoct. Chauntecleer counters his wife's quotation of Cato with a story of dreams and murder from either Cicero or Valerius Maximus (or perhaps from Robert Holcot's *Commentary on the Book of Wisdom*: the cock defines his source simply as 'oon of the gretteste auctour that men rede'). It is the story of two pilgrims and friends. One night, when they are housed at some distance, one of them dreams he hears the other shouting out that he is being murdered; the following day his body is found in 'a dong carte'. He then tells another story to the same effect, quotes the Life of Saint Kenelm, the *Somnium Scipionis*, Daniel, Joseph, Croesus, and Andromache to clinch the matter, and roundly proclaims he will have no talk of 'laxatyves'. Then, with marvellously male inconsistency, he suddenly changes the subject: 'Now let us speke of myrthe, and stynte al this.' When he gazes on the beauty of Pertelote's face (and Chaucer has him ironically declare that the scarlet of her eyes is an eternal monument to henly beauty), all his fears are forgotten. He then crowns his speech with a famous Latin maxim and his own disingenuous translation of it:

> For al so siker as *In principio*,
> *Mulier est hominis confusio*—
> Madame, the sentence of this Latyn is,
> 'Womman is mannes joye and al his blis'.

Finally, after three hundred lines, the action begins. When Chauntecleer flies down from his beam, Russell, the fox, who has been lying in wait for some time, suddenly appears before him. The cock naturally tries to escape, but Russell flatters him by extravagantly praising his merits as a singer and inviting him to show his ability. As soon as Chauntecleer begins to sing, on tip-toe, with neck out-stretched and eyes closed like an inspired tenor, the fox seizes him by the same neck and makes for the woods. A tremendous uproar ensues, animals and farm labourers launching themselves in hot pursuit of Russell and his victim. Meanwhile, Chauntecleer prompts his captor to brag that no one will catch them as they have already reached the woods. And of course the moment the fox opens his mouth, the cock flies up into a tree. There he remains, flatly refusing to come down even when his enemy asks for forgiveness and promises to explain what he really meant by his 'trespas'—Chauntecleer has had enough of flattery. And with this, to which is appended the Priest's moral ('Lo, swich it is for to be recchelees | And necligent, and truste on flaterye'), the Tale as such is over.

Littera gesta docet, moralis quid agas, as the medieval maxim has it: the letter teaches what has been done, the moral sense what should be done. Here, then, is the literal, plain sense—the relatively straightforward plot—and an equally straight-forward morality in accordance with the tradition of animal fable. But things are more complicated than at first appears. We have already seen that in the first part of the Tale, in the long discussion about dreams, Chauntecleer and Pertelote quote various exempla and authorities, and the cock, in particular, goes so far as to use a Latin proverb, linking it to the beginning of Genesis and John's Gospel which rewrites it (*In principio*, 'In the beginning'). Clearly, these are fairly special animals, and Dryden, three centuries later, has part-cloned them in his own animal farm, his 'trans-lation' of Chaucer's Tale in the *Fables*. His Chanticleer actually goes one better when, for example, he counters Partlet's quotation from Cato with a super-scholarly remark from a post-Renaissance world, when the *Distichs* were finally no longer attributed to Cato:

> Nor Cato said it: But some modern Fool,
> Impos'd in Cato's Name on Boys at School.

But of course Dryden's animals belong to a different age—
the golden, pre-evolutionary age of Animalitarism: 'In the
Days of Yore', he writes, glancing at the foreword to
Babrius's *Aesop's Fables*, 'the Birds of Parts | Were bred to
Speak, and Sing, and learn the lib'ral Arts'.

From the very beginning of the second part of Chaucer's
Tale, we realize that his narrator, the Priest, is going to run
wild in the same vein. He announces that he will now tell of
Chauntecleer's 'aventure', and his opening is a masterpiece
of solemnity:

> Whan that the month in which the world bigan,
> That highte March, whan God first maked man . . .

With exquisite deployment of the chronographical tech-
nique invented by the classics and refined from Dante to
Boccaccio, we go right back to the time of Genesis. The
rewriting begins. But at once we realize the absurdity of the
procedure: the month our Priest requires is not March, but
May, the topical month for the beginning of an adventure.
Undaunted, he adds:

> Was compleet, and passed were also,
> Syn March was gon, thritty dayes and two . . .

In other words it is the third day of May. To point this out,
the Priest has had to use two subordinate time clauses
('whan that . . . and passed were also'), plus no fewer
than three further subordinate clauses, of which two are
again temporal. We begin to smell a parodic rat, and a
rat—like his cock—of rare literary refinement. The Priest
goes further. At last comes the main clause, and with it the
subject:

> Bifel that Chauntecleer in al his pryde,
> His seven wyves walkynge by his syde,
> Caste up his eyen to the brighte sonne

Oblique syntax states a finely balanced parody. The opening was the beginning of the world and the creation of man; now Chauntecleer, in all his Sultan-like pride, raises his eyes to the sun with the demeanour of an eagle. A barnyard cock, he here poses as the lord of all creation, addressing himself to the sun, the primeval light; the sun, as the author specifies in another parenthesis,

> That in the signe of Taurus hadde yronne
> Twenty degrees and oon, and somewhat more . . .

This is really taking astronomical time-telling a degree too far, as well as being simply scientifically wrong. But as soon as we demur at the exaggeration, we return to Chauntecleer, now in his natural dress, as 'commune astrologer', who 'knew by kynde, and by noon oother loore, | That it was pryme'. Chauntecleer, as we have already seen, is more reliable 'than a clokke or an abbey orlogge', for Nature herself has planted in him infallible knowledge of astronomy. Step by step, a dual irony is constructed, aimed on the one hand at the cock believing itself lord of creation, and on the other, at man, the putative lord of creation who has to invent a complicated science ('loore') and sophisticated instruments ('orlogge') to work out what the cock knows by instinct:

> 'The sonne', he seyde, 'is clomben up on hevene
> Fourty degrees and oon, and moore ywis . . .'

Meanwhile, the register and the sphere of reference remain unchanged for four lines, with the introduction of a new element, Edenic joy:

> 'Madame Pertelote, my worldes blis,
> Herkneth thise blisful briddes how they synge,
> And se the fresshe floures how they sprynge;
> Ful is myn herte of revel and solas!'

Chauntecleer, breezily denoting his peers 'thise briddes', sounds like a splendidly paternalistic Adam: 'padre' and 'padrone'. Once more, Dryden, in the late seventeenth century, goes a step further. In surveying the flowers and birds, his Chanticleer feels that Nature herself has 'adorn'd the Year' just for him, and quite openly proclaims, 'All these are ours'. Then, with an extraordinary, almost Orwellian, leap, he adds: 'and I with pleasure see | Man strutting on two Legs, and aping me!' The cock surpasses Adam to become some kind of God walking in the garden, as it were, 'in the cool of the day' (Genesis 3: 8); an almost demonic—certainly devilish—rewriting of Scripture.

But to return to Chaucer's Tale: at this point, by a process of association akin to a stream of (narrative) consciousness, the Priest intervenes with the first of his comments, taking up the theme of joy and inserting it into the wider pattern of Fortune:

> But sodeynly hym fil a sorweful cas,
> For evere the latter ende of joye is wo.
> God woot that worldly joie is soone ago;
> And if a rhetor koude faire endite,
> He in a cronycle saufly myghte it write
> As for a sovereyn notabilitee.
> Now every wys man, lat him herkne me;
> This storie is also trewe, I undertake,
> As is the book of Launcelot de Lake,
> That wommen holde in ful greet reverence.

Here proverbial wisdom—indeed, priestly considerations on worldly transience—suddenly turns to literary allusion and anti-literature mockery: a rhetorician, the Priest says, might write us a chronicle, that is, a noble *historia* in the high style (perhaps a tragedy such as one of those just told by the Monk in his 'de casibus virorum illustrium'); but his tale, he proclaims, is a true 'storie' like that of Lancelot, to which women (witness Dante's Francesca da Rimini) are partial. It is as 'true', in other words, as a romance, which even by medieval standards is completely fictitious. We shall soon return to this problem: for the moment, let us note that the

Priest is playing with literature and with his audience—both women in general and the lady pilgrims journeying to Canterbury in particular (Dryden, for instance, makes an explicit connection with the Wife of Bath at this point). Later on he will find himself a real rhetorician to make fun of, and will continue with his women-targeted irony (women, of course, form the favourite audience of the man of letters). With momentary restraint, he here switches back to his 'sentence' ('subject'), and the fox finally makes his entrance.

The narrator, however, cannot keep out of his own story: along with the fox he introduces the subject of predestination ('by heigh ymaginacioun forncast') and of homicide, already mentioned by Chauntecleer himself in his speech on dreams: the fox is full of iniquity, like the worst sinners of the Bible, the murderers. The Priest then goes into ecclesiastico-cultural overdrive, cursing Judas, Ganelon, and Sinon (and bringing us back to sacred and profane literature, to Scripture as well as classical epic and *chanson de geste*, fastforwarding from the beginning of the world to the New Testament, from Troy to Charlemagne). He addresses the cock directly, launching into a discussion on predestination, free will, and necessity. This time, he introduces the world of the Schools—philosophy, 'clerks', 'altercacioun', and 'disputisoun', Boethius, Augustine, and Chaucer's contemporary, Bradwardine.

Chauntecleer's imminent tragedy seems to acquire a cosmic dimension, placed as it is on the level of universal destiny. But 'that', as the Sterne of *Tristram Shandy* would say, 'is another story'—the story of Troilus, or of Arcite and Palamon, which Chaucer told in *Troilus and Criseyde* and the *Knight's Tale*. The Priest 'wol nat han to do of swich mateere'. 'My tale', he firmly proclaims, 'is of a cock', a cock who followed his 'wife's' advice in spite of his dream. And the 'conseils' of women, he continues, are often 'fatal', witness that which 'broghte us first to wo, | And made Adam fro Paradys to go'.

What more astonishing *reductio* than this: 'my tale is of a cock.' But its purport is not altogether clear: is the Priest really talking about a cock, or rather about all humankind? The cock has taken the advice of his wife, not of the hen Pertelote, and this wife is immediately put on a par with all women, beginning with Eve. Where, then, does that leave us? Well, most definitely back in the Book of Genesis, where the narrator and Chauntecleer with his *In principio* had already taken us. In short, we are at the beginning of the world, in the Garden of Eden. Is this re-Scripture to be taken literally? Obviously not. Can we then consider it as a case of typology, Adam being the *figura* of Chauntecleer in the same way as he is the antitypos of Jesus, Pertelote being the fulfilment of Eve? Whilst the cock in general does of course symbolically represent Christ in medieval iconography, the notion that this cock incarnates the Messiah and this hen (through Eve) the Virgin Mary is so preposterous in the context (and context here is fundamental for any text interpretation beyond the most barely literal) that even the stoutest adherent of modern American allegorism should abandon it forthwith.

Our uncertainty is further increased by two complementary statements. The first is Chauntecleer's Latin maxim, *Mulier est hominis confusio*, which now seems to tally with the Priest's opinions about women. As the Priest quotes Eve to prove his point, so Chauntecleer authenticates his pronouncement by linking its certainty and truth to the first words of the greatest authorities, Genesis and John. But the cock then 'translates' his maxim into the opposite of the original: 'Womman is mannes joye and al his blis.' This, too, we must assume, is 'al so siker as *In principio*', and in a sense of course it is. Genesis does say that God had second thoughts about leaving man on his own, and created woman as a 'help meet for him' (in Robert Alter's translation of this 'notoriously difficult' expression, a 'sustainer beside him').

The cock thus turns out to be a fairly shrewd Scriptural exegete. He seems to carry to its extreme consequences the fourteenth-century theory of *duplex sensus litteralis*. At one and the same time he makes Genesis say the two apparently opposite things, the 'two truths' that the letter of the biblical text predicates of woman. He does it by using first Latin, then, wilfully or otherwise, an English mistranslation of the Latin. The words of Genesis itself do not change: *In principio* is immutable. But by turning the words that surround it from one language to another, by offering an apparently innocent 'sentence' or 'plain, literal meaning' of them, Chauntecleer interprets the biblical *littera* twice over and cocks—as it were—a snook at literal translation and interpretation as such, at the same time managing to cast doubt on the meaning of *In principio* for good measure.

If the propositions contained in the maxim and in its translation are epistemologically uncertain or 'not true', what value shall we give to the *In principio* that supports them? Perhaps we should not forget that the first fourteen verses of John's Gospel were very popular for devotions and were even supposed to have magical power, especially against demons. A friar such as Chaucer's in the *General Prologue* to the *Canterbury Tales* would intone *In principio* (as friars were indeed wont to do when entering a home) 'so pleasantly' that, in collecting alms, he would get a farthing even from a poor widow. Or are we to consider the two words not a quotation from Scripture, but an allusion to the canonical opening of every medieval commentary, 'In the beginning we must say that . . .'? In this case the cock would be deliberately making fun of Genesis and John—an offence for which every medieval animal would immediately have been roasted alive. Or perhaps nothing can be predicated of women—not least by a cock. The only corresponding, non-refutable, 'true' parts of the two sentences are '*Mulier est*' and 'Womman is'. The rest is silence. Yet this silence curiously reverberates around *In principio*. In the beginning what?, one may ask. Both the Creation of Genesis and the Logos of John are strangely absent. *In principio* is reduced to a word without the Word, to misquote the Eliot of the *Quartets*:

without *Verbum*. Subversive stuff, this kind of re-Scripture, for a medieval animal farm.

And the point to note here is not so much what someone has, within a different interpretative context, termed Chaucer's 'de-cock-struction', deconstruction as critical 'Bobbitting', but the fact that Chauntecleer is allowed to offer as it were a triple reading of the letter, thus in a sense shortcircuiting it, without having to resort to allegory, morality, or anagogy. Is this part of the new 'literalism' that, according to Beryl Smalley, conquered Scriptural exegesis with the advent of Aristotle and the thirteenth-century friars?

I shall return to this presently. For the moment, let me simply note that the Latin *'Mulier est hominis confusio'* stares across a significant gap at its English mistranslation. The whole of the *Nun's Priest's Tale* as ideological and cultural message (as a story with a 'sense' and a historical dimension), is as it were contained here, in the gap which Chauntecleer leaps over in a sweeping flurry of psychic suppression and wishful thinking.

This 'translation gap' looks particularly interesting if we read it in the light of the English fourteenth century, an age of translation that culminates with Wyclif's version of Chauntecleer's authorial text, the Bible, and Chaucer's own 'translations'; from the *Roman de la Rose* to *Boece*, *Melibee*, *The Second Nun's Tale*, *Troilus and Criseyde*, and *The Knight's* and *Clerk's Tales*, to his version of Ugolino from Canto XXXIII of the *Inferno* in the *Monk's Tale*. In actual fact Chaucer, whom the French poet Deschamps defined a 'grand translateur', has some indicative—not to mention bizarre—observations on his own translatorly practice. In *Troilus*, for example, he radically transforms Petrarch's sonnet 132 while stolidly declaring he is not only giving his *auctor's* sense ('sentence') but repeating the source of Troilus's song word for word and completely, give or take the odd difference between the two languages (*'save our tonges difference'*). 'Mind the gap' indeed: awareness is now complete.

Translation and interpretation do in fact share more than one problem. How does Chaucer's Priest respond to these? After quoting Eve in a none-too-favourable light, he promptly retracts:

> But for I noot to whom it myght displese,
> If I conseil of wommen wolde blame,
> Passe over, for I seyde it in my game.

So it was a joke. Or was it? With subtle malice, the Priest invites us to refer to the 'authors': read them, he says, and you will see what they say of women. Well yes: the only problem being that what 'authors', beginning with Genesis, have to say on the subject is to say the least contradictory. Thus, Pilate-like, the Priest washes his hands of the whole business, and with a triple wammy attributes what he has just said to that subtle interpreter of Scripture, Chauntecleer:

> Thise been the cokkes wordes, and nat myne.
> I kan noon harm of no womman divyne.

A Priest leaving exegesis to a cock? We have not just lost the letter (which has gone up in smoke between Chauntecleer's Latin and his English): we are losing the very foundation of Roman Catholic doctrine, which affirms the authority of the *magisterium* over all interpretation, thus conditioning the literal sense itself. Where would we end up if everybody were allowed to interpret the Bible? To which the inevitable answer is: in the fourteenth century, somewhere between Huss's Prague, Wyclif's Oxford, and the abbey of Umberto Eco's *Name of the Rose*.

As if this were not enough, from this moment on the Tale is an explosion of verbal fireworks and rapid ventriloquisms, from character to narrator and vice versa. Texts and authors are invoked by all. The fox quotes Boethius's *De Musica* and 'Daun Burnel the Asse', the animal tale of Nigel of Longchamps entitled *Burnellus*, or *Speculum Stultorum*. The Priest manages to bring in the *Physiologus*, 'Ecclesiaste', the *Aeneid* and the destruction of Troy, Hasdrubal and the sack of Carthage, Nero and the burning of Rome. After the *beginning*, the secular history of humanity starts and develops, and the tragedy of Chauntecleer unfolds in this melo-dramatic apocalypse as, in a mock-epic crescendo, men, women, and animals of the farm all rush to the scene. The style throws an ironic light on the protagonists of the action and, indirectly, on the protagonists of the Peasants' Revolt of 1381, reduced by assimilation, as in Gower's *Vox Clamantis*, to beast-like figures: the noise made by the animals when the fox captures Chauntecleer is so 'hideous' that not even Jack Straw and his mob shouted so much when they attacked the Flemings, Chaucer's text narrates. As if with a proleptic glance at Orwell, historico-political reality bursts into the story with the urgent explosiveness of the present, forcing us to ask where the Priest and Chaucer stand. Needless to say, no clue as to the answer will be forthcoming.

Yet the Narrator promptly abandons this potential mine-field and hides behind rhetoric. At one point, beginning with an appeal to destiny, with a closely interconnected series of tragicomic invocations, the Priest harangues Friday ('Venus' day'), then Venus herself, then Geoffrey of Vinsauf, who lamented the killing of Richard the Lion-Hearted, which took place on a Friday (traditionally, Friday was also the day of the expulsion from Eden, of the Flood, of Jesus's betrayal and crucifixion). Nothing is spared—neither dreams, nor courtly love ('servyce'), nor sexual pleasure and the commandment of Genesis ('moore for delit than world to multiplye'), nor the 'sentence' and the 'loore' of a 'mais-ter soverayn' of rhetoric.

Meanwhile Chauntecleer, who once was Adam, becomes Richard the Lion-Hearted, Priam, Hasdrubal, and a Roman senator. The fires of Troy, Carthage, and Rome flare up and envelop the whole scene, taking on tinges of the infernal (the men and women on the farm scream like devils in hell, the Priest informs us). The world is about to end, when suddenly, Fortune turns, and Chauntecleer, once more a simple cock, sets himself free.

But the Priest has not done yet. He now adds the moral, and then concludes with another bit of dazzling profundity, a last flash of Scripture:

> But ye that holden this tale a folye,
> As of a fox, or of a cok and hen,
> Taketh the moralite, goode men.
> For Seint Paul seith that al that writen is,
> To oure doctrine it is ywrite, ywis;
> Taketh the fruyt, and lat the chaf be stille.

This, then, finally, is the point. It was not, the Priest tells us, a simple tale about a cock, a hen, and a fox. Leave the 'chaff', and take the core, the moral. Very fine, and very appropriately medieval. A century later, in rewriting Chaucer's story for another version of an animal farm, his *Morall Fabillis of Esope the Phrygian*, Robert Henryson picks up the 'kirnill delectabill' which he says lies inside the 'nuttis schell'—the 'frute' under the 'fenyeit fabil'—and expands the Priest's short *moralitas* into twenty-one lines about pride, vainglory, and flattery.

And modern critics, particularly on the other side of the Atlantic, have rushed beyond the moral pure and simple, hunting for the *sensus allegoricus*, which is—it seems to me—quite a different thing: not 'quid agas' (what you should do), but 'quid credas' (what you should believe). Thus the Tale, they say, is an allegory of the Fall of Man; a sermon on moral obligation (with Chauntecleer representing the holy man and Russell the devil); an allegorical controversy between the secular clergy (the slothful Chauntecleer) and the friars (the fox); even a mock allegory, with Chauntecleer as the exegetical figure of the preacher-cock. Allegorical interpretation is by its nature infinite: every object, event, or word in a discourse can be attributed with any number of 'other' meanings as long as they have cohesion as a system. The imagination can chase off with any number of cyphers, particularly in trying to resolve the conflict between the two traditional genres which come together in the tale: moral fable, and amoral animal epic.

Yet, before taking any such interpretative step, there is a preliminary move we have to make in any case—a choice between accepting or otherwise the Priest's invitation to take the moral and 'lat the chaf be stille'. Suppose we decide on the first, and 'take the fruyt'. In the Priest's version, this is none too juicy, but our readerly appetite can just about be appeased, although we are still left with a high-fibre diet, and an awful lot of chaff to dispose of. And St Paul, we are reminded, maintains that all that is written is written for our instruction. On the one hand, taken 'literally' in the present context, this means the chaff as well. On the other, taken intertextually, it makes the *Nun's Priest's Tale* the equivalent of Scripture, for what Paul says in Romans 15: 4 is that 'quaecumque enim scripta sunt, ad nostram doctrinam scripta sunt, ut per patientiam et consolationem Scripturarum spem habeamus' ('whatever was written in former days was written for our instruction, that by steadfastness and by the encouragement of the Scriptures we might have hope'), a pronouncement which comes after the quotation of a Psalm.

Now all this is a bit disturbing, but we will decide to overlook our embarassment at the apparent equation between chaff and Scripture, and go ahead, remembering that scholars have proved that by the fourteenth century the 'all' in Paul's sentence comes 'to mean "almost anything", writings of all kinds'. At this point, we must ask what precisely the chaff is in our case. And the answer is obvious: the tale of a cock. This is as true a 'story' as that of Lancelot, but not a 'folye' of a mere fox, or cock and hen: i.e. cock and bull. It both is and is not the tale of a cock; it is and is not something else. We are neatly back at the beginning of the circle.

We are forced, then, to try the second course. We refuse to take the moral alone because this is too minimal for such a story (Caxton, who in his fifteenth-century *Aesop* composes yet another animal farm, makes the morality even cheaper by reading the plot as an exemplum of 'ouer moche talkyng' and 'to moche crowing'), and because St Paul and fourteenth-century literary theory apparently urge us to accept everything. With the fruit, we then eat up all the chaff. In other words, we chew over—or, more precisely, we 'ruminate'—the letter. But what, again, is the letter? Clearly, the whole crust made up of the various levels of fiction, culture, and reality: the cock, the hen, the fox, Adam, Ganelon, Richard I, Nero, Bradwardine, and Jack Straw.

Let me repeat that there is no biblical typology here. Chauntecleer does not fulfil Adam or Priam as he would in Auerbach's *Figura*—for a moment, he is Adam, and Priam. And this single, climactic, and very brief moment occurs when his narrator, the Priest (and behind him, Chaucer) decides to superimpose, by allusion, two or more of those figures. In short, for us, who are listening to or reading the Tale, and to whom it looks like a succession of such moments—a continuous explosion of names which are hurled out on the same level of speech, but which we know belong to different levels of being—for us, the letter is 'letters': *littera* is *litterae*, literature. All of it is 'true', like the story of Lancelot; all of it is written for our instruction, like the Bible, and like indeed all literature. For the Priest, the Book of Genesis and the Genesis of the cock, St John's Word and the words of the Tale are on the same level.

And we are not done with complications. In the so-called 'Retraction' which appears at the end of the last of the *Canterbury Tales*, the *Parson's Tale*, 'the makere of this book' takes his leave, asking his listeners and readers to thank Christ if they find in his work something they like, and to attribute anything they might dislike to the 'defaute' of his 'unkonnynge' and not to his will. He would have been all too pleased to put things better if he had been able to. 'For oure book seith, "Al that is writen is writen for oure doc-trine", and that is myn entente.' Whether this was actually composed by Chaucer or not hardly matters in the présent context. But what does it mean? If 'entente' stands for 'intentio', we cannot forget that the generally accepted late-medieval view is, to put it with Thomas Aquinas, that 'sensus litteralis est, quem auctor intendit': the letter is the 'intentio auctoris'. And this leads us into another neat cul-de-sac. For, whether the 'work' which is being spoken of in the Retraction is the *Canterbury Tales* or the 'collected works' of Geoffrey Chaucer, the writer of the present sentence seems to say that the intention of the author is the literal sense, and that this is, at least intentionally, all 'doctrine'. What, then, is 'true' in these works? What, in particular, is 'true' in our animal farm, in the *Nun's Priest's Tale*?

A diachronic exploration of medieval theory in animal fables might be of some help. In the eleventh century, Conrad of Hirsau had maintained in his *Dialogue on the Authors* that the 'literal explanation is when one is told how the *nuda littera* is to be understood'. He had then offered, in the tradition of Isidore of Seville, an etymology of 'fable'—*fabula*—from *fando* (speaking), adding that 'fable is fiction, not fact'. 'Aesopic' fables, according to Isidore and Conrad, 'are made to relate to a moral end, and have been invented to give pleasure'. 'Their invented stories about human events and characters correspond with the truth', says Conrad, 'albeit only in a certain sense' (the crux, of course, lies precisely in this 'certain sense', about which Conrad offers no explanation), 'but the material Aesop invented never happened, nor could it have happened.' As Isidore puts it, 'so that one may come to the thing which is intended by means of fictional narrative but truthful meaning'.

Holy Writ itself is not above this 'fabulous' or 'fabulistic' manner, and if it does not contemplate the possibility of animal farms, it certainly knows something about vegetable ones. In Judges 9: 7–15, Isidore and Conrad write, Jotham,

'the only one to be saved when his brothers were killed by
Abimelech, ascended Mount Gerizim and cursed the men
of Shechem and the king chosen by them', saying that 'the
trees of the wood, the vine and the olive and the fig, had
come together and sought to create a kingship over them
from among their own number, but all to no avail, so that in
the end they got the bramble as their king'.

The substance of this argument is picked up by Pierre
Bersuire in the Prologue to his *Ovidius Moralizatus* and, even
more interestingly, by Boccaccio in his so-called 'Defence of
Poetry' in the *Genealogie Deorum Gentilium*. In Book XIV,
chapter ix, Boccaccio declares that 'fabula est exemplaris seu
demonstrativa sub figmento locutio, cuius amoto cortice,
patet intentio fabulantis'. Fable is, then, exemplary and
demonstrative discourse under the veil of fiction ('figmento'); once you remove the cortex, the bark, the 'intention' of the fabulator, the narrator, appears evident (the
question of authorial intention, on which I have already
touched, is clearly central for both Isidore and Boccaccio).
The writer of the *Genealogie* then distinguishes four types of
fables: the first is Aesop's, which 'omnino veritate caret in
cortice', which superficially lacks all appearance of truth.
This type was accepted even by Aristotle, and we can find its
equivalent in the Book of Judges.

I could, though, pursue this line of enquiry endlessly, and
to no conclusion: it persists until the sixteenth century at
least, when Sidney, for example, takes it up in his *Defence of
Poetry*. But Boccaccio brings us to the second half of the
fourteenth century and to the emergence of a stronger
'humanistic' stance as regards the status of *litterae*. Is Chaucer's
Priest, then, a 'humanist'? Or is he merely repeating things
already to be found in Isidore and Conrad of Hirsau—or,
for that matter, in Theon of Alexandria—i.e. central to
ancient and medieval tradition? Maybe in order to appreci-
ate the distinction, in order to gain some kind of historical
perspective, we need to travel further in time.

The prince of modern animal farms and fable-telling,

Jean de La Fontaine, obviously has a lot to say about the genre. The first is that as far as Aesop's fables are concerned, 'their surface is childish, but these childish things serve as envelopments of important truths'. The second is his interpretation of Plato's account in the *Phaedo*, according to which Socrates put Aesopic fables into verse before dying. La Fontaine writes that it suddenly occurred to Socrates that perhaps the gods' advice to devote himself to music meant that he should pay attention to poetry, for 'there is no good poetry without harmony'. Yet, he adds, 'there is no good poetry without fiction, either': 'et Socrate ne savait que dire la vérité.' Socrates thus hit on a compromise, that of choosing fables that would contain some truth, like those of Aesop. None of this syllogism is of course present in Plato. But La Fontaine goes further. He argues that what he is really talking about is the 'Apologue', and that this is exactly the same as a parable in the Gospels. Finally, he distinguishes between the 'body' and the 'soul' of an apologue. The former is the fable, the latter the moral.

Where are we? In the Middle Ages or the seventeenth century? Chaucer's Priest (and let me emphasize this again, a priest) seems to be far less serious or 'medieval' than La Fontaine—he only says the story is true. No more, but no less. By contrast, look at Dryden. He follows Chaucer in holding that 'the Legend is as true I undertake | As Tristram is, and Lancelot of the Lake', but in his 'Moral' he concludes: 'The Truth is moral, though the Tale a Lie.' From his much expanded *moralitas* Dryden also eliminates St Paul's dictum, though, like La Fontaine, he alludes to Christ's parables. On the one hand, then, we have a medieval Priest who maintains his story is as true as fiction and who seems to liken it to Scripture, but in fact follows a 'modern', contemporary fashion of justifying all writing by means of a sentence in St Paul. On the other, we have two seventeenth-century writers who believe that the tale or fable is a lie, but liken it to a Gospel parable.

The two positions would seem to be similar, and indeed there is a 'historical' route whereby the latter would appear to have been 'genealogically' prepared or even produced by the former. But the purpose of this chapter is to show how subtly, and radically, different those positions really are. Dryden and La Fontaine are squarely pre-Darwinian. They believe not only that man is a rational animal, but also that, since man is the image of God, animals have some divine quality as well. This is why we can predicate about human beings in the same way Christ preached in parables. Their animal farms are, as for Theon of Alexandria, the places of false discourse giving the semblance of truth. Chaucer is both pre- and post-Darwinian. He is not quite sure whether man is a rational animal, or an animal is a rational man. And he firmly believes that human discourse about animal farms is not false, but true: as true as all fiction, as true as John's Gospel.

Chaucer's stance, to paraphrase a title of Robert Alter's, is that of a man who seems to enjoy the pleasures, and to know the pains, of writing and reading in an ideological age. La Fontaine and Dryden take the edge off both the joys and the sorrows. They make interpretation easy. Jesus, Dryden writes openly, knew perfectly well that a parable 'was a pleasing way, | Sound Sense, by plain Example, to convey'. Sound sense, by plain example? We have been looking for the 'sound' sense of Gospel parables for some two thousand years now. Dryden had clearly not read Frank Kermode's *Genesis of Secrecy*. Chaucer, on the other hand, seems to have at least glanced through 'The Plain Sense of Things', an essay in which the same critic uses translation (another animal being involved this time: 'the cat sat on the mat') to show that what the cock calls 'sentence' ('the sentence of this Latyn') is impossible. My audience will remember where Kermode's inspiration comes from. It is from one of the great poems of our age, Wallace Stevens's 'The Plain Sense of Things':

> After the leaves have fallen, we return
> To a plain sense of things. It is as if
> We had come to an end of the imagination,
> Inanimate in an inert savoir.
>
> It is difficult even to choose the adjective
> For this blank cold, this sadness without cause.
> The great structure has become a minor house.
> No turban walks across the lessened floors.
>
> .   .   .   .
>
> Yet the absence of the imagination had
> Itself to be imagined. The great pond,
> The plain sense of it, without reflections, leaves,
> Mud, water like dirty glass, expressing silence
>
> Of a sort, silence of a rat come out to see,
> The great pond and its waste of the lilies, all this
> Had to be imagined as an inevitable knowledge,
> Required, as a necessity requires.

The plain sense of things is precisely this: the cold emptiness, unreasonable sadness. His interpretation? 'Inert savoir';
'silence'. To know is to die a little. To interpret is to enter
the terminal phase. To read the plain sense is to fall ill, to
fade with the fall of the autumn leaves. But the blankness
and the silence are the first facts from which to depart on an
exegesis of the world: they represent, as it were, the *nuda
littera* of knowledge. This is why Kermode can mantain that

The plain sense is not accessible to plain common sense. That is
why it has been possible to say, 'The plain sense is hidden'. Luther
believed that 'the Holy Spirit is the plainest writer and speaker in
heaven and earth', but we may well sympathize with Erasmus,
who wanted to know 'if it is all so plain, why have so many
excellent men for so many centuries walked in darkness?'.

We can now return to our medieval narrator and his
Genesis-rewriting cock. Chaucer, who obliquely rewrites
the Bible, freely and ecumenically, in true lay fashion
accepts the letter as literature, without excluding the moral.
But in telling us to take the moral and leave the chaff, he

justifies the letter in itself—as scriptural exegesis requires—
and forces us to stay within it, to taste all the joys and the
pains of the so-called 'plain sense of things'. The 'fruyt', on
the other hand, like that of the tree of knowledge, is forbidden, and the Priest makes us put non-literal exegesis
behind us, while inviting us to pursue it. Comic rescripting
of Scripture turns out to be terribly serious: the inner doubt
behind any re-Scripture opens towards the light and in the
very same moment locks itself inside the permanent darkness of exegetical indeterminacy.

To stay with animal fables (and parables) for one last
moment, not forgetting that they are highly serious things:
when Bruce Chatwin went to visit Konrad Lorenz, the
latter commented that he had noticed a gradual *cochonifica-
tion* ('pigification') of the youth swimming in the Danube, as
they fattened like domestic pets. Let me conclude, then, by
saying that in reading Chaucer's Tale we find ourselves in
the position both of Bucephalus and those who observe
him. Once, Bucephalus was Alexander of Macedonia's battle
charger. Now, he is the new advocate just admitted to the
Bar. Though there is little in his present appearance to
remind us of his former shape, 'even a quite simple court
attendant can stare at the lawyer with the professional eye of
a modest racetrack follower as the latter, lifting his legs high,
mounts the outside stairs step by step, with a tread that
makes the marble ring'. Bucephalus's position in modern
society is a difficult one. There is no Alexander the Great,
no blazing trail to India. 'The gates have receded to remoter
and loftier places.' 'So perhaps', Franz Kafka concludes, 'it
may be best to do as Bucephalus has done' and bury oneself
in the old volumes. 'In the quiet lamplight, his flanks
unhampered by the thighs of a rider, free and far from the
clamour of battle, he reads and turns the pages of our
ancient tomes.' He is searching them—we may presume—
for the literal meaning: perhaps also for the allegorical, the
moral, and the anagogic. But above all he is perplexed by his
own strange metamorphosis. Who, or what, is Bucephalus?

Does the new advocate 'fulfil' Alexander's horse? Neither he, nor we, are allowed to know for sure. We, 'the creatures outside', as if we were the protagonists of the only *Animal Farm* which actually bears the title—Orwell's, this time—look 'from pig to man, and from man to pig, and from pig to man again; but already it is impossible to say which is which'.

CHAPTER FOUR

Why Should Moses Go Down?

Then he saw the bear. It did not emerge, appear:
it was just there.

GO *Down, Moses* is one of Faulkner's most fascinating
works: one of those books that coil round the reader and
then suddenly strike him with oblique and unexpected
revelations. A collection of seven stories, published in one
volume in 1942, it acquires fictional unity by tracing the
events of one family, the McCaslins, in the American
South. Faulkner 'goes down' three generations in direct
descent (from the plantation founder, Carothers, to his
grandson Isaac, who rejects plantation property and the
whole idea of slavery), four generations in indirect descent
(the Edmonds, who inherit the plantation after Isaac), and
five of the black descendants, the slaves and progeny of
the plantation owners, who continued to live and work
on the same land. The intricate genealogical line structur-
ing the book is reproduced through the presence, consciousness and memory of Isaac McCaslin, whose very
unlinear narration ranges with total analeptic and proleptic
freedom across past and future, childhood, adolescence,
adulthood, and old age. A series of stories are made to
revolve around him with the river-like quality that charac-
terizes Faulkner's prose (and in a very similar way García
Márquez's *A Hundred Years of Solitude*): epic, tragic, and
comic, which together bear extraordinarily striking resemblance to the Scriptures.

To enter into this spiral we should immediately catch the
powerful, biblical rhythms which are established from the
first page:

Isaac McCaslin, 'Uncle Ike', past seventy and nearer eighty than he ever corroborated any more, a widower now and uncle to half a county and father to no one.

This was not something participated in or even seen by himself, but by his elder cousin, McCaslin Edmonds, grandson of Isaac's father's sister and so descended by the distaff, yet notwithstanding the inheritor, and in his time the bequestor, of that which some had thought then and some still thought should have been Isaac's, since his was the name in which the title to the land had first been granted from the Indian patent and which some of the descendants of his father's slaves still bore in the land. But Isaac was not one of these—a widower these twenty years, who in all his life had owned but one object more than he could wear and carry in his pockets and his hands at one time, and this was the narrow iron cot and the stained lean mattress which he used camping in the woods for deer and bear or for fishing or simply because he loved the woods; who owned no property and never desired to since the earth was no man's but all men's, as light and air and weather were; who lived still in the cheap frame bungalow in Jefferson which his wife's father gave them on their marriage and which his wife had willed to him at her death and which he had pretended to accept . . .

Not something he had participated in or even remembered except from the hearing, the listening, come to him through and from his cousin McCaslin born in 1850 and sixteen years his senior and hence, his own father being near seventy when Isaac, an only child, was born, rather his brother than cousin and rather his father than either, out of the old time, the old days.

Faulkner's two opening paragraphs come rolling over us like the massive Mississippi, slow and compact. At the same time we hear them divide and branch out, like the Mississippi delta, tributary-sentences becoming rivers in their own right. The ground swell of the prose re-enacts the place and time of the narration; in the river delta, through the succeeding generations which dictate the unifying rhythm. It presents Isaac McCaslin, the centre of the current, and the method of ramification opening out from him ('this was not something participated in or even seen by himself'), and gradually reveals what are to be recurrent themes: the land and its possession, name, Black and Indian blood, the forest, hunting.

What, though, is the relation between the narratives and the title of the book and the last story, *Go Down, Moses?* The collected stories include, for example, the hunt, complete with a bet and a poker game mounted by Buck and Buddy, the two brothers, for their step-brother and black slave Turl of Tomey, who has escaped into a neighbouring property in search of a girl ('Was'); the story of the impenetrable half-cast Lucas, with his bootleg whisky-distillery, his metal-detector to search for buried coins, his old wife Molly, and Edmonds, the white man, whom Lucas definitively defeats ('The Fire and the Hearth'); the tragedy of Rider, the herculean black who takes to drink after his wife Mannie's death, plays at dice which his opponent, the white Birdsong, has loaded, slits Birdsong's throat, and is beaten to death in jail by his victim's relatives ('Pantaloon in Black'); and, lastly, the death sentence, final journey, and funeral (paid for by the community) of Samuel Worsham Beauchamp, grandson of the old black woman Mollie ('Go Down, Moses').

Then there are the hunting-stories centring on Isaac McCaslin: 'The Old People', 'The Bear', and 'Delta Autumn'. The first focuses on the initiation of the 12-year-old Isaac, against the extraordinary backdrop of the forest, 'profound, sentient, gigantic and brooding', and the epiphany of the deer; the third on a nearly 80-year-old Isaac who returns, this time by car, for another deer-hunt to a delta in which most of the forest has been destroyed by man. Between the two is the longest and most splendid piece in the whole book, the hunt for Old Ben, the elderly grizzly bear who reigns supreme in the remaining forest. He is tracked down by Isaac, his indomitable dog Lion, and the great Sam Fathers, who has both black blood and that of an ancient Indian chief, the epic incident taking on a mythical density underscored by the theologico-ethical discussion between Isaac and his cousin, and overtones of historical tragedy through the introduction of the ledgers unflinchingly recording the many sins of the McCaslins and the Edmonds against their slaves.

Now all of this is extremely interesting, but still leaves unsolved the question as to what any of it has to do with the title of the novel. *Go Down, Moses* comes from the negro spiritual which goes as follows:

> When Israel was in Egypt land,
> let my people go,
> oppressed so hard they could not stand
> let my people go.

> Go down, Moses,
> way down in Egypt land,
> tell old Pharaoh
> to let my people go.

> Thus spake the Lord, bold Moses said,
> let my people go,
> if not, I'll strike your first born dead,
> let my people go.

> *Go down, Moses, etc.*

> Your foes shall not before you stand,
> let my people go,
> and you'll possess fair Canaan's land,
> let my people go.

> *Go down, Moses, etc.*

> You'll not get lost in the wilderness,
> let my people go,
> with a lighted candle in your breast,
> let my people go.

> *Go down, Moses, etc.*

The spiritual establishes a direct relationship between the liberation of Israel from Egypt as told in the Book of Exodus, and the liberation of the blacks from slavery in America's South. Although the refrain 'let my people go' is taken from chapters 4 and 5 of Exodus, the spiritual occupies, in the Afro-American imaginary, the place occupied by the famous Psalm (113 in the Vulgate, which I here use for reasons that will become evident soon), *In Exitu Israel de Aegypto*:

> When Israel went out of Egypt,
> the house of Jacob from a people of strange language:
> Judah became his sanctuary, and Israel his dominion.
> The sea saw it, and fled:
> the Jordan was driven back.
> The mountains skipped like rams,
> the little hills like young sheep.

Now, given that *In Exitu Israel de Aegypto* is used time and again by medieval authors as the example of a text to be interpreted using the fourfold method of Scriptural exegesis, why not try to read Faulkner's *Go Down, Moses* as if I were Dante presenting the *Divine Comedy* to Cangrande della Scala? Faulkner, we know, comes from the medieval heart, the South, of the American Middle Ages, the years between 1930 and 1950. When he chose the title of his novel he was fully aware of the implications; furthermore, to each his or her interpretative own: a professional medievalist like myself will be allowed to practise medieval exegesis, albeit applied to a modern text (did Castelvetro, for example, not use Aristotle's *Poetics* to read classical, medieval, and Renaissance texts?). One can but try. Here, then, is Dante describing the polysemy of the *Commedia* to Cangrande in Epistle XIII. The first meaning, he writes, is that deriving from the letter of the text, and is designated 'literal'; the second from 'that which the letter of the text means to signify', called allegorical, or moral, or anagogical:

These diverse ways of treating a subject can for greater clarity be exemplified in the verses *In exitu Israel de Egipto, domus Iacob de populo barbaro, facta est Iudea sanctificatio eius, Israel potestas eius*. For if we inspect the letter alone, the departure of the children of Israel from Egypt in the time of Moses is presented to us; if the allegory, our redemption wrought by Christ; if the moral sense, the conversion of the soul from the grief and misery of sin to the state of grace; if the anagogical, the departure of the holy soul from the slavery of this corruption to the liberty of eternal glory.

What, then, if we were to discover a literal, an allegorical, a moral, and lastly an anagogical meaning in the black spiritual and in Faulkner's *Go Down, Moses*? Even a first glance at the sequence in the spiritual reveals some interesting similarities. Here we have the firstborn, the McCaslins and the Edmonds, all, metaphorically, being struck down. There, in the mist, appears fair Canaan's land. Under our very eyes, a number of people find their way in the wilderness (here a forest), some of them at least, like Sam Fathers and Isaac McCaslin, with a lighted candle of truth and understanding in their breast. Faulkner himself then introduces a long theological *disputatio* in the fourth section of the most important story, 'The Bear', including a history of the world from the beginning to the colonization of the New World, slavery, the American Civil War, and the years which follow it. Grandfather McCaslin, Isaac maintains in this parascholastic discussion with his cousin, could not buy the land from the Indian Ikkemotubbe because the land could be neither bought nor sold:

Bought nothing. Because He told in His Book how He created the earth, made it and looked at it and said it was all right, and then He made man. He made the earth first and peopled it with dumb creatures, and then He created man to be His overseer on the earth and to hold suzerainty over the earth and the animals on it in His name, not to hold for himself and his descendants inviolable title for ever, generation after generation, to the oblongs and squares of the earth, but to hold the earth mutual and intact in the communal anonymity of brotherhood, and all the fee He asked was pity and humility and sufferance and endurance and the sweat of his face for bread.

In the same discussion, Isaac—true prophet and unimpeachable autoexegete—announces how the Book, Scripture, is to be read. When his cousin cites the sons of Ham (traditionally identified with the blacks), cursed by Noah, as the slaves of slaves for their brothers, Isaac replies:

There are some things He said in the Book, and some things reported of Him that He did not say. And I know what you will say now: That if truth is one thing to me and another to you, how will we choose which is truth? You don't need to choose. The heart already knows. He didn't have His Book written to be read by what must elect and choose, but by the heart, not by the wise of the earth because maybe they dont need it or maybe the wise no longer have any heart, but by the doomed and lowly of the earth who have nothing else to read with but the heart. Because the men who wrote his Book for Him were writing about truth and there is only one truth and it covers all things that touch the heart.

And then Faulkner himself invites us to read his book typologically, showing us the young Isaac McCaslin listening to Sam Fathers's stories and considering them *figurae* of the present and future. In reading the following passage, one would immediately be reminded of Dante's 'allegorical' sense. *In Exitu Israel de Aegypto* pre-figures 'our redemption wrought by Christ'. We immediately think of Auerbach's fundamental essay, *Figura*, and Friedrich Ohly's more recent *Tipologia*, and the work devoted to American typology by Sacvan Bercovitch, T. M. Davis, Earl Miner, and Karl Keller. Here is Faulkner in *Go Down, Moses*, actually using that key word of medieval figuralism, *umbra*, shadow:

And as he talked about those old times and those dead and vanished men of another race from either that the boy knew, gradually to the boy those old times would cease to be old times and would become a part of the boy's present, not only as if they had happened yesterday but as if they were still happening, the men who walked through them actually walking in breath and air and casting an actual shadow on the earth they had not quitted. And more: as if some of them had not happened yet but would occur tomorrow, until at last it would seem to the boy that he himself had not come into existence yet . . .

Of course, this is a literary, narrative version of typology, not too different from the 'story-telling' figuralism practised by Thomas Mann in *The Tales of Jacob*, the first volume of *Joseph and His Brothers*. But Faulkner is surely allowed to take some liberties in his medievalism! And as for the moral and ana-gogical senses, they are there for any reader to find in the stories of *Go Down, Moses*, in that for the whole novel the main characters do nothing but expiate their original sin (the purchasing of the land, contamination, and slavery): initiation in 'The Old People' and 'The Bear', and the 'departure of the soul from the slavery of this corrup-tion'—to quote Dante—in 'Go Down, Moses'. Then, at the book's centre, Old Ben's epiphany, ending with the marvellous simile with which Dante describes Guido Guinizzelli's disappearance into the 'fire that refines them', 'come per l'acqua 'l pesce andando al fondo' ('like a fish sinking down through water'):

Then he saw the bear. It did not emerge, appear: it was just there, immobile, fixed in the green and windless noon's hot dappling, not as big as he had dreamed it but as big as he had expected, bigger, dimensionless against the dappled obscurity, looking at him. Then it moved. It crossed the glade without haste, walking for an instant into the sun's full glare and out of it, and stopped again and looked back at him across one shoulder. Then it was gone. It didn't walk into the woods. It faded, sank back into the wilderness without motion as he had watched a fish, a huge old bass, sink back into the dark depths of its pool and vanish without even any movement of its fins.

Medieval critics would be perfectly satisfied with this as a basis for their fourfold interpretative conclusions of this re-Scripture. As for twentieth-century interpreters, I would ask most of them what else they think they have done to Faulkner's book. To read some criticism of 'The Bear' is indeed to enter an allegorical wood thicker and darker than any Dante could have imagined. A parabola of the American Experience, a symbol of the man–nature relationship, a model of redemption, the pilgrimage as ritual observance of primitive instincts, the mythical model of the life–death pattern: all meanings found in the narrative, and not so far removed from the historical-moral-anagogical dear to the exegetes of the Middle Ages. A commentator by the name of Moses even manages to see in Lion, the Dog which kills the Bear, 'the mechanisation and applied science which ends up by taking the wilderness by the throat'!

Everything, then, would now seem to be settled: we have a text, its model or *typos* (the negro spiritual, and, indirectly, Psalm 113 and the Book of Exodus), and its polysemic, indeed infinite, exegesis. But things are not as rational in the twentieth century as they were in the Middle Ages. To begin with, we may have the allegorical, the moral, and the anagogical senses, but where is the first, the literal? Israel went out of Egypt: so Exodus, the Psalms, and the Afro-American spiritual tell us. But where does Moses go down in Faulkner's work? In fact, where is Moses? The only Moses in the book is a dog, in the fourth section of 'Was', and he seems to go down nowhere at all: at most 'into' something, and, in Disney cartoon fashion, finds it very hard to get out again:

Old Moses went right into the crate with the fox, so that both of them went right on through the back end of it. That is, the fox went through, because when Uncle Buddy opened the door to come in, old Moses was still wearing most of the crate around his neck until Uncle Buddy kicked it off of him.

Nor is there any Moses in the last story of the book, the title of which sharply commands, in the voice of God, and wearily asks, with the voice of American blacks, the future guide of Israel to go down into Egypt. So who is this Moses? To answer this question, we have to ask another: for perhaps, by learning something of his whereabouts, we shall discover who this fugitive character may be. The question is: *why* should Moses go *down*?

The question would be considered of paramount importance in the rational world of medieval exegesis, where one of the very first things a commentator does in examining a text is to explain its title. This is what I shall try to do from now on—no more fourfold interpretation of the book, but just an *accessus ad libri titulum*. Faulkner himself authorizes, indeed prompts, me to do this by imposing on his volume, almost as an afterthought, or gloss, from outside, an extremely presumptuous, para-Scriptural title.

Two pairs of contrasting elements make this heading somewhat uncanny. Firstly, the Voice that pronounces it is on the one hand both God's own ('Thus spoke the Lord') and that of Moses repeating God's command ('bold Moses said'), and on the other, its resonance in black America's whole despairing but hopeful choir. Thus, we have the supreme Authority, the threatening Logos or *dabhar* itself, and simultaneously two different echoes of it—the interiorized, public response of prophecy, and the entreaty of the people. On three different, but typologically related levels, God orders Moses to go down, Moses tells himself to go down, the blacks ask Moses to go down. Secondly, this 'going down' could at first sight be interpreted as both a humbling descent to earthly matters from (literally) God-knows-what heights, and as a missionary *katabasis* to the nether world. It would be easy, for instance, in the second case, to imagine Freud's Moses leading us down, introspectively, towards the depths of monotheism and fatherhood. It would however be harder to picture a similar kind of Moses in Thomas Mann's *The Law*, in the early Freud, and above all in Michelangelo. The latter's Moses might certainly go down towards the plain, but only to sit there on his throne with anything but humility, frowning, tense, and staring into an inscrutable distance. The plot, apparently, thickens.

The only way out of the maze, it seems to me, is to go back to the sources. In Exodus, which the spiritual, and by implication Faulkner are following, Moses is *never* told to 'go down, way down in Egyptland'. Moses is ordered to go down when he is on top of Mount Sinai, and God tells him to 'go down' and 'charge the people, lest they break through unto the Lord to gaze, and many of them perish' (19: 21, 24). They, the people, must not climb up the mountain: if they do and see God, they will die. It is during this, the supreme theophany, that Yahweh issues the ten commandments.

Moses is later told to go down when, after God has written with his finger the tables of the law, the children of Israel make the golden calf (32: 7). Earlier on in Exodus, Moses is simply sent 'unto Pharaoh' (3: 10), as it is put in the King James Bible, which the blacks and Faulkner will be familiar with, and he simply returns from Midian, where he had taken refuge and where he had married, 'into Egypt' (4: 19–21).

Let us temporarily conclude, then, that the negro spiritual and Faulkner superimpose two distinct episodes in Exodus, and that the mysterious Moses who 'goes down' into Egypt in both spiritual and novel comes from Mount Sinai with God's written Law in his hands, forbidding the people to look too closely at Yahweh. It hardly makes much sense, but might just be true. But to use Occam's ever-efficient razor, there is a more economical, albeit more bizarre, explanation. 'To go down into Egypt' is a frequent expression in Genesis, where we find it no less than twenty times in the story of Joseph, culminating, so to speak, in God's speech to Jacob 'in the visions of the night': 'I am God, the God of thy father: fear not to go down into Egypt; for I will there make of thee a great nation: I will go down with thee into Egypt; and I will also surely bring thee up again: and Joseph shall put his hand upon thine eyes' (46: 3–4).

In fact, we all remember—and should we happen not to, Thomas Mann is there with *Joseph and His Brothers* to remind us—that Egypt is the land of corruption and death, down into which one goes to die in slavery and out of which one escapes in resurrection. And we also remember that the last grand scene of Genesis is that of Jacob's funeral, when Joseph, his brothers, his servants, all the servants of Pharaoh, the elders of his house, and all the elders of the land of Egypt accompany the embalmed body of Israel 'up' into the land of Canaan, so that it may be buried in the cave of the field of Machpelah, before Mamre.

There is, I think, little doubt that *Go Down, Moses* as a whole resembles Genesis rather than Exodus. In more ways than one, Genesis seems actually to constitute the Scripture narrative which Faulkner's novel *rescripts*, and at the same time the prefiguration which *Go Down, Moses* comes to fulfil. An accurate stylistic analysis quickly reveals that *Go Down, Moses* is the work of at least three different sources: the Priestly figure who opens 'Was', the Elohist of 'Pantaloon in Black' and 'Delta Autumn', and above all the Yahwist of the uncanny stories of Uncle Buck and Uncle Buddy, and of the chase-like theophanies of 'The Bear'.

Like Genesis, *Go Down, Moses* contains endless genealogies. And, although its central character, Isaac McCaslin, presents himself at one point as 'I am what I am'—the Pauline version (1 Corinthians 15: 10) of God's 'I am that I am' in Exodus (3: 14)—he also clearly considers himself as God's 'foreseen', figural *anti-typos* of the Isaac whose name he bears: 'If He could see Father and Uncle Buddy in Grandfather He must have seen me too—an Isaac born into a later life than Abraham's and repudiating immolation.'

More to the point, this is an Isaac who, rather like Esau, sells his birthright for, as he himself says, 'not peace but obliteration, and a little food'. His antagonist is a Lucas who, like Jacob, plays tricks on everybody, and who becomes 'almost a Jehovah-like' figure: infinite in patience, impervious to time, incapable of forgiving others and of having to harm them. Isaac observes him one morning and sees an embalmed and slightly mummified face embodying the archetype of the McCaslins: a face which is that of the true patriarch and the Israel of his people. At the same time, he is the only human being now able to take on the connotations of the Heavenly Father:

He is both heir and prototype simultaneously of all the geography and climate and biology which sired old Carothers and all the rest of us and our kind, myriad, countless, faceless, even nameless now except himself who fathered himself, intact and complete, contemptuous, as old Carothers must have been, of all blood black white yellow or red, including his own.

Finally, the last story, 'Go Down, Moses', and thus the book itself, ends with the extraordinary funeral of Samuel Worsham Beauchamp, the funeral of a black man followed in procession by all the white elders of Jefferson, Mississippi, and a funeral accompanied by the following chant:

> Roth Edmonds sold my Benjamin . . .
> Sold him in Egypt and now he dead.
> Oh yes, Lord. Sold him in Egypt.
> Sold him in Egypt.
> And now he dead.

It might be in order to recall here that *In Exitu Israel de Aegypto* was the hymn with which early Christians accompanied the dead to the grave. What matters more, however, is that Samuel Worsham Beauchamp returns to Mississippi as a corpse—from Illinois. Instead of going up like Jacob, he goes down, from North to South.

I hope I have got my facts, and above all my geography, correct. Beauchamp is Lucas's and Mollie's last grandchild—thus, ideally, a Benjamin. Is his dead body coming back from Canaan to Egypt? Or is it returning from Egypt to Canaan? Down, or up? I am not just playing with Jurij Lotman's semiology. The fact is, as Thomas Mann would quickly point out, that Egypt is an odd country, where 'going down' really means 'going up'—southwards equals up the Nile and down to the heart of darkness, that 'darkest Africa' which is the original homeland of American blacks: Afro-Americans.

The Nile is the only great archetypal river that flows northwards. Moses, then, must go 'up' into Egypt to reach the hidden waterfalls, to find Greene's 'heart of the matter'. The 'inverted' course of the Nile, however, causes great difficulties to a typological, or figural, mind, for, at least since the discovery of America, the Mississippi, which quickly became the Nile's mythical and figural equivalent in the northern hemisphere of the New World, has been flowing from North to South. In their long-desired exodus, a re-enactment of Israel's, the blacks must indeed flee to the North, but *upstream*, if they are to gain their freedom.

Faulkner, however, resolutely denies that Canaan lies in the North. Isaac McCaslin makes this clear in the historical part of his long discussion with his cousin in 'The Bear', obliquely stating it, with geographical irony, when he visits Fonsiba and her husband on their farm a little further north, in Arkansas—a Southern state which, however, still represents freedom for the two blacks, and the possibility of owning their own farm. When McCaslin speaks to Fonsiba's husband of the 'curse' which, brought by the whites, still reigns in the entire South, Fonsiba's husband gives a post-Civil War response, the vision of the blacks who have absorbed the lesson of the Yankees, the Northerners:

You're wrong. The curse you whites brought into this land has been lifted. It has been voided and discharged. We are seeing a new era, an era dedicated, as our founders intended it, to freedom, liberty, and equality for all, to which this country will be the new Canaan.

But Isaac interrupts him: 'Freedom from what? From work? Canaan?' Then, jerking his hand in a gesture that seems to embrace all the squalor of the empty, non-tilled fields, and of the damp, heatless house where they live, Isaac asks with rhetorical violence, closing the discussion once for all: 'What corner of Canaan is this?' No, for William Faulkner the United States of America is not the Promised Land, and the North is no Canaan. And after all, the very Moses the title of the book evokes, the Moses of the Bible, never reaches the land of Canaan, but looks at it from Mount Nebo, opposite Jericho, and dies.

I hope I have duly confused my readers. It is precisely what, like Faulkner, I set out to do. 'And the way up is the way down, the way forward is the way back', Heraclitus and the Eliot of the *Four Quartets* confirm. Perhaps this is the anagogical meaning of Faulkner's title, leaping in one move from the uncertainties of the letter to the certainties of metaphysics and mysticism. Something, however, still escapes us: something relating to the moral sense of the title and the novel as a whole. Let us try, then, to read another version of the stories so far:

> Israel also came into Egypt;
> and Jacob sojourned in the land of Ham.
> And he increased his people greatly;
> and made them stronger than their enemies.
> He turned their heart to hate his people,
> to deal craftily with his servants.
> He sent Moses his servant;
> and Aaron whom he had chosen.
> They performed his signs among them,
> and wonders in the land of Ham.

So reads Harold Fisch's translation of Psalm 105, again celebrating the events of Genesis–Exodus. Egypt, it should be noted, is here the land of Ham. But the sons of Ham, as we all know and as Faulkner takes care to remind us in 'The Bear', are the blacks. Moses is being sent to Egypt, to the land of Ham, to tell the blacks: 'Let my people go.' Let them go from this 'cursed land'.

'In exitu Israel de Aegypto, Domus Iacob de populo *barbaro*', Psalm 113 sings. The barbarians can be but the Afro-Americans. Moses is the prophet of the *whites*. He should then, according to the order given by God and repeated in Faulkner's title, go down into Egypt from Mount Sinai, bearing the two tables of the Law written by God himself. He then has to smash them when he sees that the sons of Ham are slowly but inexorably becoming, in an America shaped by the outcome of the Civil War, *equal* to the sons of Israel—or, worse, when he sees that the two races, adoring the same golden calf, are becoming one people, bent on idolatry and materialism: when he sees that Egypt and Canaan are moving too close together, the South becoming too like the North, and 'up' too like 'down': near-interchangeable.

The message is of great 'moral' significance, and decidedly reactionary in political colour. Hence Faulkner's reshuffling of the cards in his title and in his novel, treacherously rewriting spiritual, Psalms, Exodus, and Genesis. Perhaps we do indeed need a medieval exegete to find his way around this fictionalized Bible which replaces the Moses of the title, immediately, within the narrative corpus, with an Isaac, and to extrapolate the perverse, purloined polysemia of *Go Down, Moses*.

Time now to face the crucial, 'overwhelming question'. Is this a reading of the novel 'from the heart', which Isaac McCaslin, as we have seen, requires of a reading of the Bible? The immediate answer is a resounding 'no'. This is not how the heart reads, nor the 'doomed and lowly of the earth'. It is the reading of an exegete, a critic, an analyst: in a word, all those our protagonist calls the 'wise of the earth'.

A reading from the heart, as Isaac himself points out, would overlook textual contradictions, and even lies (as he considers the curse of the offspring of Ham to be). It would go straight to the one, unchanging truth whose image he is ready to grasp in the lines from Keats's 'Ode on a Grecian Urn' which his cousin quotes in one of their lengthy debates: 'She cannot fade, though thou hast not thy bliss! | Forever wilt thou love, and she be fair.'

A truth of this kind, non-abstract, but made of earth and flesh and blood, comprehends all things that concern the heart: 'honour and pride and justice and courage and love'.

The forest is truth: complex, sentient, boundless, secret; brooding on itself, and able to teach Isaac, in the guise of a mother, humility. True, also, are the deer, the bear, the dog: cyphers for humanity to measure itself against, to know itself and its own codes of honour, pride, and courage. Sam Fathers is a master of the truth, his Indian and negro blood producing insight into and knowledge of humanity and the natural world, and can initiate the young McCaslin, instilling in him the yearning for solitude and independence which will make him ready to renounce his property, and therefore free.

When, years after Sam's death, Isaac re-enters the forest to visit the graves of Sam, Old Ben, and Lion, he is suddenly able to understand their truth, and the truth of earth and time. Isaac has brought with him a twist of tobacco, a new calico handkerchief, and a bag of the mints Sam was so fond of:

that gone too, almost before he had turned his back, not vanished but merely translated into the myriad life which printed the dark mould of these secret and sunless places with delicate fairy tracts, which, breathing and biding and immobile, watched him from beyond every twig and leaf until he moved, moving again, walking on; he had not stopped, he had only paused, quitting the knoll which was no abode of the dead because there was no death, not Lion and not Sam: not held fast in earth but free in earth and not in earth but of earth, myriad yet undiffused of every myriad part, leaf and twig and particle, air and sun and rain and dew and dawn and dark and dawn again in their immutable progression and, being myriad, one: and Old Ben too, Old Ben too; they would give him his paw back even, certainly they would give him his paw back: then the long challenge and the long chase, no heart to be driven and outraged, no flesh to be mauled and bled.

What he realizes is the truth of life, of the perennial transformation, of eternal return: an almost metaphysical, mystical vision of nature as the soul of the world, the heart of matter: the land as the only supreme being which is inclusive of all becoming. Apparently unchanging, it will however be demolished, as Isaac himself realizes at the end of 'Delta Autumn', by history's becoming, continuously eating into the forest to make room for human beings and their crops.

Among the 'truths of the heart' are also the stubbornness, shrewdness, impenetrability, self-possession, and dignity of the half-cast Lucius Quintus Carothers McCaslin Beauchamp who, on coming of age, reclaims his part of his white inheritance and changes his name to Lucas, 'not denying, declining the name itself, because he used three quarters of it; but simply taking the name and changing, altering it, making it no longer the white man's but his own, by himself composed, himself self-progenitive and nominate, by himself ancestored'. Equally of the heart is the near-silent message the old negro woman Mollie sends out to the whole South. Eager to have her grandson Sam's body home for burial (unaware that he had been executed for murder up in the North), she bends the entire city of Jefferson in a collective act of pity and remorse, as it follows his coffin in the novel's final images.

The gesture reveals the South for once united and in step, blacks and whites walking together towards that land of Canaan where Jacob's burial takes place at the end of the Book of Genesis. The white South is here, undoubtedly, at its best in the chivalrous generosity which has always belonged to its imaginary. It is forced into this final *pietas*, however, by the obstinacy of an old black woman, a quasi-fulfilment of Isaac's prophecy when he discusses with his cousin his vision of the two divine plans which would come about to shape the history of America and the plantations.

In the first, God would use a simple man to discover a new world 'where a nation of people could be founded on humility and pity and sufferance and pride of one another'. He would then, however, have realized that the earth had been cursed, since the time of Indian possession, by the greed, godlessness, and violence brought from the Old Continent and the whole of white history. He would then allow the earth to be emptied of Indian blood, and white blood would be used to remove the curse of the white man. In other words, he would allow the pioneers to drive out the Indians and found a Union of freedom and equality. But the plan would fail since the whites had brought into the New World the blacks, too: an 'abject' people whose exploitation could only make America's original sin blacker.

Divine wisdom then thought up a second, more complex plan, grounded in blood and suffering (the only functional *aide-mémoire* for humanity). This was to allow all the manipulating of the Unionist profiteers, and the resultant oppression, with all the illusions and courage and patriotism of the Southerners—in a word, all the laceration and horror of the Civil War and the years which followed—in order to save the New World from ruin, 'binding' the blacks for a short time more even after the war and formal emancipation:

Yes. Binding them for a while yet, a little while yet. Through and beyond that life and maybe through and beyond the life of that life's sons and maybe even through and beyond that of the sons of those sons. But not always, because they will endure. They will outlast us because they are— . . . Yes. He didn't want to. He had to. Because they will endure. They are better than we are. Stronger than we are. Their vices are vices aped from white men or that white men and bondage have taught them: improvidence and intemperance and evasion—not laziness: evasion: of what white men had set them to, not for their aggrandizement or even comfort but his own.

Here, then, is the prophecy of Faulkner's Moses, Isaac McCaslin: it is the blacks who will resist, survive, and save. This is the truth of his heart, in clear—apparently clear—contradiction to the 'wiser' reading extrapolated above.

But how to paint ourselves out of this corner? Must we choose between a 'heart' and 'head' reading, accepting a deconstructive division in every text? Must we admit that there can be two truths, as Isaac would never do? Or negotiate an agreement with psychoanalysis, maintaining that a 'heart reading' only concerns the most superficial level of authorial intention, while the intellect reaches down and retrieves repressed areas, so that two versions of truth are not only plausible, but in a sense inevitable, and that 'heart' and 'intellect' are no more than conventional signifiers for what Isaac defines the 'complexity of passion and lust and hate and fear which drives the heart', i.e. the human psyche?

The questions are hardly idle. If we were to apply them to the Bible itself, rather than to a para-biblical literary text, the results would be explosive. They would take on the aspect of an unbridgeable gap between a 'wise' and a 'simple' reading: between the truth of the poor in spirit and that of the rabbis and exegetes, which would be intolerable both for any organized Church or tradition-based hermeneutics, but also, more to the point, for any man or woman of good faith.

I shall pause for a moment before rushing into this particular abyss, although it would be wrong to lose sight of it. Let's go back to our literary text and ask ourselves if it really is as divided as it seems, considering first of all the 'heart' reading Isaac offers of the McCaslin plantation in particular and American history in general. The first reading is the foundation for the second, thus placing Isaac's reconstruction on exactly the same level as the Hebrew Bible, the Book of Genesis in particular, in that it takes a series of events regarding only one line of descent (albeit multiple) as paradigmatic of a whole people, if not the whole of humanity.

There exists, however, a very basic difference between the Bible story and Isaac's. The narrative sequence leading from Adam to Joseph, and from Moses to Canaan, or, later, from Saul to David and Solomon, is self-sufficient, self-referential: it offers itself as *the* history, with no need of documentation to endorse specific episodes or general lines. Isaac's history of the plantation, on the other hand, is based on the 'master narrative' of the masters' ledgers, frequently quoted in 'The Bear', and it is these, which represent the concrete historical

facts within the fiction, on which history is based. Furthermore—and here Faulkner's rescripting moves along a razor's
edge—they are presented to us as the books of Revelation:
the Sacred Books (including the book of life) which present
the record, the ledger, of humanity's past actions and final
destinies, to be opened on the Day of Judgment:

To him it was as though the ledgers in their scarred cracked
leather bindings were being lifted down one by one in their
finding sequence and spread open on the desk or perhaps upon
some apocryphal Bench or even Altar or perhaps before the
Throne Itself for a last perusal and contemplation and refreshment
of the All-knowledgeable before the yellowed pages and the
brown thin ink in which was recorded the injustice and a little
at least of its amelioration and restitution faded back for ever into
the anonymous communal original dust.

This is a more radical paradox, perhaps, than that of the
prophetic books of the Bible: the basis of history in *Go
Down, Moses* is Revelation, prophecy, which, however—
paradox-cum-scandal—make outright claims to be objective fact and documented proof. And are they the basis of
history, or, rather, of historical interpretation? Every histor-
iography has its own thought-structure, the guiding lines for
the [hi]stories it narrates, but Isaac's is actually a theological
interpretation of the history of the plantation and the whole
of America. The plans he reads are the work of providence,
or, more precisely, of soteriology, in that they promise
salvation. In this Isaac is, for the early twentieth century,
in line with all those Europeans and Americans who,
between the sixteenth and seventeenth centuries, believed
that their contemporaries' discovery of the New World was
fulfilling Scripture's prophecies (the new heaven and new
earth of Isaiah and Revelation), and represented a peak in
the West's *Heilsgeschichte*, the 'sacred history' which saw in
America its paradise lost.

On the other hand Isaac is decidedly behind the culture
of his own time: positivist, idealist, or materialist, whatever

it chooses for itself within its own definition of history; nor does a precedent exist anywhere in the traditional imaginary for his theory of the original curse on the land, or of a change in God's original plan. In other words, Isaac shows himself to be a canny exegete: a passionate reader from the heart, certainly, but at the same time, with the right mixture of traditionalism and originality, a hermeneut, one of the wise of the earth. Medievally speaking, if in renouncing all possessions he is something of a St Francis of Assisi, simple and radical, the complexity of his theology is worthy of a Bonaventure: a Franciscan but also a man of the Schools and *disputationes*: 'seraphicus', indeed, but equally a 'doctor'.

Lastly, the final impulse in Isaac's *Heilsgeschichte* will certainly come from the heart, but it is also most definitely ambiguous. To see the blacks as superior to the whites, able to survive and save themselves and the whole South, at the same time as proclaiming that God will still 'bind' them for a time, until the third generation and beyond, means visiting on them an election as potentially tragic as that conferred on the children of Israel over the centuries, with the additional irony of total temporal indeterminacy: 'a little while yet, but not always'.

Isaac McCaslin's truth of the heart proves, then, to be considerably more complex than at first sight, he himself admitting that aspects of it escape him. Not only is it rooted in a knowledge of the earth, but ultimately it also moves towards that truth of the exegete which it putatively denies. This, then, is the reason Moses has to go down: to order Pharaoh to let his white people go, and confirm for the blacks, for the non-eschatological present and future, the yoke they have been under for more than two hundred years. In Italian one would say this is an undoubtedly *di razza* re-Scripture, the expression meaning both 'first-class' and 'racial', possibly even 'racist'.

The final link in exegetical logic, in this *accessus ad titulum*, is now almost inevitable. Moses, tradition dictates, is also the writer of the Pentateuch, the inspired author of the Book. It is this Moses, too, whom God orders to 'go down'. A Book–book analogy, then, would allow us also to order William Faulkner to 'Go down, way down in Egypt land, tell old Pharaoh to let my people go'. This is the mask of the writer who rewrites the Bible to announce its scandalous and embarassing truth. It would have been perfectly understood by a refined medieval exegete. Dante, who put on a similar, though less sardonic, writer–prophet mask, would have understood it at once, and would have recognized without a second's hesitation one of the meanings which, with and beyond the literal, give the Bible and the *Comedy* their polysemic, polyphonic fullness. For us, para-biblical, post-medieval readers of a book by William Faulkner, this Moses will go down once again to hold back the Exodus of American blacks, forcing us to add our own counter-melody and ask, with all the sorrow and anger which Primo Levi puts into the words of the Talmud's *Maxims of the Fathers*: 'Se non ora, quando?' If not now, when?

Shall we try to find a partial answer, or at least a counterpoint, to this question dictated by rightly impatient waiting, in a re-Scripture that might at the same time prepare us for the present volume's conclusion? In the Bible, Exodus is of course a crucial book: open to the most sacred of dimensions, but also to history and to the definition of personal and national identities, it explores with tremendous dramatic strength the exaltation and the pains of Israel's relationship with God (it is here, as everyone will no doubt remember, that he reveals himself to Moses and proclaims the Law). Exodus is also all-important in Christian interpretation (Dante's Epistle to Cangrande, quoted above, representing but one significant example out of many one could mention from the last two thousand years), and in the Islamic tradition (in the Koran, Moses, the first Muslim believer, constitutes a predecessor of, and a model for, Muhammad). Its figural value has never ceased to fascinate entire cultures: in the Gospels, Jesus is opposed to, and fulfills, Moses; the

Puritans see their migration to America as a new Exodus, and we have just seen how the American blacks dream of leaving the Egypt of slavery in the South for the new Canaan of the North. It will come as no surprise to discover that the second book of the Bible has produced infinite— both direct and oblique—rewritings, from Jewish legends to the Arab Thalab, from medieval mystery plays to Drayton, from Schiller to Chateaubriand, from Steinbeck's *The Grapes of Wrath* to Leon Uris's (book and movie) *Exodus*, from Handel to Rossini and Schönberg.

Here, I will choose, and very briefly examine, a recent work of fiction as a contrast to Faulkner's and as a foreshadowing of Joseph Roth's *Job*, the last novel I examine in this book. This is Michel Tournier's *Éléazar, ou la source et le buisson*, published in 1996. Tournier is not new to rewriting: besides publishing an original *rifacimento* of *Robinson Crusoe* with his *Vendredi, ou les limbes du Pacifique*, he has tackled re-Scripture itself in the opening story of *Le Coq de bruyère*, 'The Adam Family' (where he reconstructs Genesis from the creation of woman down to the children of Cain and Abel with surprising reversals of the traditional perspective), and in *Gaspard, Melchior & Balthazar*, recounting with great brio the stories of the (four) Magi who come to adore the child Jesus in Bethlehem, projecting that of the fourth, Taor, all the way to Good Friday, and making Herod as well as the ox and ass speak up.

In *Éléazar* Tournier presents a young shepherd of the Irish West, Eleazar O'Braid, who becomes an Anglican priest, a 'pastor of the people' (in Jewish tradition, Eleazar is the name of a series of priests, beginning with Aaron's son in Exodus). He marries a Catholic girl, Esther, whose right leg is withered but who sings and plays the Irish harp beautifully, and has two children, Benjamin and Coralie. With his serpent-shaped crook, Eleazar, who has himself been branded for life on his cheek by a whip, kills a man who is whipping a poor young shepherd. In 1845, when the potato famine devastates the land, Eleazar flees from hunger and remorse, with the whole family, to America, where they arrive after forty days' sailing. Having landed in Virginia, the O'Braids decide to reach California by crossing the deserts and the mountains of the Far West. They encounter an enormous herd of buffaloes, the Indians, and Mexican outlaws. As they sight the new Canaan from the heights of the Sierra Nevada, Eleazar, who has been wounded by the bandits, chooses not to continue on his journey and, entrusting his wife and children to the hands of the repentant outlaw, José, leaves them, dies, and is buried on the last mountain summit.

The novel is clearly built by interweaving various themes and genres and modernizing them: for instance, emigration from Europe to America (here, from Ireland, which Joyce, in *Ulysses*, had already shown as an Israel slave to British Egypt), the Western movie tradition, the mysterious opposition between spring and burning bush. Although at times *Éléazar* flirts with the popular *feuilleton* and exploits its resources, although it is often surcharged with sudden, brief deviations from its main plot line, it also reads like one of the most enlightening rewritings of Exodus one may encounter. The whole story of Eleazar is recounted in a bare hundred pages with the lightness, quickness, exactitude, visibility, and multiplicity recommended by Calvino in his *Six Memos for the Next Millennium*. In every chapter the events follow on each other's heels as if we were in an action movie, but in every chapter there always emerges a distinguishing feature, a pause, a meditation that suggest, evoke, or foreshadow something deeper and higher.

The narrative, for example, opens with 'an immense wave of soft, silvery mist' breaking from the West on to the Ocean and overflowing it. This fog, which penetrates Ireland from the Atlantic, dominates the whole first part of the novel, where the island appears as the place of 'imperfect vision' and of water, its fire, that of turf, being 'dim, flameless, almost wet', while its songs, impersonated by Esther, speak of the streams, fountains, and springs that give life to the earth, the

Irish soil. Only when Eleazar leaves behind Ireland's (and Europe's) extreme West to move on to the American Far West, do we understand that Ireland has laid before the protagonist's eyes 'a veil of rain, fog, and chlorophyl' which hides truth, whereas 'the desert's perfectly dry, transparent air respects the brutal clarity of biblical law'.

Eleazar's voyage is thus a journey through the primal elements as well as through history and Scripture. The three levels are never separate, but always cleverly fused into each other. To grow up in Ireland means being destined to become a shepherd and being branded on the face by a master's whip; it means experiencing the famine and the constant division between Protestant and Catholics. With a leap, it means living between the Old Testament of Moses and the New of the Good Shepherd. Obsessed by the former's powerful figure, Eleazar soon asks himself four crucial questions derived from exegetical tradition: why, being a Jew, should Moses be brought up by an Egyptian princess and return among his people by betraying his adoptive family; why must he kill with a blow of his club the Egyptian overseer smiting a Jew; why should his brother Aaron take advantage of his absence to forge the golden calf; and why (here Tournier explicitly draws on André Chouraqui's *Moïse*), 'above all, above all, why Yahweh's incomprehensible, inexorable prohibition to let him, leading his people, enter that Promised Land where milk and honey flow'.

Eléazar answers these questions with an exegesis which becomes part of life: in other words, it harmonizes a reading from the heart with that from the intellect. Little by little, the protagonist understands the events of Exodus by experiencing them, his journey thus becoming one of initiation as well as of 'interpretation' of the biblical text. Eleazar is not a fool, he does not believe he is a Moses, nor even his typological fulfilment. But his personal history appears to him 'strongly attracted, forged, and endowed with meaning by the prophet's own destiny, as the iron file dust takes order and direction by strength of a magnet's field': Moses's grand adventure 'worked as a reference to decipher his life's humble facts'. Like Moses with the Egyptian, Eleazar slays the man whipping the young shepherd. The Irish famine refers back to the plagues of Egypt. The forty-day long crossing of the Atlantic echoes the forty days of young Moses on Mount Sinai. The serpent-shaped shepherd's crook which Eleazar inherits from his O'Braid ancestors and which he always carries with him can be compared to Moses's rod, which God transforms into a serpent.

The theme of the serpent lies at the novel's very centre and constitutes its enigmatic keystone. According to legend, there are no snakes in Ireland because they were all banished by St Patrick. Now, when the O'Braids, having parted from the other pioneers, start crossing the American desert in complete solitude, Benjamin is bitten by a rattlesnake. The boy would soon die were it not for the intervention of an Indian chief, Serpent-of-Brass, who lightly touches the lad's eyelids and cures him.

The conversation between the native American and the Irish priest reveals that the serpent represents a multiform symbol of the divine. It is Lucifer, who shone in Heaven as 'the most perfect of the Great Spirit's creatures', but who, perverted and fallen, taught his dark science to Adam and Eve. The serpent's 'perfect, fascinating head, beyond all beauty or ugliness', is like the desert: if the desert shows us 'the face of God turned into a landscape', the serpent's head constitutes its 'animal symbol'. Like those of snakes, Serpent-of-Brass's eyelids never lower, whereas 'the closing eyelid, the warm and dark humidity is the very organ' of Ireland.

At the end of the conversation, Eleazar opens up his Bible and reads the episode in Numbers (21: 6–9) in which God sends 'venomous serpents' to bite and kill his people, who are complaining against him and Moses for having led them into the wilderness only to let them die of hunger and thirst. When, implored by his repentant followers, Moses prays

God to take the serpents away, Yahweh orders him to make for himself a serpent and set it upon a pole, 'and it shall come to pass, that every one that is bitten, when he looks upon it, shall live'. Moses makes a serpent of brass, and the children of Israel survive. At this point, Eleazar's initiation is completed, and the complex, evocative mysteric ritual becomes revelation: '"Je suis visage partout", avait dit l'Indien. Ce regard nu qui blesse à mort et qui guérit, c'est tout le mystère de Dieu': '"I am visage all over", the Indian had said. This naked sight which wounds to death and cures is the whole mystery of God'.

The sea breeze that blows on the novel's first pages becomes now like the breath of that Paraclete which dominates Tournier's autobiographical essays. On the desert plateau, Eleazar stands still before a bush. He *sees*. Numbers (20) narrates (rewriting Exodus with a significant variation) how the Jews complained to Moses for having taken them into 'an evil place', 'no place of seed, or of figs, or of pomegranates; nor is there any water to drink'. To the imploring Moses, the Lord gives power of speaking to the rock so that it shall 'give forth its water'. Moses strikes the rock twice with his rod, and water comes out 'abundantly'. According to traditional interpretation (based on Numbers 20: 12), it was in fact Moses's second blow that irritated God, because it showed his (and Aaron's) lack of faith. For this reason Yahweh forbade his prophet to enter the Promised Land.

Eleazar, however, receives from his bush a wider revelation: the spring is water, a land to till, all that is profane, all that produces the golden calf; the desert is fire, the sacred. Moses, 'saved from the waters', shall have a life divided between the spring and the bush, for the bush and the desert are the places of God and the signs of his love. God wants to keep his prophet there, by him, and that is why he makes him die on Mount Nebo before he can enter Canaan. Eleazar, then, consciously chooses the bush, while his people, led by José-Joshua, descend into the valleys of

California, the pure, serene, fertile Ireland of America. God and the world go their separate ways: not that the latter is wholly ungodly—it is still the Lord who will guide Esther, Benjamin, and Coralie to the land of life and plenty—but to be wholly his a human being must choose solitude, wilderness, and death.

This Moses, then, does not go down: neither into Egypt nor, more importantly, into the Promised Land. Tournier's re-Scripture is not as perverse as Faulkner's. He rewrites Exodus (and Numbers) with sadness, fury, and *hope*, composing a true *midrash* which reads the Bible ascetically, with an almost sacred inspiration, entering history and exploring its many cunning, painful passages, but also looking at them, as it were, *from the other side*—from that of God's fiery, serpentine, unfathomable sight.

CHAPTER FIVE

To Recognize Is a God

Helen, Mary Magdalene, Marina—Menuchim

Rabbunì!

HELEN, whose face launched a thousand ships and burnt the topless towers of Ilium, never went to Troy. Paris never swept her into his chamber. It wasn't Helen the city leaders contemplated on the walls. Furious at her defeat in the most fatal beauty contest of all time, Hera fobbed Paris off with a phantom, an image made out of air: a *quasi*-living-and-breathing, identical copy: Helen's double. The flesh-and-blood Helen had been carried off by Hermes and hidden in a cloud in some fold in the ether, then removed safely to Egypt, to the house of the chaste Proteus, to preserve Menelaus' bed inviolate. The first ever East–West clash, the First World War—the Trojan War—was fought for an illusion. Zeus simply wanted to ease the earth of some of its burden by thinning out the human population, and at the same time give the most heroic of heroes, Achilles, the chance to shine.

This is Helen's own account when she appears at the opening of the play Euripides devoted to her a few years before his death. This admirable fiction manages at a single stroke, following a tradition which possibly goes back to Hesiod and Stesichorus, to rewrite the founding myth of Greek civilization, and, seventy years after the most recent East–West skirmish at Salamis, in the middle of the Peloponnesian Wars which were to devastate Greece, to destroy the very idea of war. Helen is removed from sight and mind, conveniently relegated to the shores of the exotic Nile; yet she is, for the first time, moved centre-stage, and Euripides'

Helen is not a tragedy in the modern sense of the word but the enacting of an astonishing rehabilitation of the first adulteress, the story of her reunion with Menelaus, and their return to the marital bed and home: a romance play with a happy ending.

The plot is relatively simple to the spectator; more complex to a careful reader. Divided into two parts, the first shows Helen at Proteus' tomb, where she is imploring his protection against his son Theoclymenus, her undesired suitor. Teucer appears before her, having returned from the Trojan War only to be exiled by his father as punishment for not dying when his brother Ajax killed himself after the contest for Achilles' arms (which went to Odysseus). From questioning Teucer (who, on recognizing her, initially hurls his hatred at her before deciding that it is not Helen), she learns that Troy is destroyed and Helen returned to Menelaus; that the latter, however, has been missing for seven years, while Helen's mother has committed suicide in shame at her daughter's conduct, and her brothers Castor and Pollux have either become gods or have killed themselves, again on her account. Left alone with the Chorus after Teucer's hasty escape (Theoclymenus is killing any Greek to set foot in Egypt), Helen mourns the fate of Troy and of her relatives: all the death and despoiling caused by her name and beauty, which she now vehemently rejects ('Oh that I might, like a painting, be cancelled out and shed my beauty, receiving in exchange some hideous semblance'). Her immediate, desperate response is to consider suicide but the Chorus persuades her to enter the palace and consult the king's sister, the omniscient virgin prophetess Theonoe who will be able to reveal the fate of Menelaus. Helen moves away, again giving in to despair and again bewailing the calamities caused by illusion:

> Weep for the tears of Troy!
> For Troy, deeds without name have bred
> Pain without end. Aphrodite, goddess of joy,

Gave, and I was her gift; thence without respite sprang
Anguish and blood and tears and deep despair;

. . . .

But my curs'd beauty damned with deadly power
Trojan and wandering Greek to sufferings untold.

At the precise moment Helen enters the building,
Menelaus appears; he has lost his ship in a storm, and,
having left the person he believes to be Helen in a cave
with a small guard, he has come to the palace to ask for
assistance. The Old Woman who receives him warns him
that he is in Egypt and explains that he should depart
without ado, given the new king Theoclymenus' hatred
of the Greeks on account of Helen, who is here and
whom he has every intention of taking for his own pleasure.
The dazed Menelaus asks when Helen arrived, imagining
she has been abducted from the cave; on hearing she came
from Sparta before the Greeks set sail for Troy, he can only
presume that she is referring to a different Helen, the
daughter of some Egyptian Zeus, from some other Sparta.
He has just taken the decision to tackle Theoclymenus in
any case when Helen comes running in to announce
Theonoe's vaticination: Menelaus is alive and wandering
the seas and will shortly arrive in Egypt, or has already
been washed on to the shore. The man in question stands
stunned at her words, while she takes in every detail of his
face. After endless questions to establish their identity, she
recognizes her husband and attempts to embrace him, but
Menelaus' mind is still on the woman in the cave, and he
wants nothing to do with her. A Messenger now arrives,
however, from his surviving companions, to inform him
that the Helen in the cave has vanished into the air, revealing Hera's trickery. Menelaus is now able to believe his eyes
and recognize his own wife. After seventeen years they
finally embrace and recite an extremely moving 'recognition
duet', narrating their various misadventures and exchanging
impressions with the Messenger, too, although Helen is

careful to warn him that Theoclymenus wishes to marry her and will attempt to murder her husband.

This begins the second part of the play. It is imperative that Helen and Menelaus escape, but they must first prevent Theonoe (who, as her name states, is a 'divine mind' and thus all-seeing) from revealing Menelaus' identity to her brother. Through a series of varying but convergent arguments—Helen appealing to Proteus' memory and the prophetess's sense of justice, Menelaus threatening to kill himself and his wife—they manage to procure Theonoe's silence. Helen sets out a plan of escape: Melenaus, in the tattered clothes he is wearing, must pretend to be the sole survivor of the shipwreck, and announce to Theoclymenus Menelaus' death at sea; Helen, her head shaved in mourning, is to promise to marry the king in exchange for a ship to perform the funeral rites at sea for her husband, according to Greek custom. Then, once they have set sail, with the help of the men left in charge in the cave, they will seize command of the ship and head for Greece. This is precisely what happens: Theonoe reveals nothing, and Theoclymenus, deceived by the couple, grants them a ship which the Chorus bless in an extraordinary speech, wishing it a safe 'flight' over the waves. Shortly afterwards the Messenger announces the couple's escape. A furious Theoclymenus rages that he will kill Helen, but the Twins, Castor and Pollux, appear *ex machina*, revealing the plans of the gods and of destiny to take Helen up into Olympus, and Menelaus to the Blessed Isles. The Chorus ends the play with the considerations on the nature of the divine which also conclude Euripides' own *Medea*, *Alcestis*, *Andromache*, and the *Bacchae*.

In departure from the usual practice in classical drama, in *Helen* the recognition scene—Aristotle's anagnorisis—does not take place towards the end of the plot, nor does it coincide with the *dénouement*. Here it occurs towards the end of the first part, an anomalous but cardinal point in the action given that, without Helen's and Menelaus' mutual agnition, there can be no flight from Egypt, nor the complete rehabilitation of Helen which is celebrated on her return home. It also, clearly, constitutes the turning-point of the plot: the moment when the phantom Helen, the *eidolon*, disappears to make room for the real Helen; when Menelaus finally accepts that he has fought ten years for a mere illusion. It is, lastly, point zero for the two characters, reduced from mythical heroes to human beings with no designation other than that of simple 'husband' and 'wife'. Abducted not by Paris but by Hera, Helen is nothing: a supplicant at Proteus' tomb, she appears as a wretched woman with her reputation in shreds, pursued by a man she despises: the shadow of her own past. Menelaus, for his part, is no longer one of the greatest Achaean leaders, the conqueror of Troy, but, like Ulysses on approaching the Island of the Phaeacians, a simple survivor of a shipwreck, a Nobody of shreds and tatters.

On this nothing Euripides constructs an initial, delicate, but persistent certainty: the recognition which seals seventeen years of separation (almost as long as that between Penelope and Ulysses) and dispels all illusion while sanctioning the union between man and woman as the nucleus for all hope, redemption, and salvation. The move towards agnition is similarly delicate, faltering and slow, as if we had wandered into a second *Odyssey*. If Helen, lamenting her fate to the Chorus after Teucer's flight, had mentioned that husband and wife would recognize each other through signs known only to themselves (like Penelope and Ulysses), Menelaus has to grapple with the possibility—absurd in the light of all empirico-rational evidence—that his Helen exists, on this very shore where the shipwreck had landed her husband. When the Old Woman informs him, he simply refuses to believe it: he has, after all, fought for her for ten years, and for seven has wandered the seas with her! It is almost easier to believe that there exists another Sparta, 'another', *pace* Yeats, 'Troy for her to burn', and that another Helen lives in Egypt, the daughter of a man called Zeus.

Immediately afterwards, however, Menelaus is shaken

when Helen appears. As soon as he sees her emerging from the palace, he is turned to stone, unable to pronounce a syllable. In her turn Helen, seeing a man in rags approach her, runs to the tomb of Proteus to implore protection. Paradoxically, it seems to be Menelaus who first recognizes her, while she is as if blinded: the supreme moment hanging by a hair. But seeing is one thing, recognizing quite another. Helen has no need of secret signs, reasoning, or memory: she simply observes and understands. At the same time, each asks the other who he/she is: the one is too similar to Helen; the other to Menelaus! Prepared by Theonoe's prophecy, Helen is more open to recognition, and immediately accepts that her husband is he, exclaiming, 'Come to me—I am your wife!' He, however, is far from ready to reciprocate: 'Wife? What do you mean? Leave my clothes alone!' The facts simply fail to square, and when Helen asks him to believe his own eyes, he replies that while it is most certainly true that she resembles Helen, the evidence (*saphēs*: 'that which is clear') prevents him from believing it: he already has one Helen. And when the real Helen informs him that the other is an image created out of air by some god, and that there are not two Helens, as he seems to believe, but only a name endowed with ubiquity, Menelaus decides to leave her: 'The memory of what I went through at Troy is more convincing than you are.'

Seeing is most certainly not knowing, nor believing: what speaks directly is life, experience, suffering felt on the pulse, in the soul, and in the flesh. What is certain, for Menelaus, are the long years spent doggedly battling to win Helen back: defamation, death, destruction. This constitutes life. Accepting *this* Helen means believing in the unknown, in the unowned: accepting as one's own a different story invented by the gods, and another level of existence independent of oneself: in a word, it means making the leap of faith.

In Euripides' *Helen* Menelaus can afford not to run this risk. The Messenger informs him of the 'prodigy': the Helen of the cave has vanished into the air, explaining the divine plan as she departed. And he who was sceptical of the evidence of their eyes, faced with this wonder (*thauma*), can now yield: 'Then all concurs, and the woman speaks the truth! Ah long-desired day that brings you back into my arms!' 'That is this', is what Menelaus says literally: a paradox indeed, that two divergent realities are now recognized as one ('all concurs'), when one of the two is annulled by a 'miracle', and a *thauma* is accepted as proof! Helen had required considerably less. After a moment's hesitation, given the 'stranger's' condition, she was more than ready to welcome him back. Bursting with desire and longing ('Oh, Menelaus, when will you come? How I yearn for your arrival!', she had exclaimed on leaving the palace), Helen looks and believes. 'Oh gods!', she murmurs, 'Because to recognize those we love is a god.'

To recognize those we love is a god. The original, *theos gar kai to gignōskein philous*, leaves no room for doubt: in recognizing our loved ones (and the sentence could also be translated, 'it is a god that makes us recognize those we love') there is, or there comes into play, something divine (*theos* could also be an adjective). It makes little difference whether the divinity is the cause or the thing: what Helen proclaims when she understands who is standing in front of her is that to love is human, to recognize divine: that the agnition between two human beings linked through love has something of the life of the gods in it, and is in itself a *numen*. This is a truth of no small significance. It places the divine within the process of awareness and the love between husband and wife, and at the same time makes that awareness, when accompanied by this love, an emanation of the divine. Apparently a small, but in reality a huge certainty. Helen has no need of the leap of faith: prepared by desire and longing, she perceives the divine immediately, within herself, an instant flood of feeling the moment she perceives her husband. Helen has no need of the leap of faith because she herself represents faith: that between husband and wife which here is a seamless part of her faith in god.

Menelaus, with shared tears of joy, now echoes his wife's words after the proof of the miracle announced by the Messenger. He, too, now 'believes' in his wife and in god:

> No dearer sight than this! All grief forgotten!
> Daughter of Zeus, you are mine to have and hold.
> I claimed you once, when the Heavenly Twins your
>   brothers
> Rode their white horses under the torchlit night,
> And their shouts of blessing echoed, echoed again—
> Once, long ago; and then
> Hera stole you away, and my house was empty.

This moment, when Menelaus too is moved by the certainty that the divine exists in the recognition of those who love, is the moment of supreme balance in the whole of the play. This human-based certainty is the only one *Helen* offers concerning the divine. The moment over, the divine nature becomes the object of doubt. When Menelaus attempts to clarify the whole issue with the Messenger, he denies that Helen was the cause or even the divine instrument of human suffering at Troy: 'It was not Helen', he states, 'for the gods deceived us, leaving in our hands the sorrowful image of a cloud.' This statement in itself constitutes one of the most important signifying *nuclei* in the play: the opposition between reality and illusion, the futility of war, and divine deceit. The Messenger then turns to Helen with a reply that marks the beginning of the impassioned meditation on the nature of the divine which the play now becomes:

My daughter! The ways of the gods are involved and mysterious; they send us good and bad fortune in turn, and all is for the best. One man suffers, but soon his suffering is over and he prospers beyond his hopes; another man does not suffer, but when his turn comes the luck he enjoyed so long deserts him, and he perishes miserably. So you and your husband had your share of suffering— you were ill spoken of, and he was caught in the storm of battle. As long as he struggled for what he wanted, he gained nothing; now good fortune has come to him of his own accord.

Human and divine: no longer interacting, but separate and parallel. Changing, uncertain, and unequal the destiny of humans, in the hands of *tykhē*, fortune: multifaceted, oblique, and resistant to all understanding and interpretation, the divinity. How far we have travelled, in one hundred and fifty lines, from the luminous certainty of Helen, 'Recognizing those we love is a god'! Is this, then, the only god we are to know?

Helen's reply is long and complex. When the Messenger launches into a tirade against the prophecies of soothsayers—predictions based on fire or birdsong—arguing the merits of reason and common sense, he simultaneously recognizes the benefits of offering sacrifices to the gods to ensure their benevolence. Some time later Theonoe actually announces a council of the gods, presided over by Zeus, on the question of Helen's and Menelaus' return to their homeland, disagreement existing between Hera (for) and Aphrodite (against). This seeming rehabilitation of Homer's Olympus, however, is immediately qualified, Theonoe adding that the decision rests neither with Zeus nor with destiny: she herself, a human being, will decide, either revealing their presence to Theoclymenus as Aphrodite desires, or hiding the truth as required by Hera. The gods, then, exist, their wishes can be known, and tensions among the gods can be represented anthropomorphically, as long as this task is left to a human being with *nous*, a woman called 'divine mind'—the mind which for Euripides, following the teachings of Anaxagoras, 'is us and within each of us is god'. She it is who must decide the solution (*telos*) of the gods' controversy, and, in judging, she will most certainly draw on her knowledge of the divine; ultimately, however, she will rely on her moral good sense and human sense of justice. When Helen and Menelaus appeal to her in speeches which are structured like legal pleadings to sway the judge, Theonoe pronounces both the sentence and the criteria adduced: extreme piety, naturally—i.e. awe and veneration of the gods—but principally love and self-consideration,

TO RECOGNIZE IS A GOD   139

which means honouring the good name of her father and avoiding the ignominy which would be hers should she favour her brother; and then *dikē*, the justice to which she has raised a magnificent inner temple, and which eschews human life to survive within the immortal knowledge of the dead:

By nature and by choice I venerate the gods. I respect myself; I am anxious not to cloud my father's good name; while to my brother I must refuse any service that would turn to his dishonour. Within my soul I have consecrated a great temple to justice . . . So I will try to save Menelaus; and since Hera wishes to help him, I will cast my vote with hers. For Aphrodite—may she forgive me; but I have had no dealings with her in the past, and I will grow old a virgin as I am now. . . . I should indeed commit an injustice were I not to return Helen to you; for if my father were alive he would certainly restore you to each other. Such wrongs must be expiated by all, both the dead and the living. The mind of the departed is without life; but it has become one with immortal spirit, and therefore has immortal understanding.

Just as it had previously been for a woman to assert the divine presence in the act of recognition, so now it is for another woman to preach supreme moral awareness, an awareness encompassing the divine, but privileging human reason; and it will again be for a woman, Helen, to elaborate an efficient stratagem of escape (Menelaus meanwhile producing plan after unrealizable plan), although it means repudiating her celebrated beauty, shaving her head to fake bereavement. It will again be Helen who recognizes as 'providential' the seeming disaster of the shipwreck which has reduced Menelaus to rags, whereby Theoclymenus may be convinced of the truth of his presumed death, and persuaded to agree to a sea burial. In short, it is the woman, and Helen in particular, on whom the action hinges; hers is the intellect which plans, and hers the capacity to sacrifice her self-image of beauty to obtain safety. If not exactly divine, woman is the earth's nearest manifestation.

Divinity in its non-terrestrial form, on the other hand, remains for men an inscrutable enigma. When, immediately after the hatching of their escape plan, the Chorus appears in the first stasimon of the play, invoking the nightingale in painfully plaintive lines, and evoking the sufferings of Helen and Menelaus, the Greeks and the Trojans, and all those who seek glory through war only to find themselves under the ground and in the power of Hades, there again surfaces the questioning of the divine:

> Shy nightingale, mistress of woodland music,
> Rapt votress, sweetening with each anguished note
> The green leaf-curtained chambers of the forest,
> Come to my call, and share my sorrow's burden
> With shrill grief rippling from your russet throat.
>
> Sharp was the pain of Helen, hot the tears
> Troy's women shed, cursing the Hellene spears,
> Since Trojan oars raced the rough Malean water,
> And Paris, doomed in love, brought home from
>   Sparta,
> With mocking Aphrodite as his guide,
> The phantom Helen for his fatal bride.
>
>   .   .   .   .
>
> What is god, or non-god,
> Or that which is in between?
> Who among mortals could ever claim,
> For all their searching, to have found it,
> When the matters of the gods toss now here, turn
>   now there
> To reach unlooked for, contradictory ends.
> You, Helen, are Zeus' own daughter,
> In Leda's firm womb swoopingly planted.
> Yet your name, unjust, unfaithful, flies—
> The name of impiety, the name of treachery,
> Throughout your native Greece.
> Among mortals I see
> Nothing that is clear,
> But the divine word I have
> Experienced as true.

The invocation to the nightingale acts as a prologue to a lyrical rewriting of the whole system of myths surrounding the Trojan War and the 'return' of the Greek heroes (issues examined in the two antistrophes omitted above), but is also a more strictly philosophical meditation. The question, preannounced in the human–divine separation in the Messenger's speech, is the *alternative*, now posited as a *distinctio*, in directly dialectical terms: the Chorus asks what constitutes god (*theos*) or non-god (*mē theos*), or that which lies in between (*to meson*). Basically, the Chorus is extending the terms of the question, inserting the negative term (being—non-being) and the middle term which links them, as indeed Protagoras and Gorgias had already done. Thus: it is not given to know whether the gods are or are not (Protagoras); if something is, it is either being or non-being, or being and non-being together (Gorgias). Humanity finds no answer to the Chorus's question, not even from philosophy: no mortal can ever claim to have 'solved' or found it out even after a long search, both because the actions of the gods frequently thwart human expectations, proceeding obliquely or subject to rapid change, and because human vicissitudes (cf. Helen, Menelaus, the Greeks, and the Trojans) are on a contradictory switchback ride. But the impossibility of a reply is endemic to the human condition, as philosophy demonstrates. Carlo Diano, in his extremely lucid analysis of the passage and its context, writes: 'God, non-god, and God and Non-god together, i.e. a cause operating under an order and sense of justice, or the absence of any finality proper to *tykhē*, or causes which operate each time with an aim, but lack order or any sense of justice, merely following wilful, immediate desire.' This, precisely, is still our dilemma.

The alternative is radical in the extreme: without justice there is no divinity. The consequence of this is that nothing can be predicated of the gods, because nothing can be understood, to which we should immediately add that very little can be said of humanity either. *Among mortals no clarity exists*. Paradoxically, however, the 'word' of the gods can be affirmed as 'true'; but the Chorus, while claiming personal experience of this, fails to clarify exactly how and when. *Helen* has so far produced no proof of it at all, and the only 'true' words have been Theonoe's, a 'divine mind' only in that she is human and with a keen sense of justice, and Helen's, the female by definition.

The Chorus plunges the audience into total uncertainty. Even if we accept that it really believes in the word of the gods, we have to recognize that it does so *after* discovering in transcendence nothing less than God, or Nothing, or God and Nothing together. Shortly afterwards, in the second stasimon, the Chorus further complicates matters by celebrating the mother of the gods, identifying her, in a totally exceptional rewriting of myth, with Demeter, the goddess of the hills who 'Ran to and fro frantic over the mountains, | Through green glades of the forest, | Scanning the swirl of every river, | Scouring the deep-voiced swell of the salt ocean, | Searching in anguish for her lost Persephone, | Maiden of mysteries'. The Chorus possibly believes in some new cult—Dionysian, perhaps—such as that which pulses through the *Bacchae* and brings about a terrifying recognition. Or perhaps it is intrinsically uncertain as to the whole problem of the divine, wavering between philosophical analysis, canonical religion, and a new 'mysticism'. When Menelaus invokes Zeus and the gods, pleading their assistance in the coming flight, the Chorus adds its voice in a powerful stasimon which first re-enacts the ship's flight across the waves, then evokes the Twins:

> Oars of the East,
> Winged Sidonian galley,
> Flash through the foam-spray!
> Darling of Mereus, dance,
> While the dancing dolphins follow!
> Now in the soft season,
> The sea smoothed with the wind's caress,

When the voice of Calm, the grey-blue daughter
  of Ocean,
Quietly sings,
Now spread sails to the breeze,
Good-bye to the sheltering port,
Grip and pull on the pinewood sweep,
Crew of Menelaus, and carry in triumph
Helen to the harbours of home and the city that
  Perseus built.

  .   .   .   .

O for wings to tread the air
Where the cranes in ordered flight
Shun the wintry rain-storm,
Seek their southern homeland;
Swift, obedient to their eldest leader's cry
Rising shrill, triumphant,
As they near the frontiers
Of this land, where rainless valleys teem with corn!

Turn, you long-necked travellers,
Who run winged races with the dancing clouds,
And while the Pleiads still are in mid-course
And Orion rides the darkened sky, swoop down,
Alight on Eurotas and proclaim your news
That the taker of Troy, Menelaus, is coming home.

Speed along your airy path,
Riding sons of Tyndareus,
You whose home is heaven
And the stars' bright orbits!
Helen's brothers, Helen's rescuers, ride on,
Skim the green and foam-white ridges
On the dark face of the ocean,
Bring soft breath of welcome winds, the gift of
  Zeus . . .

The movement from the ocean to the gods is part of the same élan: as the sea opens at the passage of the Phoenician ship, across the horizon of the whole Mediterranean, from Egypt to Argus, up into the crane-crammed sky of Libya and through the constellations, in the same way the Chorus invokes the flight of the Twins through the ether to land, smooth as a breeze, on the milky green of the sea. The exhalation of humanity, gods, and nature is, for a moment, in the piercing nostalgia of the Chorus—though not in reality—all one.

And yet, their prayer is answered. The Twins appear to appease Theoclymenus' anger and produce the play's *dénouement*. And although theirs is an 'artificial', *ex machina* epiphany, as lambasted by Aristotle (Euripides being first in his firing-line), it provides an adequate reply to the Chorus's invocation, also making its contribution to the general problematics of the play. What can the Messenger's words regarding divine impenetrability, and those of the Chorus as to god, non-god, or god and non-god possibly mean in the light of this apparition of Castor and Pollux? Is all that questioning, all that passionate, desperate investigation to be swept under the ontological carpet by the divine Twins? Well no: if anything, their appearance on the scene at this point can only serve to underscore the unpredictable, unfathomable nature of the gods, which the whole of *Helen* proclaims, and which even emerges in the Twins' words to Theoclymenus: 'We, now raised by Zeus to godhead, | Would long ago have contrived to rescue her from your land, | But bowed to Fate, and the divine purpose thus fulfilled.' It should also be noted that Helen, with Theonoe, has so far seemed the only truly 'divine' character in the play; now her own brothers, basing themselves on the Helen cult existing in several places, and possibly on the Pythagoreans' *Helene–Selene* (Helen–Moon) identification, predict her future deification, 'for such is the will of Zeus'.

Helen, then, like many of Euripides' plays, ties Gordian knots around the nature of the divine. Small wonder that the Chorus round off the question (and the play) by admitting only a minimalist, if marvellous, transcendency:

> Many are the forms of the deity,
> And unforeseeable the god's decisions.

> The things we thought would happen do not
>   happen;
> The unexpected, god makes possible.

The only certainties, it would appear, are represented by Theonoe's mind, divine because human and justice-orientated, and the sudden illumination which leads Helen to exclaim: recognizing those we love is a god.

It has been maintained that the scenes of the disciples' recognition of the risen Christ in the fourth Gospel (traditionally attributed to John) echo the human–divine agnitions developed by the Alexandrine romance, and, ultimately, by classical theatre and epic. If this is true—and elements in common there most certainly are—then John has rewritten Graeco-Roman literature in a wholly new way, at the same time performing an extraordinary re-Scripting of the Hebrew Bible for good measure.

The Gospel according to Mark, generally considered the oldest, ends mysteriously (at 16: 8: the following verses are a later addition) without Jesus's appearance after the resurrection, and, in an explosive silence, with the fear of the women at the tombside. Mary Magdalene, Mary the mother of James, and Salome discover the tomb open, with a young man sitting inside. He informs them that Jesus is not there because risen, and that they should tell the disciples he has 'gone before' them to Galilee, where they shall see him. The women flee in silence and terror. In the canonical forms of all four Gospels there exist episodes after the crucifixion and burial when Jesus appears to his followers, first, and most of all, to the women. John, however (and the Marcan appendix), reduces the female figures to one only, Mary Magdalene, and it is John, with Luke and his scene on the road to Emmaus, who constructs the most astonishing, and astonishingly beautiful, scenes of the whole tradition.

The last two chapters of the fourth Gospel, 20 and 21 (the

latter considered an epilogue added by a redactor) are cases in point, the first constituting one of the finest dramatico-narrative masterpieces ever written. Chapter 20 is clearly divided into two sections, each in its turn based on two intersecting episodes which together mark an ascending—and unique—line of passage from ignorance to awareness, *recognition* (it will be remembered that John and Matthew give neither the Ascension of Luke, the Acts composed by Luke, and the appendix to Mark, nor the Pentecost of Acts).

Chapter 20 of the fourth Gospel, then, opens in the pre-dawn darkness of the first day of the week, Sunday. Mary Magdalene (who, with Jesus's mother, her sister, and 'the other disciple, whom Jesus loved', had been present at the crucifixion) goes to the tomb where they had placed the body and finds the stone removed. She runs to Peter and 'that other disciple', Jesus's favourite (whose name is never given in the Gospel, although tradition takes him to be John himself, the putative author), and tells them that someone has taken the Lord away from the sepulchre 'and we know not where they have laid him'. The scene here changes: Peter and the much-beloved disciple rush to the tomb, at first in step, and then Peter is overtaken by 'the other disciple', who is thus the first to arrive. He stoops down and sees the shroud which had covered the body, but does not enter. Peter then arrives and enters immediately, spotting the shroud and the 'piece of cloth' which had covered the head (not on the ground with the shroud, but set apart). The disciple who had been the first to arrive now enters, 'and he saw, and believed', to which the Evangelist adds: 'For as yet they knew not the scripture, that he must rise again from the dead.' The two then return home.

The account is both dramatic and enigmatic. The first person to be presented to us is Mary Magdalene; in the darkness she notices only that the stone has been removed before running to tell the two disciples simply that someone has removed Jesus's body. This, of course, is only her personal conviction (or deduction?), leading the reader naturally to extrapolate (though with no certainty) that the tomb is now empty. Mary then uses a curious plural: '*we* know not where they have laid him.' But the text shows her alone at the tomb. Was she, then, as in the other Gospels, accompanied by other women, the plural documenting a slip on the part of John or a redactor, a slip that would presuppose an earlier version, and the as yet mysterious reduction of three women to one? Or is Mary pre-emptively including the two disciples in her unknowing? Whatever the reason, the phrase expresses all her anxiety and ignorance. That Jesus's body had been removed by someone might appear a logically plausible, if hasty, conclusion when faced with a missing tombstone: an emotional leap fuelled by fear and non-understanding.

The tension mounts, the canny director moving the action abruptly to other characters. The pace accelerates in the second half of the scene, with the two disciples neck and neck, then one pulling away in the race to the sepulchre. Why does 'that other disciple', the favourite, overtake Peter? Because he is younger? Or because, as Bultmann has it, he represents Hebrew Christianity, which precedes that of the Gentiles? Like Mary Magdalene, he, too, does not enter the tomb (why? Is he recognizing Peter's right of precedence?). Some glow of daylight must in the meantime have appeared, however, since on going closer to the tomb than she had, he stoops down to look inside and notices the shroud on the ground. Until now we had seen only the stone removed; now, slowly, we make out some of the objects within the tomb. We move nearer, and see more, in the next 'frame' when Peter arrives and rushes in and spots the head 'cloth' (the whole scene echoing, and counterpointing, that of Lazarus at 11: 44). When he is followed by 'the other disciple', the objects suddenly take on the value of *signs*. It becomes clear, as the oldest exegesis maintains, that if anyone had wanted to carry away the body, they would certainly not have stopped to unclothe it, far less gather up the cloth and place it to one side. Yet these objects are signs only for the beloved disciple, not yet for Peter: he 'sees' (and the verb, in John, connotes much more than the merely optical) and, instantly, without transforming the signs into material proof, *believes*. The beloved disciple has neither time nor need to reason (what Aristotle, within the context of recognition, would call a *syllogismos*): signs are necessary not for agnition, but to push him into taking the leap of faith.

Yet even here the text is not totally clear. The next sentence, 'for as yet they knew not the scripture, that he must rise again from the dead', brings its own problems. Minimal textual cohesion would surely require something such as 'for they knew the scripture, that he must rise again from the dead', or 'for Peter as yet knew not the scripture'. Why the negative, why the plural? Who does this subject stand for? Peter, as we would imagine, or Peter and the beloved disciple, who, however, we have just been reliably informed, 'believes'? The sentence is not the completion of the preceding one, and shrouds the object of the second disciple's faith in some obscurity. What has he believed? Probably what Jesus had repeatedly promised in his last great sermon before the Passion (John 14: 28; 16: 9; 16: 17, etc.): 'I go away, and come again unto you . . . I go unto the Father.' Was this, though, a definite promise of the resurrection from the dead? The Gospel tells us that the disciple believed (*episteusen*), but that they failed to understand (*ēdeisan*) the scripture (or script, writing: *graphēn*). Believing is one thing, understanding what is written is another: particularly if the written text is *the* Scripture.

The beloved disciple believes, pure and simple. The text has so far thinned out into gaps and silence. Now, the question marks intact, it assumes a strange fullness. All uncertainty seems swept away by the disciple's believing. Whether or not we join him in his faith, the account has not a shadow of doubt: he sees and believes. His certainty is, however, not shared by Peter, nothing of whose reaction is communicated to us, and it radically contrasts with Mary

TO RECOGNIZE IS A GOD   149

Magdalene's 'belief' that 'they have taken away the Lord'.
With no further explanation, the two men return home.

Mary, for her part, is now outside the sepulchre, weeping
(did she, then, return alone, afterwards, or with the disciples? Did they address her?). While she weeps, she too
finally bends down to see inside the tomb, although without
entering. But she does not see, or does not notice, the
shroud and head cloth. What she sees are two angels *en
leukois*—'in white garments', or, simply, 'in white'—sitting
one at the head and one at the feet of where the body of
Jesus had been. Like Abraham at Mamre, in our first chapter,
the Magdalene is totally unperturbed by the two who are
here—unlike the Mamre episode—clearly identified as
superhuman beings. The angels should, as *angheloi*, messengers, be there to announce something; they appear, however, as two lights framing an emptiness, two whitenesses
underlining an absence at the very moment they mutely
imply a presence: something—an event—absolutely out of
the ordinary. What the angels do is not announce but
question: they ask Mary why she is crying (an insistence
on tears, as shortly before and shortly afterwards, which
underlines not only the emotional charge but the words
of Jesus at 16: 20: 'Verily, verily, I say unto you, That ye
shall weep and lament, but the world shall rejoice'). She, in
all candour, gives as her answer what she has thought from
the beginning and will shortly repeat, for the third time, to
Jesus himself: 'Because they have taken away my Lord, and I
know not where they have laid him.' The problematic
plural, 'we know not', of verse 3, is now replaced by the
more logical singular, '*I* know not', but this firm conviction
would imply she has had no contact with the two disciples,
least of all with the beloved one. Mary's anxiety and ignorance now appear as anguish and despair, as if she were
grieving Jesus's double disappearance: that into death, and
that of the dead body.

Then, suddenly, the dramatic reversal occurs: no sooner
has she pronounced these words than she turns round and

finds Jesus standing there, presumably in full light, outside the sepulchre. Mary Magdalene fails to recognize him ('and knew not that it was Jesus'). He immediately addresses her, however: 'Woman, why weepest thou? whom seekest thou?'; and, believing him to be the gardener, she replies from the depths of her obsession: 'Sir, if thou have borne him hence, tell me where thou hast laid him, and I will take him away.' Mary Magdalene does not recognize—she *mis-recognizes*. Her blindness is total. But why does Jesus put these questions to her at all, the first reiterating the words of the angels, the second repeating the words which were the first he ever spoke in the Gospel (1: 38) when questioning and 'calling' the disciples? Surely he already knows the answer. Is he testing her faith and love? The writer is clearly dramatizing the scene with a series of questions whose implied addressee is the reader.

The agnition seems about to implode. But then Jesus speaks to her again, simply pronouncing her name: 'Mariàm', 'Mary'. Then, turning round (but had she not turned round already? In what direction does she now turn? Significantly, at least two versions read 'recognizing' instead of 'turning'), the woman replies 'in Hebrew' (but what language have they been speaking until now?): 'Rabbunì', 'which is to say, Master'. Recognition has taken place. And suddenly we understand why 'the women' in the other Gospels have now, in John, become one only: an ingenious invention which gives us an agnition scene worthy of Sophocles and Euripides (and which, incidentally, contributes to the whole legend of the Magdalene which grows over the centuries to come). The questions, however, remain (and abound): why did Mary not recognize Jesus when she saw him, having been so close to him in the past? Was he disguised as a gardener, as if he were an Athena disguised as a shepherd to appear to the newly returned Ulysses? Or has his appearance radically changed? And then is the fact that he knows her name, with the suggestive circumstance of the two white angels, enough to prove that the man is Jesus? Might it not be the tone and timbre of the voice that make her turn her head, astounding her and flooding her with the truth? And if so, why is the particular tone not described?

Enough questions: let me try to give some answers. Jesus appears as a human being: he is taken for the gardener. But he is no longer, in appearance, the Jesus Mary Magdalene knew so well. Of course, he has been through dying, death, and burial, yet none of the pallor, *rigor mortis*, or decomposition of a corpse are indicated, nor the indefinable inconsistency of a ghost (far less the luminous, numinous beauty of a god, transfigured). Jesus appears as a normal, flesh-and-blood being, but different ('in another form', as the addition to Mark has it). The voice would seem to be the same, but only when pronouncing her name; when he had spoken a few moments before, Mary had failed to recognize him.

Few answers are forthcoming, then—fewer, in fact, than in the case of the apparition to the two disciples on the road to Emmaus in Luke's Gospel, where they at least recognize him when he breaks and blesses the bread, thus repeating the rite of the Eucharist. Here, in John, there are no such sacramental pointers, although Jesus's words concerning the good shepherd (10: 3 ff.) are evoked, when he opens the gate of the penfold, calls the sheep one by one, by name, and is recognized and followed on account of his voice. Some readers may wish to associate this *Mariam* with the *Miriam* who, in Exodus 2: 8, recognizes and saves Moses (her brother) for Pharaoh's daughter; just as that Miriam was the prophetess of the first redemption, so this Mariam (the same name, in Aramaic) announces the second (and John rewrites not only himself, but the second book of the Pentateuch too). The alert reader of John will thus recognize in Mary Magdalene's recognition an underlying theological dimension. A shadow of this could even be seen as prefigured in Isaiah (42: 1) when the Lord promises Israel: 'Fear not: for I have redeemed thee, I have called thee by thy name; thou art mine.' When God calls, he possesses and saves: those who truly listen to him recognize him. The ultra-canny reader will remember that the theme of 'recognition' is present from the beginning of John's Gospel, in the Prologue: 'He was in the world, and the world was made by him, and the world knew him not . . . But as many as received him, to them gave he power to become the sons of God.'

All this, however, has little to do with the agnition as such. At this moment Mary—unlike the beloved disciple—does not believe, but calls him 'master', recognizing him as nothing more than he had been before his death. The agnition is the focus of narratorial attention here, but a shroud of mystery surrounds it: a human phenomenon which, however, has something of the unfamiliar, disturbing, and even other-worldly. Mary Magdalene is not able to exclaim, with Helen, 'to recognize those we love is a god': she can only accept Jesus for what he was and is—someone, a man, who has returned from the dead. To stage the recognition between a human being and an unchanging, ever-transcendent God, is simple by comparison: Moses and the Burning Bush, or Elijah and the 'still, small voice'. The problems arise when God appears in human form, as to Abraham, at Mamre, and are compounded when the God is to be represented as mortal man—mortal to the point of death, and then again mortal, from beyond death. It is hard to imagine what the Yahwist would have thought of it, or Euripides and *Helen*'s Chorus!

To recognize this man we must look death in the face and become that face: recognizing those we love means dying a little, to use Proust's expression, rather than meeting the god within the process. At the same time, to recognize this man in the present circumstances means a journey beyond death, recognizing that he is beyond the becoming to which he is subjected. To recognize Jesus now implies the discovery, in the flesh, of the *being-this-here*, on the threshold between metaphysics on the one hand, and theology on the other. We can hardly forget that this is precisely one of the central messages of the Gospel according to John. Jesus has on several occasions proclaimed his being (following Isaiah 43: 10). 'If you believe not that I am [*hoti egō eimi*], you shall die in your sins', he warns the Jews (8: 24), adding (8: 28), 'When you have lifted up the Son of man, then you shall know that I am', and finally proclaiming: 'Before Abraham became, I am' (8: 58). These statements are to be taken as absolute: not so much metaphysical as directly theological. When Jesus says *I am*, what he is declaring is *I Am*, and applying to himself the formula God uses to reveal himself to Moses (Exodus 3: 14): 'EHEYE ASHER EHEYE; Egō eimi ho ōn'; 'I AM THAT I AM . . . I AM hath sent me unto you'. Jesus is preaching his own supreme *Being*.

It must be admitted that in this scene of recognition John rewrites with extraordinary drama and sense of theatre not just the recognition scenes in Graeco-Roman literature, but those of the Hebrew Bible and the Synoptic Gospels themselves. He suggests that his readers open their eyes on the dizzying concept of God made man, and does so with narrative devices of disarming simplicity and disturbing perception, by *questioning*: the head twice turned, a gardener, a voice, and a name. And all this is done in defiance of tradition, placing centre-stage a *woman*. John possibly intended to fulfil the words of the bride in the Song of Songs (3: 1–4): 'By night on my bed I sought him whom my soul loves: I sought him, but I found him not. I will rise now, and go about the city in the streets . . . and I will seek him whom my soul loves . . . The watchmen that go about the city found me: to whom I said, Have you seen him whom my soul loves? Scarce had I passed from them, when I found him whom my soul loves: I held him, and would not let him go.' What we can be certain of is that if the beloved disciple is the first to believe, it is a woman who first recognizes: 'e ciò non fa d'onor poco argomento'—no small honour, this, in Dante's words.

The scene, however, continues, and if hitherto it has been suspended between the human and the divine, the metaphysical and the theological, it now takes a purely prophetic and theological turn. As soon as Mary Magdalene exclaims 'Rabbunì', Jesus adds the famous 'Noli me tangere', a clumsy mistranslation of the Greek, and more closely 'do not hold me back, or cling to me': 'For I am not yet ascended to my father', he explains, 'but go to my brethren and say unto them: I ascend unto my Father, and your Father; and to my God, and to your God.' So far we have witnessed a being-this-here and being and Being. We now hear proclaimed the *being-where* which Jesus had announced to the Pharisees and to the disciples. When a number of the inhabitants of Jerusalem had asked with scepticism whether Jesus was the Messiah of whom 'no man knows whence he is', while Jesus's origins were adequately known, he had stated: 'You both know me, and you know whence I am: and I am not come of myself, but he that sent me is true, whom you know not . . . Yet a little while am I with you, and then I go unto him that sent me. You shall seek me, and shall not find me: and where I am [*hopou eimi egō*], thither you cannot come' (7: 25–34). To the disciples, on the contrary, he had promised: 'And if I go and prepare a place for you, I will come again, and receive you unto myself; that where I am, there you may be also.' And to Thomas's question, 'Lord, we know not where you go; and how can we know the way?', he had replied with one of the crucial statements of the fourth Gospel: 'I am the way, the truth, and the life: no man comes unto the father, but by me' (14: 3–6). The *being-where* of Jesus is beyond time and the world of humans (8: 23; 17: 14), with the Father, *in* the Father (14: 20), in the fullness of life (14: 19), and of his glory (17: 24), and where the disciples will also go. It is this that he orders Mary to announce to his followers: the recognition is extended to the Father and to the *God* of all, to the *where* of the ascension which 'is coming to pass' (human time is short-circuiting) even as he is speaking with the woman. The agnition ends in an indirect revelation of glory; and Mary is quick to apprehend this. When her brief, normal, and most bizarre conversation with Jesus is over, she rushes to the disciples to tell them she has seen not the 'master', as she had denoted him a few minutes ago, but— thereby fulfilling the prefiguration in the episode of the blind man healed (9: 35–8)—the *Lord*.

The beloved disciple believed without seeing; Mary Magdalene recognizes while seeing a different Jesus. Her agnition is indispensable for establishing a continuity between the previous Jesus, the Jesus of the here and now, and the Jesus of the here, now, and forever. Mary's recognition is the human basis of faith, and can be extended into a more ample awareness, a superior revelation. The evening of that same day, while the disciples are gathered together behind closed doors 'for fear of the Jews', Jesus comes and stands 'in the midst', saying 'Peace be unto you'. The nature of Jesus has obviously changed: his body, the Gospel implies, can pass through closed doors (or walls) and materialize suddenly within a room. But his is not the apparition of a ghost. Having greeted them, he then shows them his hands and side: the (seemingly) material parts of his body where the wounds and scars of the crucifixion are still visible. At the sight of these, the disciples are 'glad': the signs are those of recognition, and the subsequent rejoicing. In dramatic terms, this is the point which is closest to Euripides' *Helen*.

Jesus is both different and the same: a similar, and similarly impenetrable message was implied in the scene with Mary Magdalene. Only Paul, in the famous chapter 15 of the First Letter to the Corinthians, attempts to give an explanation—not rational, but by analogy. 'If there be no resurrection of the dead', he passionately writes after listing Jesus's many appearances after the resurrection, 'then is Christ not risen: And if Christ be not risen, then is our preaching vain, and your faith is also vain.' As to the bald facts of resurrection, Paul can only offer a simile: that which is sown cannot come to life unless it dies; that which is sown is not the body which will be born, but a simple grain of wheat. The resurrecting body is of the same substance but different in form. And there are earthly and celestial bodies, but the splendour of the one can bear no comparison with that of the sun, the moon, and the stars. 'So also is the resurrection of the dead. It is sown in corruption; it is raised in incorruption . . . It is sown a natural body; it is raised a spiritual body.' Continuity and transformation: what the scenes in John and the exposition in Paul are trying to show is the supreme mystery of the *being-in-becoming* and the *becoming-towards-being*; in John's case, he is reconciling the opposition between being and becoming announced in his Prologue.

Having shown the disciples his hands and side, the Jesus of the fourth Gospel, now recognized as 'Lord', repeats the sign of peace (one of John's central messages), and charges the disciples with their apostolic mission: 'as my Father hath sent me, even so send I you.' Jesus the man, the master, now acts as God. In the following verse he actually repeats the gesture of Genesis (2: 7), breathing life into Adam's nostrils so that 'man became a living soul'. He breathes over them, saying: 'Receive a holy Spirit. If you forgive men's sins, their sins are forgiven; if you hold them, they are held fast' (there is, of course, no Pentecost in the fourth Gospel). Recognition has again produced re-Scripture. John, who had dared to rewrite the first verse of the Bible in his Prologue ('In the beginning God created the heaven and the earth'—'In the beginning was the Word'), now reformulates the creation of man as 'living soul' and has Jesus create the new Adam.

What is still missing is the definitive recognition of the divinity, which finally takes place in the last scene of chapter 20, when his fellow disciples inform Thomas, absent that Sunday evening, that they have seen the risen Lord. Thomas, already dubious after the death of Lazarus, and uncertain as to the 'where' of Jesus, replies with the famous words: 'Except I shall see in his hands the print of the nails, and thrust my hand into his side, I will not believe.' Thomas asks for material proof, like the scar Euriclea washes on Ulysses' thigh. And he seems to be about to receive it: appearing a week later, again behind closed doors, Jesus openly invites him to touch the marks of the nails, and to thrust his hand into his side, and 'be not faithless, but believing'. Jesus's expression is significant. Thomas had said he would not believe unless he saw and touched; 'Look, touch, and believe' is Jesus's reply. Recognition is still the objective, but as a means to the faith which is the end. And the Evangelist, with another mesmerizing silence, makes no mention of seeing and touching, but simply tells us that Thomas replies: 'My Lord and my God' ('ho kyrios mou kai ho theos mou')—an expression which coincides with the Septuagint standard translation of YHWH (*kyrios*) and Elohim (*theos*) in the Old Testament. John, again rewriting, pro-claims through Thomas's ecstatic exclamation that Jesus is the same God as that of the Hebrew Bible. The last word is therefore Jesus's, to be projected towards its ultimate addressees, the readers—us: 'blessed are they that have not seen, and yet have believed.'

'The disciple whom Jesus loved' believed; Mary Magdalene recognized and then proclaimed him Lord; the other dis-ciples rejoice to recognize him and again declare him as such; Thomas confesses the *God* within this man risen from the dead. The twentieth chapter of the fourth Gospel, in its bold rewriting, has passed from the dark dawn of the beginning to its glorious final proclamation, from enigmatic uncertainty to literally palpable evidence, re-enacting the gradual dawning of awareness in which the human leads to the divine so mysteriously, so subtly as to give the impres-sion that the narrative is not only factually true but at the same time, in some way, divinely inspired. We reach the ultimate threshold at which to decide, each of us, whether to recognize, or recognize and believe; where recognition can be a god as long as we give ourselves to him: as long as, like Mary Magdalene, we listen to his voice.

I would like to believe that whoever continued and con-cluded the fourth Gospel with chapter 21 did it not only for

ecclesiastical reasons, but because he was still under the spell
of the preceding scenes, captivated by the recognition and
rewriting in John, and wanting to prolong it for one more
chapter. The first part is the account of the risen Christ's
'third' apparition to the disciples. This time Peter, Thomas,
Nathanael, the sons of Zebedee, and two more disciples are
at the sea of Tiberias. Peter decides to go fishing for the
night, and the others go with him. They catch nothing,
however, and the nets remain empty. In the morning, on the
shore, stands Jesus, unrecognized by the disciples, who asks
them if they have caught anything to eat; hearing that there
has been no catch, he suggests they cast the net over the
right side of the boat. On so doing the net is immediately so
full that they are not able to drag it in again. The beloved
disciple informs Peter: 'It is the Lord.' When he hears this,
Peter hitches his coat up and jumps into the water, the
others following in the boat. On the shore they see a brazier
with fish and bread. Jesus tells them to bring a little of their
catch, Peter jumps into the boat to draw up the net, 'full of
great fishes, an hundred and fifty and three', and Jesus invites
them to eat. None of the disciples dares to ask who he is,
'knowing that it was the Lord'.

The scene fulfils and completes the previous chapter, not
least in landscape terms: from a sepulchre and adjoining
garden, from a closed room, to the sea of Tiberias, night-
fishing, the dawn apparition of Jesus, the boat, and the
brazier. The scene is set in a wider horizon and a time-
scheme which is both more homely (their fishing) and more
'romantic' (darkness, incipient daylight, and glowing coals).
The signs are changed or extended: from shroud, cloths,
wounds, and voices to the out-and-out miracle of the fish.
Thirdly, the agnition is repeated ('the disciples knew not
that it was Jesus') and concentrated on the beloved disciple,
he who had simply believed. Now he is the one to recognize Jesus and proclaim him *Kyrios*: 'It is the Lord' (and with
this he takes us back to the scene of Joseph and his brothers
in our first chapter). Peter, for his part, now does what in the

previous chapter he had failed to do: he recognizes, believes, and, throwing himself at Jesus, loves. Lastly, the awareness extends mysteriously to all of them: no one dares to ask who it is because they all *know*.

The author or redactor who continues the fourth Gospel rewrites John, and he does so by using the Gospels themselves. The allusion to the miraculous fishing through which Peter is chosen by Jesus in Luke (5: 1–11) is indubitable. The echo of the episode in which Peter, in Matthew (14: 28–33), walks over the waves, is indirect but surely present, as is the oblique parallel between the 'fullness' sketched in here and that foreshadowed by the wine at Cana. The eucharistic symbolism, underlined by the similarity of this scene with the miracle of the multiplication and distribution of bread and fish in John (6: 11), is certain. The author or redactor who continues the fourth Gospel does all this not only in order to proclaim Peter's rehabilitation, call, and martyrdom (in the second section of the chapter Jesus asks Peter three times if he loves him and when the disciple answers affirmatively, he orders, 'Feed my sheep', then adding a prophecy on the way in which Peter will die), nor merely to clarify the future of the beloved disciple (who presents himself here as the witness and writer of these events). He does it also to celebrate recognition in the joy of its being repeated and exalted. The protagonist of the scene is not another person—Mary Magdalene, Peter, Thomas, the beloved disciple—but Jesus alone. Human and divine at once, he shapes everything by himself. The chapter had significantly opened with the sentence, 'After these things Jesus *showed* himself again.' The writer who, following John's programme, continues and concludes the fourth Gospel, wants to crown recognition with *revelation*.

These scenes from the fourth Gospel cling forever to the Western imagination, with their description of recognition and faith; humanity's encounter with the fullness of being, God made man and returned to life from death. At their best, even scenes of recognition between merely human beings will be (oblique) rewritings of these. And always, as in Euripides and John, they will centre on a woman. Thus Shakespeare's last plays, those 'romances' which, along the prefigured lines of the Lear–Cordelia encounter, contain sublime scenes of deferred recognition between fathers and daughters and/or husbands and wives. I am referring, of course, to *Pericles*, *Cymbeline*, and *The Winter's Tale*.

I shall take *Pericles* as my example, both because its closing agnitions are among the most magical Shakespeare ever created, and in order to follow the oblique and shadowy ghost scripting a fascinating intertext, a point of encounter between Pericles and Mary Magdalene. *Pericles* is the dramatic version of the much-rewritten story (existing in dozens of variations and languages) of Apollonius of Tyre (Shakespeare simply changes the names, but openly refers to the account in the *Confessio Amantis* of John Gower, who appears in the play as Chorus). Between the two plots, the Middle Ages has intervened with a splendid contamination. In Jacopo da Varazze's *Legenda aurea*, for example, Mary Magdalene has become the sister of Martha and Lazarus (and sinner *par excellence*). She washes Jesus's feet with her tears, dries them with her hair and anoints them with a precious ointment, repents, is present at the crucifixion, anoints Jesus's body after his death, and is the first to see the risen Lord. Thirteen years after the Ascension, with Lazarus, Martha, and others, she is herded on board a ship by infidels and abandoned to the mercy of the waves. The divine will propels them towards Marseilles, where Mary preaches faith in Christ. The provincial governor and his wife are ready to convert if Mary will obligingly perform the small miracle of making the woman fertile. When the latter finds that she is indeed pregnant, her husband immediately heads for Rome, to verify the facts of this 'Christianity' preached by Mary. His wife begs to go with him, and refuses to be gainsaid. Blessed by the saint, the two depart. On the second day, however, a violent storm arises, and amid the pitching of the ship the woman gives birth to a male child, and dies. The sailors are anxious to placate the waves with the woman's body, but her husband dictates that mother and son be left, covered by a mantle, on a 'hill' arising from the waves. Roundly cursing Mary, he continues his journey to Rome, where Peter advises him patiently to allow his wife to 'sleep' and their small son to 'rest', assuring him that, as the Lord gives, takes away, and returns, so he may transform his tears into joy. Two years later, having been instructed in the faith and gone with Peter to Jerusalem, he again sets sail for Marseilles. He stops at the 'hill' where he had left his wife and son, and discovers a small child playing on the sea-shore. The child is frightened and runs to his mother, still lying under her mantle, and suckles. The man recognizes his son and wife, and invokes Mary Magdalene to make her breathe once more. The miracle is granted, and all three set sail for Marseilles, where they tell the saint the whole story before she moves to a hermitage in Aix-en-Provence. The story was staged in England as a miracle play, *Mary Magdalene*, during the late Middle Ages.

The central nucleus of the Apollonius and Pericles plot contains clear parallels with this secondary motif of the Magdalene legend: Pericles' wife, Thaisa, insists on accompanying him to Tyre, and dies in giving birth to Marina during a storm at sea. Thrown overboard (like Jonah, because of the sailors' superstition), in a coffin carrying all identifying details, Thaisa is 'resuscitated' by the music and medicine of Cerimon in Ephesus, where she takes refuge in the temple of Diana. Pericles leaves the tiny Marina at Tharsus, with Cleon and Dionyza. Years later, out of envy, Dionyza decides to have Marina put to death, but pirates 'save' her in time, and sell her to a brothel in Mytilene. The girl firmly refuses to have any part in its activities, and gets permission to be housed in an honest establishment where she earns her living by singing, sewing, and teaching the daughters of the nobility. In the meantime Pericles has returned to Tharsus to retrieve his daughter, but

Cleon and Dionyza answer his request by showing him the tomb where she supposedly lies. Racked by grief, Pericles puts on sackcloth, grows his hair and beard, and wanders, stunned, over the seas, finally reaching Mytilene where a mysterious young girl is brought before him to heal him with her wondrous voice.

Shakespeare's version (Shakespeare's in spite of the well-known 'textual collapse' of *Pericles*) naturally rewrites the plot into a frame which belongs even more to romance than the legend of Magdalene: that of Apollonius. All the misadventures of Pericles, Prince of Tyre, begin when he journeys to Antioch to win the daughter of Antiochus the king; she will be his if he can answer a riddle: the penalty for failure, death. Pericles decodes the horrendous secret of the incest between father and daughter, and returns to Tyre, followed by an assassin in Antiochus' pay. Handing over the government of the city to Helicanus, he flees, like Jonah, towards Tharsus, governed by Cleon and Dionyza and now ravaged by famine. Pericles offers all the provisions he has on board, then, on receiving a letter from Helicanus recalling him to Tyre, he sets sail. Shipwrecked by a violent storm, he is cast up in rags on the shores of Pentapolis where the waves also vomit up the armour entrusted to him by his dying father. Donning it, he takes part in the tournament to win the hand of Thaisa, daughter of the king of Pentapolis, Simonides. Thaisa falls in love with him and they marry. A further message then arrives from Helicanus, recalling Pericles to Tyre: at the pregnant Thaisa's insistence, husband and wife set sail, but are caught in the tempest which will be the backdrop to Thaisa's delivery, and death.

Guided by the ancient voice of Gower, whose choral account links the different episodes, and instructed by the dumb shows which silently, 'like motes and shadows', make clear a number of plot junctures, spectators and readers follow Pericles over the sea, a second Ulysses buffeted by fortune and the tides, in the grasp of an incomprehensible divinity whose actions, however, are to prove providential.

Pericles has every imaginable situation hurled at him, like a character from late-antique romance, or a medieval knight: enigma and flight, the salvation of a starving Tharsus, the eternal journeying, shipwreck, the tournament, the loss of his wife in a further storm, and the presumed death of his daughter. He acts with energy, nobility, and generosity throughout: everything is endured with patience until the final blow: the sight of Marina's tomb. Then, like Lear after all his maltreatment and misusage, Pericles too 'bears a tempest which his mortal vessel tears', lost within himself, all awareness swallowed by pain, allowing 'his courses to be ordered by Lady Fortune'.

And like Euripides' Chorus, Menelaus, and Helen, Pericles also invokes and interrogates the gods. When, for example, the ship carrying him to Tyre, with his wife in labour, is splintered by the storm, he appeals to the gods of the sea and the wind, and then Lucina, goddess of labour:

> Thou god of this great vast rebuke these surges,
> Which wash both heaven and hell. And thou, that hast
> Upon the winds command, bind them in brass,
> Having call'd them from the deep! O, still
> Thy deafening, dreadful thunders; gently quench
> The nimble, sulphurous flashes! . . .
>
> . . . .
>
>   Lucina, O
> Divinest patroness and midwife gentle
> To those that cry by night, convey thy deity
> Aboard our dancing boat, make swift the pangs
> Of my queen's travails!

No reply is forthcoming, however, from either the gods or the elements, and 'The seaman's whistle | Is as a whisper in the ears of death'. And when the reply finally arrives, it announces, through the earthly midwife, Thaisa's death and the new, tiny life of Marina: 'this piece of [his] dead queen'. Pericles then calls into question the very honour of the gods, comparing it with that of mortals who at least never take back what they have given:

> O you gods!
> Why do you make us love your goodly gifts
> And snatch them straight away? We here below
> Recall not what we give, and therein may
> Use honour with you.

Yet on turning to his newly born child, to wish her a life less troubled than her birth, Pericles entrusts her to the 'best eyes' of the 'good gods'; and later, in Tharsus, in speaking of his dead wife to Cleon and Dionyza, he acknowledges that 'We cannot but obey | The powers above us': even if he could 'rage and roar | As doth the sea she lies in', 'yet the end | Must be as 'tis'. Like the hero of romance and the Jesus of the Gospels, Pericles bows to the *telos*, the end in the sense both of conclusion and objective. Only when he hears the news that Marina, 'all his life's delight', flesh of his flesh and the beloved daughter of a beloved wife, has passed from the bloom of her young beauty directly to death does Pericles—like Job, in this prefiguring of a person soon to emerge from the shadows—dress in sackcloth and give way to despair.

Pericles, already become Nobody after the first ship-wreck, dies inside. His wife and his daughter are both dead to him: Thaisa has indeed passed through death, and Marina enters it, having been nearly murdered and then consigned to a brothel. But Thaisa, as we have seen, rises again with the ministrations of music and Cerimon's med-icines, and consecrates herself to Diana; Marina survives all the scheming of the pimps by virtue of her words, expres-sive, Lysimachus observes, of all her goodness and purity. Marina, as Gower informs us at the beginning of the last Act, 'sings like an immortal, and dances | As goddess-like to her admired lays'; her knowledge 'dumbs deep clerks', and with her needle she 'composes | Nature's own shape, of bud, bird, branch, or berry, | That even her art sisters the natural roses'. Marina is the goddess of art and knowledge, the quickening enchantress, Spring: *Life*.

Through the last Act she will by degrees also become the Way and the Truth. The scene of recognition between Marina and her father, which T. S. Eliot describes as the finest ever written, and a perfect example of the 'ultra-dramatic', 'a dramatic action of beings who are more than human, or rather, seen in a light more than that of day', is enacted in an atmosphere resonant with the fourth Gospel. Marina is presented to Helicanus as a creature who, with her sweetness and harmony, could enchant Pericles and open a breach in his sense-deafness: she is both thaumaturge and *kalogathos* supreme, 'all goodness that consists in beauty'. Convinced by Lysimachus, Helicanus bids her board the ship where Pericles lies in a stupor. Marina approaches him, singing, and invites him to listen to her, but his only reply is an unconscious, phatic 'Hum! Ha!'. Marina takes this as encouragement to speak, and begins her story: she is a young girl who, although 'gaz'd on like a comet', has never invited the glance of strangers ('I am a maid': *Virgo* Mari[n]a); one who has suffered as he has, of noble birth but reduced to the condition of the world's and adversity's slave. Getting no reply, she is about to desist, but 'something'—a *daimon*?—makes her cheeks 'glow', whispering to her to remain until he speaks. And speak Pericles finally does, muttering a garbled version of her words and asking her to explain herself. Marina has restored his speech. She now stirs his wandering memory and sluggish consciousness: he asks her to look on him, as if she were some divinity, because she is, he murmurs, 'like something that . . .'. The shred of memory then suddenly urges him to ask what country she is from: 'What countrywoman? Here of these shores?', to which Marina gives a totally natural and honest, yet allusive and near-transcendental reply: 'No, nor of any shores; | Yet I was mortally brought forth, and am | No other than I appear.'

Marina is telling the precise truth: she is not from

Mytilene, nor from any other 'shore', because born at sea. Yet 'nor of any shores' suggests an other-worldly provenance, and Marina quickly adds that she was brought into the world 'mortally', humbly concluding that she is precisely what she seems. A *being* which coincides completely with an *appearing*, then? A being who is not 'of any shores' but 'of woman born'? Only the Jesus of the Gospels can claim such fullness and such birth.

Pericles remains on the ground, 'great with woe' and about to 'deliver weeping'. Emerging from his long sleep, he notices the resemblance between the girl and his wife: the wide forehead, the same height ('to an inch'), the same body, straight as a rush, silver-voiced and jewel-eyed, Juno's step, and her words, enticing, appealing (the importance of Voice!). His questions tumble out: where do you live? where were you raised? how did you learn such skills? 'Where I am but a stranger', is her answer to the first question, shrugging off the others with the words, 'Should I tell my history, it would seem | Like lies, disdain'd in the reporting'. The human and superhuman again come together. Pericles is now ready to believe. The woman standing before him is Pallas (as the quarto has it), Wisdom, Justice, and *Truth*:

> Prithee speak.
> Falseness cannot come from thee, for thou look'st
> Modest as Justice, and thou seem'st a Pallas
> For the crowned Truth to dwell in. I will believe thee,
> And make my senses credit thy relation
> To points that seem impossible; for thou lookest
> Like one I loved indeed.

If it is the superhuman at play here, then it is rooted in the most human of emotions, love—love for a wife (Helen and Menelaus once more). Belief, certainly: but arrived at through the senses, finding resemblance through physical appearance, and being through appearance. Pericles has to make the same leap as Mary Magdalene: Thaisa and Marina, he is convinced, are dead, and for him, too, recognition lies beyond the mystery of death. Yet it also encompasses facts, proofs, and signs: relatives, blood, line, history, and sufferings endured:

> Tell thy story.
> If thine consider'd prove the thousandth part
> Of my endurance, thou art a man, and I
> Have suffer'd like a girl; yet thou dost look
> Like Patience gazing on kings' graves and smiling
> Extremity out of act. What were thy friends?
> How lost thou them? Thy name, my most kind virgin?
> Recount, I do beseech thee. Come, sit by me.

Two parallel Passions are represented, making of the man and girl, father and daughter, one person, as if foreshadowing the Christian God. It is the girl, however, who here incarnates the infinite capacity for suffering and enduring: *patiens* like Jesus on the cross, and simultaneously a statue of Patience—like those placed on the funeral monuments of the period—on the tombs of kings, and on the tomb of *this* king, Pericles, whose painful story she smiles down on. The image is both passive and active: endurance, and a smile which annuls the most extreme misfortune ('smiling Extremity *out of act*'); Olympian contemplation, and com-passion: a detached, but restorative smile.

The girl simply speaks her name, like Jesus calling 'Mariàm': 'My name is Marina.' Pericles, echoing Lear on recognizing Cordelia, exclaims: 'O! I am mock'd, | And thou by some incensed god sent hither | To make the world to laugh at me.' He is beginning to perceive the god in recognition. But Marina—and Shakespeare—exacts patience. Every sentence of hers is an oracle, an enigma eliciting further questions. The game of agnition is slow and gradual, retarded as in Mann to emphasize all the joyous *Freude am Wiedererkennen*. This is the patience that gazes on kings' graves. Marina slowly goes on, revealing that the name was given her by her father, a king. When Pericles starts with amazement, slowly composing the fragmented tesserae of signs behind this revelation, she further retards with the comment: 'You said you would believe me; | But, not to be a troubler of your peace, | I will end here.' The question, then, once more, is to believe or not to believe:

> But are you flesh and blood?
> Have you a working pulse? And are no fairy?
> Motion as well? Speak on. Where were you born?
> And wherefore call'd Marina?

In order to believe it is necessary to recognize, re-establish the continuity of being-in-reality, identify the *being-this-here*, and pass through death: to find not a phantom or an elf, but flesh, blood, pulse, and movement—a living being. Everything, then, must fit: 'Call'd Marina | For I was born at sea.' Marina fails to clarify whether or not she is flesh and blood—anyone's flesh and blood; she simply evokes her birth at sea, and not 'of any shores'. But the sea is now, for Pericles, fast becoming that particular sea: who was your mother? And when she replies that she too was the daughter of a king, and had died giving birth, he self-enforces an ultimate doubt: 'O! stop there a little! | This is the rarest dream that e'er dull sleep | Did mock sad fools withal. This cannot be | My daughter, buried!' Belief in a dream is easier: no one survives death. But this dream speaks, moves, and tells of wondrous but credible adventures. Pericles asks for further details, promising to hear her out in silence, and to believe (again) every syllable she utters. Marina further delays: then, as he weeps, she tells her tale, ending in the name of the father: 'I am the daughter to King Pericles, | If good King Pericles be.'

Now the gradual revelations and delayed epiphanies shape towards awareness: but not immediately, not directly. Pericles calls Helicanus and asks if he knows this girl who has caused his tears. Helicanus, not knowing Marina, is obliged to ask Lysimachus, the governor of Mytilene. But when he, too, is unable to answer, it is up to him, Pericles, to fulfil the act both of recognition and faith together. Pericles feels himself awash in the sea which had so harrowed him, but it is now a sea of happiness: *to recognize those we love is indeed a god.*

> O Helicanus, strike me, honour'd sir!
> Give me a gash, put me to present pain,
> Lest this great sea of joys rushing upon me
> O'erbear the shores of my mortality
> And drown me with their sweetness. O, come hither,
> Thou that beget'st him that did thee beget;
> Thou that wast born at sea, buried at Tharsus,
> And found at sea again. O Helicanus,
> Down on thy knees; thank the holy gods as loud
> As thunder threatens us. This is Marina.

Marina has risen again. Born at sea, the earth buried her and the sea now returns her, alive. Pericles becomes—to paraphrase Dante in *Paradiso* XXXIII—'figlio di sua figlia', his daughter's son, and, at the opposite extreme from the incest of Antiochus with which the play opens, Marina is presented as the shadow of Christ made man, the parent of his mother: 'god-like perfect' and 'another life | To Pericles thy father', as he will state a few lines on. Marina, then, is the *Way*. Yet she is flesh and blood: Thaisa's daughter, as she herself replies to the last of her father's serried questions, thus producing the ultimate proof. Pericles, and Shakespeare with him, is careful to leave the theological subtly balanced, and fully ambiguous: Helicanus is to kneel and thank the 'holy *gods*'. And it is Pericles who now, after revealing his name to her, is raised again, a father once more, and blesses, requests fresh clothes, and consecrates her as his daughter, like the Holy Spirit which, in the guise of a dove, pronounces above Jesus's head, 'This is my beloved son, in whom I am well pleased':

> Now, blessing on thee! rise; thou art my child.
> Give me fresh garments. Mine own, Helicanus!

Father and daughter are becoming what Lear had wished for himself and Cordelia, God's spies, who have taken upon themselves, have experienced, and are still experiencing, in the first person, the 'mystery of things'. Pericles returns to full awareness of the world around him and of himself: 'I am wild in my beholding' (both perhaps 'beside myself at what I see', and 'wild in my appearance'). Then, as soon as this final act of recognition is over, the shadow of the other-worldly returns. Pericles again asks for his garments, invokes the benediction of the heavens on Marina, and suddenly hears notes: 'But hark, what music?' He asks Marina to go on with her tale, detail by detail, to Helicanus, who still seems in some doubt. Then he again breaks off: 'But what music?' And to Helicanus, who claims he hears nothing, Pericles replies: 'None? | The music of the spheres! List, my Marina.' To the others' astonishment, he repeats: 'Rarest sounds!' Then the celestial music assaults him, wounds him, enchants him, and makes him drowsy:

> Most heavenly music!
> It nips me into listening, and thick slumber
> Hangs upon mine eyes. Let me rest.

Only Pericles hears this transcendental music, and Alessandro Serpieri is quite right when, glossing the phrase 'It nips me into listening', he writes that 'the metaphor is . . . particularly pregnant because it makes *physical* this *metaphysical* hearing'. Knowledge of the flesh, in the flesh: experience of the other-worldly. To recognize those we love is indeed, finally, a god.

Shakespeare, then, is rewriting Euripides with his attention concentrated upon John the Evangelist? In all its philological absurdity, this seems to me the only answer feasible in literary terms. Shakespeare as divinely inspired? I think the only critically consistent answer in all its theological enormity is that, like John, he does all he can to make us believe so.

And apropos of rewriting Euripides with an eye on the

Gospels, we find Shakespeare, at the end of the play, bringing in Diana *ex machina* to the sleeping Pericles, who is
instructed to go directly to Ephesus, make sacrifices at her
altar, and reveal to her priestesses all the 'crosses' born by
himself and his daughter. This the pious Pericles promptly
does, in the next scene; Thaisa faints at the recounting. But
here, too, Shakespeare defers. If Thaisa, like Helen, recognizes her husband on the spot, by his voice and appearance,
he needs proof and an intermediary. Cerimon, who had
'raised' Thaisa from the dead when her body arrived in
Ephesus, now reveals that the priestess of Diana is in reality
Pericles' wife, as implied in Pericles' own account in the
temple, adding the 'jewels' found in the coffin as definitive
proof. But if John was reluctant to allow Thomas to touch
Jesus, Shakespeare, while not disallowing it, has no intention
of adducing merely material proof. When Thaisa comes
round, it is again Pericles' voice and appearance which strike
her, and it is her voice, pronouncing his name—like Jesus's
with Mary Magdalene—which stops his heart for a second:
'O, my lord, | Are you not Pericles? Like him you spake, |
Like him you are'—'The voice of dead Thaisa!'

Thaisa thus twice returns from the dead. This time there
is no music of the spheres, no sleeping fit; now Pericles
experiences the ultimate threshold between life and death,
between 'the utmost realization of happiness and the van-
ishing of all':

> This, this: no more, you gods; your present kindness
> Makes my past miseries sports. You shall do well,
> That on the touching of her lips I may
> Melt, and no more be seen. O come, be buried
> A second time within these arms.

This, then, is the supreme moment, when rediscovering a
wife, recomposing the human family, and perpetuating it (in
the marriage announced between Marina and Lysimachus)
coincide with the recognition of divine action; when kissing
the lips of a woman means 'melting', and burying her

within one's arms means 'no more being seen', so that this most human gesture of affection and union which subverts death becomes one with the act of passing beyond: a transfiguration. *This* is the time, here and now, on the earth, *this* is the thing—here, in the theatre. *This*, to reply to Euripides' Chorus, is god, non-god, and god and non-god together.

Hercules returns from Hades with Cerberus, at the end of the last labour inflicted on him by Juno, jealous of the stepson imposed on her by Jupiter's unfaithfulness. He is greeted by his father, Amphitryon, his wife, Megara, and his children. Suddenly a fit of insanity overcomes him: a Juno-sent fury which cracks his brain, seizes his heart, and clouds his eyes. Before the powerless gaze of his father, aghast with horror, the great Hercules kills his wife and children, believing them to be Juno and the offspring of his enemy Licus in person. Then, falling to the ground, he falls asleep. When he wakes, the fogs still clinging to his brain (as with Lear and Pericles) are such that he fails even to recognize his surroundings, and his home city, Thebes. He mutters:

> Quis hic locus, quae regio, quae mundi plaga?
> ubi sum? sub ortu solis, an sub cardine
> glacialis ursae? numquid Hesperii maris
> extrema tellus hunc dat Oceano modum?
> quas trahimus auras? quod solum fesso subest?
> certe redimus . . .

[What place is this, what district, what region of the world? | Where am I? Beneath the rising of the sun, or beneath the course | of the icy Bear? | Is this the confine which the farthest earth | of the Western sea marks to the Ocean? | What air do I breathe? What earth stretches beneath my tired body? | I have surely returned . . .]

Thus Seneca, rewriting Euripides' *Madness of Heracles*, presents us with strength personified and made hero, lying senseless on the ground, despoiled of his arms, at the beginning of the last scene of his *Hercules Furens*. We wait in horrified anticipation for the moment he recognizes the butchered bodies of his wife and children, learns from his father, after frantic, frenzied questioning, that he is responsible, and realizes that he has been annihilated, made less than a Nobody, an Oedipus who seeks death or desperate flight and will find refuge only in the Athens of Theseus.

It is the first line of this scene—'Quis hic locus, quae regio, quae mundi plaga?'—which T. S. Eliot uses as the epigraph for 'Marina', one of the *Ariel Poems* published in 1930, his own rewriting of the recognition scene in *Pericles*. He used it, he explained in a letter, because he intended 'a crisscross between Pericles finding alive, and Hercules finding dead—*the two extremes of the recognition scene*'. In his rewriting of Shakespeare, Eliot places 'Marina' between death and rebirth, interlinking the two by means of the slow, mysterious process of the dawning of consciousness: making poetry on the scene of Shakespeare and agnition itself, or, to put it more precisely, on the threshold between the two.

'Marina' is a monologue pronounced by an anonymous voice which the title and some lines imply to be that of Pericles. Its resonance, however, is at least triple: the words emerge from the nameless breath of an 'I' seemingly in search of itself, filtered through the echo of Shakespeare and reverberating between the Seneca quotations which open and close the poem. Rewritings of *Hercules Furens* immersed, as it were, in the sea of *Pericles* (also evoked by Seneca) actually frame the poem:

> What seas what shores what grey rocks
>   and what islands
> What water lapping the bow
> And scent of pine and the woodthrush
>   singing through the fog
> What images return
> O my daughter.

> What seas what shores what granite islands
>   towards my timbers
> And woodthrush calling through the fog
> My daughter.

Hercules' sleep-drugged questions have become, as indicated by the absence of punctuation, both evocation and interrogation, directed at his daughter, here seemingly recognized, and at himself and his own failed memory. Out of this, there emerges some northern shore, known and lost, identifiable but mysterious. Eliot apparently based himself on the shores of Rogue Island, in Maine, on the Atlantic Coast of the United States; for the poetic 'I' of the poem, these are vague, amorphous memories, a horizon of water and rocks suspended in time and space. The 'images return' with the perfume of the pines, the woodthrush song, and the water lapping the prow; past and present are coterminous, suggested by the poem's temporal dimension, the reader moving in to supply the text's tacit association. This is not yet knowledge, in the opening lines (the last, as we shall see, contain a subtle but vital variation), but a threshold of associations, a 'fog' of echoes, radical doubt as to what is actually seen and what remembered (*what* seas, *what* shores?), and intertextual doubt as to the *being-where* (*ubi sum?*).

But consciousness is not inactive: we are informed that it is roused by 'those who sharpen the tooth of the dog', 'those who glitter with the glory of the hummingbird', and those who wallow in animal contentment: all 'meaning Death', because all pernicious personifications of Evil and capital sins: gluttony, pride, sloth, and lust. It is from spiritual death that this Pericles-Hercules must rise again, and knowledge must emerge from awareness of his own sins. Yet the purification is through no tortuous inner process, but seemingly divinely dispensed: the stains spotting his soul are stated in the present 'confession' but seem of no consequence because washed 'by a wind, a breath of pine', while the fog singing in the wood appears to be dispersed in space by abundance of grace:

> Are become unsubstantial, reduced by a wind,
> A breath of pine, and the woodsong fog
> By this grace dissolved in place.

In the context, the mysterious wind (*a* wind) cannot fail to evoke the divine *pneuma* of the beginning of the world, and the breath of John's Jesus on his disciples after the Resurrection: not accidentally, Eliot associates this with a *breath*. At the same time, this breath is that of the pines, the 'scent' pervading the first lines. Evil is annulled by the Spirit and by the scent. Meanwhile, the woodthrush singing in the fog disappears, leaving a concretion of voices and a scene dimly glimpsed through the darkness, an incorporeal sublimation, a *woodsong fog*: fog-of-the-song in/of-the-wood. Are we to take this fog as the object of the grace which dissolves it, as grammar, punctuation, and logic would argue, or in apposition to the wind and the breath of pine, as would be far from unfeasible in a poet like Eliot, who has taken care to have fog lingering over the punctuation and the definite and indefinite articles of the first lines? Are we to read the wind, pine-breath, and woodsong fog as variations and progressive intensifiers of the same 'thing'? Or should we read them as a series of agents of the 'grace' which wipes out evil and Death? And does 'dissolved' then refer to the listed personifications of sin in the previous verse, or the 'woodsong fog', or only to 'grace'?

Let me attempt a word-by-word paraphrase: i.e. an interpretation. First: 'Have become without substance, reduced by a wind, | A breath of pine, and the fog of the song in the wood | [Fog] dissolved by this grace in space.' Second: 'Have become without substance, reduced by a wind, | By a breath of pine, and by the fog of the song in the wood | [All of which are] dissolved by this grace into space.' Third: 'Have become without substance, reduced by a wind, | a breath of pine, and the fog of the song in the wood | by means of this grace [which has been] dissolved in space | in this place.'

At the heart of 'Marina' there lies a question which might apparently solve all questions: a mystery which can open out or close in on itself. In the first and second readings above, the text preludes an inner process of awareness, and a higher process of illumination, possibly ending in recognition. In the third, however, a dream is described, an illusory vision: 'the rarest dream that e'er dull sleep | Did mock sad fools withal', as Shakespeare's Pericles exclaims in disbelief a few seconds before agnition. The difference is nothing less than the alternative between salvation and resurrection granted by an external 'person' on the one hand, or by a mere inner illusion, 'unsubstantial', on the other.

The text moves in various directions simultaneously: towards an opening up, if the woodsong fog clears; towards closure, if it remains dense; towards the progressive action of grace dissolving sin by means of the wind, the breath of the trees, and the fog reverberating in the forest (that is, by divine, natural, and, through memory and sensations, human means); or towards the sudden melting away of grace itself, into space, or in space, or even *in loco*, here and now. Eliot ensures that his poem is more enigmatic than the Scriptures, creating a rewriting which is elusive, hermetic, and evocative.

The next three lines can, for instance, be read in two radically different ways, according to whether we listen to the echo of *Pericles* ('But are you flesh and blood? Have you a working pulse?') or of *Macbeth* ('Lesser than Macbeth, and greater; not so happy, yet much happier') which they undeniably contain. The voice takes up the questioning with Herculean and Periclean insistence:

> What is this face, less clear and clearer
> The pulse in the arm, less strong and stronger—
> Given or lent? more distant than the stars and nearer
>   than the eye.

Recognition is close at hand, or out of sight? Is the face given permanently, once and for all, or a temporary gift?

Pericles himself was still uncertain at this point: 'But are you flesh and blood? | Have you a working pulse? *And are no fairy?*' To what reality does the entity called 'Marina' in the title, then, belong: flesh and Spirit, or illusion of the mind, or of theatre, literature? Might she even be oracular enigma, that with which the witches hail Banquo in *Macbeth*?

The problem, of course, is that in 'Marina' the interlocutress defined 'my daughter' never replies, and there is no *being*, more or less human, giving counterweight to the returning images, thereby creating an objective consciousness. Pericles-Hercules' questions drop into the well of silence inside him, and reverberate only there. To the questions just quoted, for example, the voice replies in a series of near-incoherent fragments: whispers and 'small laughter' among the leaves, and hurried steps (memories of youth? Of married happiness?), but '*under sleep*, where all the waters meet', submerging everything. Then there appears a first shred of self-awareness: 'I made this, I have forgotten | And remember'. But this 'doing' is predicated on a 'bowsprit cracked with ice', heat-cracked paint, weak rigging, rotten sails, a leaking garboard strake, uncaulked seams—a phantom ship, in other words, the ship of an Ancient Mariner condemned to life-in-death. Between one journey and the next, one adventure-labour and another, 'Between one June and another September' nine or infinite months have passed (one June, *another* September): time to conceive and give birth to a daughter; time to age, be lost at sea, or in the underworld.

Then comes the turning-point. Like a man-god whose memory returns, or who himself returns from the dead, the voice now claims to have 'made this', and to have 'made this my own', as if he recognized that, 'unknowing, half conscious, unknown', he had generated a Daughter, fashioned his own vessel in his own image. Now, suddenly, there appears before his eyes 'This form, this face, this life'. Whether 'Marina' (her name is never pronounced) be dream or human being, she is, as in Shakespeare, *Life*, and, as in John, *this*. The voice has found her within himself, with super-Herculean labour, and abandons his old age to her, beyond himself and his own power of speech. *Not* an agnition, then, but the promise of faith which is the necessary prelude:

> This form, this face, this life
> Living to live in a world of time beyond me; let me
> Resign my life for this life, my speech for that unspoken,
> The awakened, lips parted, the hope, the new ships.

'Marina' is, more precisely, the hope of *new life*: the hope of the future of the single individual, on earth, and that of eternity, of the ineffable and the arisen; the hope of new, unending sea voyages in 'the new ships', leaving the old, cracked vessel to rot away: of the living-for-the-life-of-others—the total commitment of love and charity. Pericles and Hercules lay down the whole of themselves to possess *this life*: 'He that loves his life', John's Jesus preaches (12: 25), 'shall lose it; and he that hates his life in this world shall keep it unto life eternal.' Everything seems to centre on a 'this-ness' of form and, above all, face (in the middle of the line), as if this Pericles-Hercules, who had already wondered over it, perceiving it 'less clear and clearer', were positing a forthcoming trajectory cognate with that of the First Letter to the Corinthians (13): now he sees 'through a glass, darkly', but then he will see 'face to face'; now his knowledge is imperfect, but then he will know completely, as he himself is known.

The voice of 'Marina' potentially opens, then, to the word and the Word, uttered through 'parted lips'. Within Eliot's personal trajectory we have passed the penitential *Ash Wednesday* to reach the Christmas-related *Ariel Poems*: the poems of the 'altar of God' and of Jerusalem (according to the etymology of *'ari'el* and its associations in Isaiah 29), *and* of the aerial sprite of creation and salvation evoked by Prospero and Shakespeare in *The Tempest*. But we are also heading for the *Four Quartets*, where Marina's granite islands, northern and fog-bound, will become the *Dry Salvages*, where travellers are greeted not with a 'fare well' but with a 'fare forward', and where the present 'daughter' will become, quite explicitly, Dantesquely, 'Figlia del tuo figlio' ('Daughter of your son'): the Christian Queen of Heaven. This now casts a retroactive light on 'Marina', revealing its tensions and ambiguities as tormented stages on an inner journey of conversion which is also Eliot's own. Suspended one second before the moment of recognition, 'Marina' is the most resonant prelude to it (Western) poetry has ever produced: a lyric not of being and knowing, but of the whisper of being, and the shadow of knowing: the re-Scripture of waiting and *expectation*, beyond which it opens up the potential in each individual of the divine that lies in recognition. Thus the final questioning of the poem's voice remains open, re-echoing that of the beginning, and on the threshold of awaking it returns to wonder 'what seas what shores what granite islands'. But the same voice now moves these seas and shores and islands '*towards its timbers*', while, through the fog, the woodthrush *calls*.

Waiting and expectation, then, are our lot: has the god ever been, will he ever be re-cognized, known again? Let us return, in conclusion, to the first chapter of this book, to rewriting and recognizing, revisiting it after our reading of Euripides, John, Shakespeare, and Eliot. For all of these, it is woman who possesses the particle of divinity which lies in recognizing and which makes recognition possible. My last example is a man: a 'simple' man, a 'most common Jew': Russian, devout, god-fearing, pure of heart, chaste of soul, and 'just'. His name is Mendel Singer and he is the protagonist of what I consider one of the finest and most moving of the century's novels, Joseph Roth's *Job*, published in 1930, the same year as 'Marina'.

Job is a rewriting not only of the Book of Job, but, as we shall see, also of Genesis and Exodus, and, like John and Shakespeare's *Pericles*, is centred on the final recognition scene, offering the ideal forum in which to observe the process we have been following throughout the present work. A twentieth-century novel written in German by a Galician Jew, it has the cadence and resonance of an epic dictated by the winds; of a tragic, beatific Scripture moving between two worlds, Russia and America, separated by an ocean and by history: the small, rural, ancient town of Zuchnow, and the huge modern metropolis of New York, before, during, and after the Great War and the October Revolution. Before we can return to our specific theme it will be necessary, then, to reread it, to hear, with the echo of the biblical text, the blasts which devastate the family of Mendel Singer. I shall therefore practise criticism as rewriting.

Mendel is 'insignificant' in appearance and, indeed, existence: in the large kitchen which constitutes his entire home, he teaches children the Bible, as thousands of Jewish teachers have done before him. His eyes, beard, and cap are black, and he walks quickly, the skirts of his caftan flying and flapping against his leggings and long leather boots 'like the beat of wings': an Everybody-Nobody, Eastern European Jew, in appearance part-tramp, part-angel. Mendel has a wife, Deborah, and four children: Jonas, Schemarjah, Miriam, and a little handicapped son, Menuchim, who sleeps in a basket hanging from the ceiling by way of a cot, and who, a doctor has declared, will one day become epileptic. From that day fear squats in the Singers' house 'like a monster', pain insinuating itself into their hearts 'like a hot, piercing *wind*'. Menuchim is seen as a disease eating away their collective flesh. He becomes their torment, their obsession, like the wind that here begins to blow, now to sweep over the entire novel.

Deborah takes her son to the holy rabbi in Kluczysk, the nearest small town, for his blessing, receiving instead a prophecy of biblical import:

Menuchim, Mendel's son, will be healed. There will not be many like him in Israel. Pain will make him wise, ugliness good, bitterness mild, and sickness strong. His eyes will see far and deep. His ears will be clear and full of echoes. His mouth will be silent, but when he opens his lips they will announce good tidings. Do not leave your son even if he is a great burden to you. Do not send him away from your side; he is yours even as a healthy child is.

The mother's silent wait begins, while Menuchim's brothers and sister try to drown him, the canker among them, in the water butt. A tenacious witness of life, beyond evil and pain, Menuchim refuses to succumb, shortly afterwards pronouncing his first word, 'Mama', the only word he will utter for ten years, 'sublime as a revelation, mighty as thunder, . . . gracious as Heaven, wide as the earth, fertile as a field': the voice of God and human rootedness, of promise and survival.

Life goes on, slow and inexorable, enacted in the pace of the novel. Miriam, pretty and sensual, devotes all her energy to men. Jonas and Schemarjah are called up. All demonstrations of love between Mendel and Deborah are one day converted into indifference or irritation. When, to his parents' horror, Jonas decides to become a professional soldier, his mother buys Schemarjah's passage to America for twenty-five roubles. Mendel begins to resemble Job for the first time, as his children disappear one by one. Only Menuchim remains, and Mendel takes him frequently on his knee to feed him, or sits him on the table, scrutinizing his wrinkled parchment face and trying to see through his eyes into his brain. He repeats his name scores of times, but the child remains inscrutable. He then taps a spoon against a glass, and the child turns immediately, a glimmer in his 'large, grey, liquid' eyes. Mendel continues to chink the spoon, accompanying the noise with a song. Menuchim becomes uneasy, turning his head and waving his legs. Again he calls 'Mama, mama!' His father takes down the big black Bible and recites the first verse, as he would with his pupils: 'In the beginning God created the heaven and the earth.' There is no reaction beyond the 'listening' glimmer in Menuchim's eyes. Heavy-hearted, Mendel addresses him:

Listen to me, Menuchim, I am all alone! Your brothers have grown big and strange . . . Your mother is a woman, what can I expect of her? You are my youngest son, my last and most recent hopes are all planted in you. Why do you remain silent, Menuchim? You are truly my son! Look, Menuchim, and repeat after me the words: 'In the beginning God created the heaven and the earth.'

In reciting the Creation, Mendel is attempting to mould his son and breathe him the word through the Word. At the same time he consecrates him as his one true Israel, his Joseph and Benjamin, and, met with his obstinate silence, with infinite, painful, painstaking patience he again takes up the chinking of the spoon, and his chanting of the beginning of Genesis. Then, despondent, he opens the door for his pupils, while Menuchim drags himself behind him and waits, curled up on the threshold like a loyal dog. The tower clock strikes seven notes, four deep, and three high, at which Menuchim cries 'Mama, mama!', stretching out his neck 'as though he breathed in the music of the bells'. His father, however, like Job, asks himself, 'Why am I so afflicted?', searching for some sin committed and finding 'none that is grave'. Life goes on.

Schemarjah leaves, passes the border, and manages, eventually, to reach America, where he makes his fortune, like a second Joseph. After a time he sends his parents ten dollars through his new-found friend Mac, with a letter inviting them to join him, promising tickets for New York. The pattern of the last part of Genesis now begins to emerge in *Job*, albeit almost inverted. Just as Jacob and his sons are unable to turn down Joseph's invitation to Egypt, so the Singers are unable to reject the promised abundance of the New World. But Mendel and Deborah immediately pronounce, in small voices, that Menuchim, with his slowness of mind and deformed body, cannot accompany them to the land of health, beauty, and intelligence. As soon as the heavy sentence of exclusion and abandonment has been pronounced, the sun sinks rapidly, a black shadow advances, 'as a lake rises over its boundaries with the beginning of a flood', and a sudden *wind* rattles the shutters.

Menuchim must remain behind, and while the Singers are making arrangements to leave him with the son-in-law of their neighbour Billes, in exchange for the use of their house, his sister Miriam shares her favours among the many Cossacks stationed in the town. Menuchim must remain behind, and for two weeks Deborah awaits the miracle (*Wunder*) that God will surely perform to heal him and allow his departure. Hope and faith are still alive, as is expectation.

Menuchim must remain behind, and Deborah weeps the tears of a mother in whose memory the rabbi's words are still ringing, 'Do not leave your son, stay with him.' Mendel refuses to return to Kluczysk to consult him, since 'No Jew needs a mediator between himself and God'; God will answer the prayers of the righteous, punishing only those who sin. 'Why does He punish us now?', Deborah asks in the tones of Job's wife; 'Have we sinned? Why is He so cruel?', to which Mendel replies, with Job's voice, 'You blaspheme Him, Deborah.' Shortly afterwards, returning from Dubno without the necessary documents, Mendel falls into a ditch when his neighbour Sameschkin's waggon breaks, and lies there, contemplating the stars which 'conceal God'. The only sense of brotherhood he now feels is with this Gentile peasant, who accuses him, jokingly, of belonging to a race which the devil drives wandering around the world. Mendel's answer is a steady weeping, at which the good Sameschkin, himself close to tears, puts his arm round his friend's bony shoulders and tells him: 'Sleep, dear Jew. Have a good sleep!' At this moment Mendel knows in his heart that his land is here, here are his roots, where good can grow and love blossom towards his fellow beings.

Menuchim must remain behind, and Mendel thinks of nothing but his son and the place he is about to leave, where he, his father, and his grandfather have all been teachers. Menuchim, 'the idiot', is agitated and uneasy. The soul which God has 'buried in the impenetrable fastnesses of his feeble mind' is disturbed by anxiety and fear. He drags himself to the door, where he curls like a sick animal, or he pounds the locks of the trunk in an 'unholy rattling'. His mother takes him in her arms, inwardly hearing the rabbi's words, and gazes hopelessly at his dull, flabby face, immersed in sleep, and the white spittle at the corners of his mouth. Deborah loses 'the strength which belongs with faith', and gradually 'the strength which is needed to endure despair' also abandons her. No miracle takes place. Menuchim remains behind, stammering 'Mama, mama' while the cart rolls away his mother, father, and sister.

The Singers travel for days by train before embarking at Bremerhaven. Here Mendel is comforted by the immensity of waving water around him, recognizes (*erkannte*) it as eternal and God-created, imagines Leviathan writhing on the bed, and blesses the green rollers. Like a Job who has already heard the Voice of the whirlwind, he recognizes the Creator and his works, which contain even the abyss of water, and even Leviathan, who is not represented as primeval chaos, but 'the holy fish, whom the pious and the righteous would eat on the Day of Judgment'. Then at last, the ship pulls out of port.

We now move from Genesis to Exodus. After a fortnight the three Singers land in the New World, before the Statue of Liberty holding an inextinguishable, electrically lit torch: such are the 'tricks' America has up its sleeve. Schemarjah is waiting for his father, mother, and sister. He now calls himself Sam, and is so changed—so Americanized in looks, smell, language, and gestures—as to be *unrecognizable*. After four days' quarantine, the Singers are released by Mac, and New York welcomes Mendel with a hot *wind*, made up of clamour and shouting, 'a floating noise', 'the fiery breath of hell'. Ground and annihilated by America, the poor Russian Jew on the verge of disappearing consciousness sees not the Promised Land but the desert his forefathers had wandered through for forty years.

This, then, is the new earth and the new heaven trumpeted by Isaiah: God's own country, as its citizens proclaim it! And is New York not known as *the wonder city*, as Jerusalem once was? In actual fact it looks to Mendel Singer like nothing so much as a 'large Kluczysk' and at the same time an unfamiliar world in which he is alone, without family, 'cast out of himself'—above all, deprived of his son, Menuchim. His heart begins slowly to turn to ice, beating 'like a metal drum-stick against cold glass'.

And yet Mendel soon begins to be at home in America: after all, he is the descendant of one who, some few hundred years earlier, had been forced to emigrate from Spain to Volinia, and is all too familiar with the centuries-old art of adapting, waiting, and smiling at adversity. Certainly he would love to return to Zuchnow and retrieve Menuchim, but Sam insists it is not 'practical'. He lives in the hope of a letter announcing that Jonas is leaving the army and that Menuchim has been healed, and one day, on one of his walks to pass time and a lifetime, he takes a young boy curled up on a doorstep for his handicapped son. In a word, Mendel lives in guilt and anguish and expectation, obstinately loyal to the life he left behind in Russia.

But America is keen to have him forget the past, and eager to thrust its munificence on him. Sam is happily married and getting steadily richer, and Deborah seems to rely increasingly on Mac's friendship. One day a letter arrives from both the Billes family and Jonas: fire had broken out in the house and Menuchim had rushed out through the flames shouting 'Fire!' and continuing with a few words more: the doctors were keen to treat him in a Petersburg hospital. Jonas, meanwhile, was glad to be serving the Tsar in the army. Mendel gives thanks to the Lord, and celebrates by exchanging glasses of mead with his wife, glowing with the idea that they could very shortly send Mac for Menuchim:

From his trunk, he fetched his old prayerbook, so familiar to his hand. He opened immediately to the Psalms, and sang one after the other. He had experienced grace and joy.

God's broad, wide, kindly hand arched protectively over him, too. Sheltered by it, and in honour of it, he sang the Psalms, one after the other. The candle flickered in the gentle but fervent breeze kindled by Mendel's swaying body. With his feet he kept time to the rhythm of the Psalms. His heart rejoiced, and his body had to dance.

We would appear to be at the end of the Book of Job, Mendel almost an exultant David. But then war breaks out in Europe, Jonas is involved, and any chance of communicating with and bringing over Menuchim seems impossible. Mendel continues to sing Psalms, but does so now with an alien voice. Fear shakes him 'as the *wind* shakes a tender tree'. Ever restless, he is tormented—like many Jews during the Holocaust—at the idea of not having done enough: what can Psalms do against the 'great storm'? The cannons thunder, the flames shoot up, and 'my children are perishing. It is my fault, my fault! And I sing Psalms! It is not enough! It is not enough!'

The novel now speeds up in pace, as does the history of the world after 1914. Sam leaves for Europe, with Mac, to fight for his new 'fatherland'; Jonas is officially declared missing; Miriam announces that Mac has returned with Sam's personal effects and his last wishes and farewells; at the news, Deborah tears her hair, begins to sing, emits a heart-splitting groan, and dies. While Mendel is imagining that Menuchim too must now be dead, and while he grieves for Deborah, accusing America of killing them both, and reproving himself and his wife for having ceased to love each other ('perhaps that was our sin'), Miriam loses her mind.

Only his own life now remains to Mendel, as to Job. Now, while he paces about the neuropsychiatric hospital

which is treating his daughter, he observes the yellow cow-
slips in their pots and thinks of the Russian meadows, lost
with Menuchim, 'the most loyal of all the dead, the farthest
away of all the dead, the closest of all the dead'. Pulverized
by fate, and driven by the new, hard wisdom of one who has
'seen a few worlds perish', he advises Sam's widow to marry
Mac, in this way absolving himself of all family responsibility. Finally revelling in his tragedy, he attempts to break
the ultimate tie, that with God: he lights a fire and is about
to burn the red velvet sack containing his phylacteries, his
talèd, and his prayer-books. Like a crazed David, he chants
his terrifying litany, beating time with his boots until the
floorboards rattle, accompanied by the pots on the wall:

It is over, all over; it is the end of Mendel Singer! . . . He has no
son, he has no daughter, he has no wife, he has no country, he has
no money! God said: I have punished Mendel Singer! For what
has He punished him? Why has He not punished Lemmel, the
butcher? Why not Skovronnek? Why not Menkes? He punishes
only Mendel. Mendel has death, Mendel has madness, Mendel
has hunger—all God's gifts are for Mendel! All, all is over—it is
the end of Mendel Singer!

But if his lips and feet are ready with their sacrilege, his
hands refuse to obey his anger. Every day for fifty years
Mendel had used those same objects to call on his God:
he cannot now simply burn them. A conditioned reflex
towards the sacred holds him back: his heart is 'angry
with God', but 'in his sinews the fear of God still dwells'.
His friends Menkes, Skovronnek, Rottenberg, and Groschel
come, alerted by his neighbours (and taking on the role of
Eliphaz, Bildad, Zophar, and Elihu in the Book of Job).
When they ask Mendel why he wants to burn the house
down, he replies that he wants to burn 'more than a house
and more than a person', and when they press him, he
finally shouts: 'Gott will ich verbrennen' ('I want to burn
God').
At this ultimate blasphemy the four feel their hearts seized

by sharp claws, but, like their biblical predecessors, attempt to reason with Mendel. Skovronnek reminds him that God's blows have 'a hidden purpose', and men can never know the reason for their chastisement. But Mendel knows very well: 'God', he spits out bitterly, 'is cruel, and the more one obeys Him the more brutally he treats one.' A powerful bully, he enjoys annihilating the weak because weakness excites his sense of power. He is an *isprawnik*, a great, brutal Tsarist police-chief. Rottenberg and Groschel then evoke the example of Job in person: he, too, blasphemed God, 'And yet, it was only a test, after all', and Mendel, like Job, has hitherto had issue and prosperity. 'Why do you break my heart?', is Mendel's not unreasonable reply, 'Why do you tell me all that was, now, when I have nothing left?': and his friends can only agree.

Rottenberg tries again, arguing that Mendel had disturbed the divine plans by leaving behind his handicapped son as if he were a child of evil. A long silence follows his comment, which has clearly touched the rawest of nerves. Mendel then replies, not to Rottenberg but to his previous interlocutor, asking why he had given the example of Job. Had they, then, 'really seen miracles' like those at the end of the Book of Job? Will Deborah and Schemarjah, then, rise from the dead, will Jonas return alive and well, will Miriam be healed, will Menuchim arrive from Russia, even supposing he is still alive? And then, he goes on, finally answering Rottenberg, it is unfair to say 'that I left Menuchim behind out of unkindness, to punish him': they had been forced to leave for other reasons, because his daughter was running around with Cossacks. And then, he concludes, why was Menuchim ill? 'His sickness itself showed that God was wroth with me. It was the first blow, which I did not deserve.'

Menkes, like Elihu 'the most thoughtful', then speaks, insisting that, although God was almighty, he considered the world no longer deserving of miracles, and even if he wanted to make an exception for Mendel, 'the sins of the others would count against you'. He is obliged to limit himself to small-scale miracles: Deborah and Schemarjah will not return from the dead, but Menuchim is probably alive, and Mendel may well see him again after the war; Jonas may have been taken prisoner; Miriam might get better; and, lastly, Mendel has a grandson, Schemarjah's son, on whom to pour his love, and comfort himself. Mendel replies in tones of closure to this 'most thoughtful' voice of human wisdom, which advises keeping the doors of the possible open but which is unable to grasp the nakedness of the being in front of him and offer adequate consolation. He begins, as always, with the last point made by his interlocutor. There can be, he insists, no relationship between himself and his grandson, because their natural link, Schemarjah, is dead; the doctor has said that medicine cannot cure Miriam; Jonas is, in all likelihood, dead; and Menuchim was not well at the best of times, and will certainly not have survived the war in Russia.

Mendel is, and wishes to be, alone. He has loved God for years, and has been hated in return. Now all that God can do is kill him, but he is too cruel for that: 'I shall live, live, live', Mendel howls. When Groschel warns him that God's power extends beyond death, to the next world, Mendel laughs and denies any fear of hell. He has already been through every imaginable hell, and since the devil is less mighty than God, he will necessarily be less cruel. Job prefers the Enemy to the Lord. Unlike his biblical counterpart, he does not call Yahweh to judgment—he seems already to have condemned God to death. His friends fall silent.

At dawn they take him to the Skovronneks, where he then stays, steadfastly refusing to pray or touch his red velvet sack. Gossips report that, to annoy God, he forays into the Italian section to eat pork. But his fellow Jews take his part in his battle against heaven, feeling for him not only pity, but admiration and reverence. Mendel has become one of the elect, the incarnation of 'holy madness':

In the midst of those whose laborious days were undisturbed by terrors he lived as a pitiful witness of the cruel power of Jehovah. For many years he had lived his days like all the others, observed by few, by many not even noticed. Then one day he had been set apart, in a dreadful way. There were none, now, who did not know him. He spent the greater part of his days in the streets. It was as though it were part of his curse not only to suffer misfortune but to set an example, to wear the sign of his agony like a banner.

Mendel is now the Job of Western tradition: a *vir sanctus* but equally a blaspheming madman; the elect and the rebel, victim and idol, humanity itself suffering without cause. But beneath the pain, rejection, and blasphemy, a thin thread, a never-severed umbilical cord links him to his God: the lack of prayer hurts him, and his anger and impotence torment him. Mendel is angry with God, but has to *recognize* that 'God still rules the world. Hate can move Him no more than piety.' Remembering the many days of his life which had opened with prayers and a familiar greeting to his 'strong but smiling' Father, who had always, he believed, returned the greeting, Mendel now considers he has been 'deceived'. The Father is 'strong but harsh', and from his lips comes 'no sound, but thunder'.

Mendel's days are spent running small errands for others, and rocking the cradles of others' children, dredging atrociously from painful memory, perhaps as a bitterly mechanical token of faith, the old chant, 'Say after me, Menuchim: In the beginninng God created the heaven and the earth. Say after me, Menuchim!' He is impervious to the many items splashed over the newspapers, such as the outbreak of revolution in Russia. On feast-days, among his fellow Jews, his heart is a stone, his lips closed. His black caftan is now green, and the seam visible down his back, 'like a tiny drawing of the backbone'. Mendel Singer is a skeleton, a death's head that shrinks daily, bent crookedly towards the ground, 'a wreck of a creature, with crooked knees and scuffling soles': a dying life, a tiny wandering Jew, a being-towards-nothingness which nothing—neither the world, nor time, nor mankind—can in any way touch.

Mendel Singer has become vanity of vanities, the infinite void of Ecclesiastes. His is the story of a simple man, and, so far, the simple-complex story of a common man: a tragedy, to define it more precisely, which has taken us through a peak (material prosperity and 'grace' after the arrival in America), two reversals, or *peripeteiai*—the loss of his children and homeland: then the loss of everything—and a difficult but fulfilled anagnorisis (between Schemarjah-Sam and his family). Everything in the tragedy is perfectly 'simple', natural, and all too human: the sick son, destiny's games with a family, the bitter, *Kunststücke* America, producing technical marvels which are a ghastly lay version of miracles and *Wunder* (Roth's slaughtering of this particular golden calf is even more savage than Kafka's), emigration, war, and revolution. Events seem entirely the result of all or any of these. Yet history appears to be relegated to brackets, while other realities, the instinct and emotions of the protagonists, occupy the foreground: Jonas's bellicosity, Miriam's lasciviousness, Schemarjah's capitalist passion, and the decay of love between Mendel and his wife. This is why the wind which arises suddenly and blows continuously over events, marking and magnifying them, penetrates into Mendel Singer's body and soul.

Above all, the tragedy is dominated by two inexplicable enigmas: Menuchim and God. Both are obsessive, unyielding, secretly interlinked presences. Menuchim is creation's misfit, 'nature's mistake', as Montale puts it, 'the world's dead point, the link that fails to hold'. But he is, and is there, not to be unmade: the life and sickness of the world, from its beginning. His father seems obscurely to perceive this, when he chants to him, 'In the beginning God created the heaven and the earth.' At the same time he is unfathomable: why does he exist, why does he not speak? The 'listening light' is in his eyes whenever he hears any elementary form of music, but his only words are 'mama', and then, years on, 'fire'. Menuchim is the child of the origins of the human race, animal-made-human, a 'thing' (the 'thing itself', Lear would say) with a soul. An ugly, dull, flabby, crawling creature, curled on the threshold like a dog, Menuchim is a pathetic, resilient, horrendous, beautiful, inexplicable mystery.

His companion is God, his creator. God never acts in the first person in *Job*: no event is directly attributed to him by the narrator as cause and effect. It is Mendel and Deborah, and Mendel and his New York friends, who discuss God constantly and try to establish some indissoluble link between his reasons and events: between Creator and created. Between the two parallel and independent lines which emerge in the story it is the human being who, in Hebraic manner, finds the plot and is caught up in it. If God is made responsible for everything, it is God who must be constantly discussed. But to reason why with God is a thankless task: why is he punishing us?, Deborah asks; why is he persecuting me?, Mendel wants to know; and all the clever answers of his four friends will crash against a wall of mystery.

Just as Menuchim cannot be killed, in the same way God cannot be burned: flesh of the same flesh and spirit of the same spirit, they brand and elect Mendel who chooses them in his turn. Good and evil are present in both for those who have eyes to see: God is a 'benign hand' and cruel *ispravnik*. Menuchim and God constitute the two opposite but complementary extremes of the unfathomable, of the ultimate inscrutability of being. To abandon one means losing faith in the Other; desiring to burn the First means considering the second irrevocably dead. They are linked by way of the expectation they arouse and nurture in those near to them—the as yet vain expectation of the miracle, the *Wunder*.

God cannot be known, he can only be *re-cognized*. This is what Mendel is doing when he tinkles the spoon against the glass for Menuchim, and intones the beginning of Genesis; when, on board ship, he contemplates the sea; when he sings his songs of thanks to America; when, bereft of everything, he admits that God cannot be annihilated, and still governs the world; when, lastly, he blames God for speaking only as the thunder does—and indeed, the Yahweh of the Book of Job speaks out of the *se'arā*, the whirlwind, the storm, with the voice of the thunder. And the God of *Job* speaks through the wind which blows through the pages of the novel, thick, hot, dark, and freezing; through the creaking of a window, the hell-house hum of New York, the breeze of fear: the *ruah Elohim*, the breath which breathes over the waters of primordial chaos. 'Look, Menuchim, and repeat after me the words: "In the beginning God created the heaven and the earth".'

Mendel, curled in on himself, ready to disappear into the earth he bends towards, an empty cypher, fails to hear the voice of God from the whirlwind. When the war ends, the first phonogram records begin to arrive, 'new songs from Europe'. In one of these, Mendel hears a tinkling of water which then swells and roars like the ocean. To him it is 'the whole world . . . engraved on such a little disk'; a silver flute then winds its way in to accompany the 'fabric' of the violins 'like an accurate little hem': a round, flat microcosm promising the entire Earth: small voices announced in mystery. Uncomprehending, Mendel cries for the first time in years. Skovronnek then reads the record label: the song is called 'Menuchim's Song'.

With the arrival of spring, Mendel is another man: he hums to himself, and allows a slight smile to remain on his lips. As the days lengthen and the community awaits the Messiah for Passover, one of his neighbours reads Mendel's transformation as the onset of a second childhood: holy madness, and joy at the onset of death.

The pages of *Job* uninterruptedly recount Mendel's gradual reduction into nothingness and the arrival of the record: life simply goes on. And the waiting begins anew, intensified and piloted by Roth, who accelerates the narrative rhythm with the skill of an Eliot, Shakespeare, John, and the Yahwist of the Joseph story. 'Menuchim's Song' safely lodged in his brain, Mendel now perfects his grand plan, to return to what had been his house and find the money Deborah had hidden, with which to purchase his return ticket to Europe. This he successfully does, and although the money is not enough, he will add to it over the next few months: now he has time, and the ocean, Zuchnow, the forests, stars, and Sameshkin 'wait' for him. If Menuchim is dead, then he too will be waiting for him in the tiny graveyard, and Mendel will lie beside him on the naked earth, and wait to sleep there 'for ever'. But his plan fails: ready for death, he is overtaken by life, which prolongs his wait, fulfils it, and renews it. Then, finally, the recognition takes place, unfolding in three scenes of increasing intensity, each prepared by the preceding one.

Scene one. The ice-cream seller, Frisch, announces to Mendel that the previous evening he had been at a concert where 'Menuchim's Song' had been played. The conductor of the orchestra came from Europe, was called Alexis Kossak (and therefore a possible relative of Deborah's: Kossak was her maiden name), and was looking for Mendel Singer. Frisch shows Mendel the concert programme with the musician's photograph. Mendel grips it, staring at the eyes which look right back at him; large and clear, simultaneously old and young, they seem to know everything, and, like the record, to contain the whole world. Mendel himself feels younger in their gaze, becoming a youth who needs to learn everything. The only thing he understands is that he knew these eyes, and had dreamt of them as a boy: 'years ago, when he had begun to study the Bible, these had been the eyes of the prophets. Men to whom God Himself had spoken had such eyes. They knew all, they betrayed nothing; they were full of light.' Mendel re-enters the primeval ocean of space and time, revisiting his past, rediscovering the Book, and recognizing that he knows nothing any longer. He takes the photograph, immediately stopping outside to re-examine it. It now seems to him that infinity has elapsed since he entered the ice-cream parlour: 'The couple of thousand years which shone in Kossak's eyes lay between, and the years when Mendel was still so young that he could imagine the countenances of the prophets.'

The strange light of those eyes is both concentrated and dilated: the light of the total knowledge granted by the word of God; the secret, enigmatic light of prophecy; the time of youth, and of Exile; the time of Bible study, and of waiting *within* the Bible; the time (and the reference is indirect but unmistakeable: *die paar tausend Jahre*) of Jesus of Nazareth. Kossak, the all-knowing, has the eyes of Mendel as a child, but they are equally those of Isaiah, Jeremiah, Ezekiel, Daniel, and Christ. They are the eyes of those announcing salvation, of those who prophesy, or present themselves as the Messiah. After Job, Genesis, and Exodus, Roth rewrites the Old Testament with an allusion to the New. Is everything, then, about to come to pass?

Scene two. The evening of the Passover. Mendel is with the Skovronneks, seated at one end of the table on which a snow-white cloth glows, with six silver candle-sticks each holding a white candle. Skovronnek, also dressed in white, 'a purified king upon a purified throne', begins to chant the legend of the Exodus from Egypt. All present join in, with the exception of Mendel. The melody 'numbers over and over again' the 'miracles' of God's goodness, greatness, and compassion towards Israel, and his anger with Pharaoh, and eventually caresses and draws Mendel, too, into its net so that he hums in spite of himself, and rocks backwards and forwards, 'cradled in the song of others'. It is as if, 'because of God's love for his whole people', the old man, too, were 'almost reconciled to his own, small fate'. His heart quietened, and well disposed 'towards heaven which four thousand years ago had generously lavished such marvellous miracles', Mendel recalls when he, too, had headed the table and intoned the chant celebrating Exodus and the Passover which commemorates it. He would be the only one to glance now and then at poor Menuchim, the one evening of the year when he joined them at the festive table, and he would see the 'listening light' in his eyes, and how 'the little one tried in vain to express what sounded in him, and to sing what he heard'. *This* is the rewriting of Job: this using of tradition and its rites, retracing Exodus, and re-evoking of music (as in *Pericles* and 'Marina'); this making of the biblical past and personal memory a symphony, merging memory and anticipation, reawakening the echo of the song heard on the record, perhaps of the chant repeated in far-off Zuchnow: 'Look, Menuchim, and repeat after me the words . . .'

Then the moment in the ritual arrives when the red chalice is filled with wine and the door opened to admit the prophet Elijah, announcing the arrival of the Messiah. The glass is ready, 'waiting', reflecting the six candle-flames. Mendel stands, glides to the door, and opens it. Skovronnek chants the invitation to the prophet. Mendel waits for him to finish, then closes the door. At this point a knocking starts. They all think they are mistaken, and that 'it was certainly the *wind* which knocked'. Mrs Skovronnek nags that the door was not properly closed. But then the knocking is heard again, 'longer and more clearly'. They all hold their breaths, 'perplexed and pale': the smell of the candles, the wine, the candle-light, and the old melody has brought adults and children alike 'to the point where they almost await a miracle', and they look at each other 'as though they asked themselves whether the prophet were indeed at the door'. Silence takes over the room, and no one dares move. Then Mendel stands up again, and again glides towards the door. The whole scene is a marvellous Hebrew rewriting of John, totally human and wholly miraculous: a counterpoint to the Last Supper by means of a return to the original which the Last Supper rewrites, the Jewish Passover and Exodus; a variation on Jesus's sudden appearance to the disciples after the Resurrection, in the closed room (here making him knock at the door): a recomposition in the waiting of Elijah, the Messiah, and the wind.

Scene three. When Mendel opens the door, no prophet or Messiah enters. Into the semi-darkness of the passage strides a tall, elegant stranger who presents himself as Alexis Kossak and asks to speak to 'a certain Mendel Singer'. Mendel introduces himself, and the guest is invited to sit. Kossak and Singer look at each other in silence, like Penelope and Ulysses; while the others continue praying, each seeks the other's eyes. Nothing of the man's face is known to Mendel except his eyes, which his gaze constantly strays back to, 'like a homecoming to well-known lights behind windows'. Mendel takes out the concert programme with the photograph of Kossak and hands it to the stranger, who smiles only momentarily, and 'thinly'. We are being invited, indirectly, to remember and conclude that these are the eyes Mendel has already recognized as those who have heard the word of God and know all, betraying nothing—the eyes of the prophets: no longer in a photograph, but in the flesh, they now seem partially to eclipse Exodus and Exile with the shadow of a *nostos*, foretelling the return to the native land.

The singing stops and dinner begins, eaten in increasing, 'unfestive' haste. The singing resumes, again the recitation of miracles; then the Psalms are intoned, the voice, the words, and the melody so enchanting that even Mendel joins in with 'Hallelujah! Hallelujah!' at the end of each strophe. Then dinner ends with the traditional 'Next year in Jerusalem!'.

The anticipation is nerve-racking, but the pace is now slowed down. Mendel, bewitched by the music and led towards his true 'home' in Israel, puts the first question. 'Now, Mr Alexis, what have you to tell me?' The stranger apologizes for not having sent his news earlier, and announces that Billes's son-in-law has died of typhus. Mendel mutters regrets, but thinks of Menuchim. Kossak goes on to say he has bought Mendel's old house for the equivalent of three hundred dollars, which he would now like to give him, then confirms that Jonas has been missing since 1915, quickly adding, however, that there is news that he is alive and fighting with the White Guards: tiny fragments of hope begin to glimmer. Mendel is now about to ask of Menuchim, but Roth, like Shakespeare, is a master of delaying; Skovronnek anticipates the question and likely tragic answer, and deflects the conversation on to the stranger's own life. Taken aback, he replies in few words: the son of a teacher, he was for many years sick as a child, and had been sent to a public hospital in a large city. One day he had sat down at the piano and played his own songs out of his head. The war had made his fortune: his military music had been an enormous success, and he had played for the Tsar himself, after the Revolution taking his orchestra abroad (the theme of music again).

Kossak's story—'not anything special', as he himself puts it—has a strange effect on his listeners, however; his words linger in the room and 'descend' on his audience gradually, and singly. He speaks Yiddish badly, interspersed with half-Russian sentences, so that his account has to be translated into English before they understand the whole, after Skovronnek's retelling. A singular, marvellous mixture of languages and interpreters is evoked (as between Joseph and his brothers), which, however, 'naturally' summarize the vicissitudes of the entire novel. The word is enigmatically suspended, echoing through the air like a winged spirit before descending to each individual. The knife-edge of expectation sharpens.

Meanwhile, the candles have burnt down and the room darkens. Everyone is reluctant to leave. Mrs Skovronnek 'reopens' the evening, lighting two more candles, while her husband asks Kossak if he is the composer of 'Menuchim's Song'. His affirmative is reluctant, and in his turn he immediately asks Mendel if his wife is dead, and if he has a daughter. Mendel nods; Skovronnek answers that the death of her mother and brother caused the daughter's mental illness. Tremblingly, the destinies are about to touch. Mendel rises and goes out: he yearns to ask after Menuchim, but dares not; he already knows the answer, and is already tasting its bitterness to pre-empt the shock of pain; finding a shy hope still inside him, he tries to kill it. Deferring the moment, he goes towards the kitchen to help their hostess prepare tea. She sends him back. The truth is calling, and the question can no longer be delayed. To save unnecessary misery, it is Skovronnek who puts it. 'My friend, Mendel, had another poor, sick son, named Menuchim. What has happened to him?'

The stranger makes no reply, but chinks his spoon in the bottom of his glass, and stares fixedly at it. Suddenly he cries: 'Menuchim is alive!' At these words (which rewrite those of the brothers to Jacob about Joseph), Mendel bursts into demented laughter which violently shakes his white beard and detonates around the room. Skovronnek is scared, and rises to hold his hands. Then Mendel starts to weep, the tears flowing from his half-veiled eyes into his beard. Calming down, he again asks: 'Menuchim is alive?', and equally calmly the stranger replies, 'Menuchim lives. He is alive, he is well, he is even prosperous.' Mendel folds his hands, lifting them towards the ceiling trying to rise, feeling 'he must stand up, stand straight, grow, become taller and taller': the man who had bent towards the earth is about to 'touch the skies'. Skovronnek knows what he must now ask on behalf of his old friend: 'Where is Menuchim now?' And slowly Alexis Kossak answers: 'I am Menuchim' ('Ich selbst bin Menuchim').

What unfolds is not recognition but progressive revelation: life, healing, being-here: a small, human, and mysterious resurrection which rewrites and Hebraically corrects the Gospel; a great and marvellous epiphany which there, in America, and now, in the twentieth century, fulfils that of Joseph himself. It is underscored by a rhythm which is alternately suspended, then taken up again in threes: three scenes—record, eyes, Passover. Three stages in the last scene—he is alive, he is well, it is I; three questions the text asks within the wider, lingering one as to *how* the recognition will take place: when will readers start to suspect Menuchim will come? When do they understand that 'Menuchim's Song' is the annunciation? When do they begin to conceive that Kossak might be Menuchim? Roth is closer to the Yahwist than Thomas Mann: M, for all the mystery, is expository, rationalizing, midrashic: a hyperconscious re-elaborator, and rewriter; R is romantic, allusive, symphonic, possessed by the spirit. The shadows of all present flicker over the walls. The candles waver, 'as though moved by a sudden *wind*'. Is God in this breath, as in the still, small voice heard by Elijah on Oreb? Evoking the wind which has braced the narrative at crucial points, *Job* suggests precisely that answer: Menuchim, surely, has come like the Elijah of the Passover?

For his part, Mendel falls on his knees before his seated son, seeks his hands with his lips, and reads his face with eager fingers, like blind Isaac. Not for a second does he take Menuchim for a god, far less for the Messiah: what he touches is the flesh of his flesh, as underlined by the anxious scoring of his son's face with his hands. But the son sitting quietly, immobile, in the general silence, surrounded by the encroaching darkness which merges those present into a 'dark cloud', and in which the candles continue to flicker, is the *shadow* of the divine. When, immediately afterwards, Menuchim says to Mendel, 'Stand up, Father', he sounds for a moment like Jesus speaking to Lazarus. But here, the son takes the father under his arms, lifts him up, and sits him on his knee, like a child, fulfilling by inversion the gesture with which, two lives ago, Mendel had taken his son to himself. Father and son find each other, a reciprocal Abraham, each in the other's bosom. The Creation attempted by the Father in his chant, 'Look, Menuchim, and repeat after me the words: "In the beginning God created the heaven and the earth"', now seems fulfilled by the Son.

For now, however, these are simply oblique suggestions, Eliot's 'hints and guesses'. A certain fact is that, sitting on his son's knee, and looking at his face, Mendel whispers the rabbi's prophecy to Deborah: 'Pain will make him wise, ugliness good, bitterness mild, and sickness strong.' For the 'simple, most common' Russian Jew, Mendel Singer, what is now achieving fulfilment is simply the far-off blessing of the holy rabbi. But both Mendel and his Passover companions go beyond this recognition of the *truth* pre-announced by a man. Unanimously his friends proclaim that 'a miracle has happened!'. The *Wunder* awaited throughout the novel has at last come about. Menkes, 'the most thoughtful', again takes up the reasons for consolation which he had offered to Mendel's despair, but subtly rearranges them into a significant recognition: the miracles perfomed by the Eternal, today as thousands of years ago, are not now 'modest', but 'great'. Then, finally, Mendel himself recognizes God, like Job, by confessing him:

I know that thou canst do every thing, and that no purpose of thine can be thwarted. Who is he that hides counsel without knowledge? therefore I have uttered that which I did not understand . . . I have heard of thee by the hearing of the ear, but now my eye sees thee. Wherefore I abhor myself, and repent in dust and ashes.

I have committed grave sins, God has closed His eyes. I called Him an *ispravnik*. He held his ears. He is so great that our badnesses seem to Him very small.

Rediscovering the Son means recognizing the Father: *'Ijjôb* probably means 'where is my father?'. Mendel, the elect of pain, has now become 'a disguised king', a little Job, a little David; possibly a little Jesus. He takes the sack of red velvet, gets into Menuchim's car, gives his three hundred dollars to the poor, and departs for the Astor Hotel, on Forty-Fourth Street and Broadway. The Passover is gone, the angel has passed, and the true Exodus—the *return* to the

Promised Land—can now begin. The tragedy has ended and a kind of divine comedy can begin.

The recognition of God can now be the start of the recognition of the world and of humanity. Up in the hotel room, Mendel sees 'for the first time America's night close at hand': its noisy 'song', and the images of health and happiness it emanates. He listens bewitched as his son tells the story of his genesis through music: the remote tinkling on the glass, the sound of bells, the violin of Billes's son-in-law, the fire, the hospital organ, the doctor's wife's piano: the story so far known through hints and guesses is now known in its entirety, recognized. Then, taken to a promenade overlooking the sea, Mendel contemplates the ocean, sun, and sky. For the first time in his life he dares to remove his old cap, and as a 'spring wind' moves the few hairs on his head he 'greets the world'. In the same moment he recognizes possibility, and the Scriptures: it is now easy for him to 'believe' that Jonas will one day be found and Miriam healed and returned to them, 'in all the land no woman so fair'. 'He himself, Mendel Singer, would have a good death, after many years, surrounded by grandchildren, "old" and "full of days", as was written of Job.' Shortly afterwards he recognizes the promise, and the shadows of the future springing from this and the other world. He gazes at the photographs of Menuchim's wife and children, and calls down on them—like Jacob on Joseph's children—God's blessing. He sees in the little girl's face that of his wife, 'dead Deborah', and considers that she, too, is perhaps living this 'miracle' with 'strange, otherworldly eyes'. Then, out of the brown background of the photograph emerge Jonas and Miriam, beside 'the new children'. And Mendel sleeps, resting 'from the burden of his happiness, and the greatness of the miracle'.

To recognize those we love is a god, we can only repeat with Helen: it is *Wunder* and *Glück*, miracle and marvel, happiness and fortune: the hope of life and fulfilment. Recognizing the son means recognizing the Father (and

Menuchim too, like God, cannot be perceived by 'cognition' but only 're-cognition'). But to recognize the Father, to recognize God—and here we rewrite Euripides, John, Shakespeare, Mann, and the Yahwist—is *a god*. We can only emerge from this tiny, irremovable tautology, within *Job's* perspective, by means of a further tautology: *to recognize God is to rewrite the Scriptures*, as Mendel Singer does when, having rejected the example in his discussion with his friends, he then identifies himself with Job by twice citing the Book, explicitly and consciously. But this re-Scripture of one book of the Bible is a rewriting of all Scripture; as Genesis appears in the Book of Job through Yahweh's voice out of the whirlwind, so Genesis, Exodus, Psalms, Prophets, and even a shadow of the Gospels are superimposed in *Job*, through hint and gesture and situation. On the other hand this re-Scripture is a continuously 'new testament', the testimony of *living*—and not just reading and writing—within the horizons of the Scriptures, thereby renewing them.

Here, however, an essential problem emerges from a contrast which refuses to be ignored. Mendel (and Deborah and their friends) always speak of God, and place everything within a God-centred, biblical perspective. Menuchim, however, whom the novel presents as the 'figure' of Elijah and the Messiah—a small-scale messiah, who will bring salvation not to a whole people, but to one man alone—*never does*. In recounting the story of his life to his father, Menuchim never once mentions the Almighty, and never once speaks of 'miracles': his healing, his 'genesis', are through music, the fire, the doctor and his wife—through natural and human causes which by chance or by deliberate application touch his mind and his psyche. When he thinks of Miriam's future, Menuchim gives himself as an example to counter his father's pessimism ('Wasn't I healed, father?'), but it is to the doctors he will turn.

This curious absence of God in Menuchim's words opens a significant gap in the novel, in re-Scripture, and in recognition, in that the narratorial voice itself, as we have already noticed, equally never attributes an event directly to God. At the same time, this is also the voice which creates the wind and, through the ritual and the books of the Bible, constantly alludes to the shadow of transcendence. Menuchim is *inside* the narrative; he is the son of a Bible teacher, of a Jew who, bereft of his God, would be unable to draw breath (even while trying to burn his God): yet he pays no attention to Yahweh. It is also true that he was abandoned as a child and raised and healed outside the Jewish community; but when he enters the Skovronneks' he keeps his hat on 'out of reverence for the ceremony' in which he finds himself. And he too is present—as cause and object— at the jubilation celebrating the miracle. Yet when he recounts the tinkling of the glass, the sound of the bells, and his father's song, Menuchim does not remember that this song began with the Beginning, the Creation.

What are we to make of this absence, this recognition *manqué*? Does it point to a gap between generations, to as it were the death of God in history? Does *Job* deny the miracle as it manifests itself? I think not. Roth's *Job* is re-Scripture, and like the Scriptures it is open or closed according to the inclination, disposition, and faith of its readers. In calling Isaiah, God orders him to announce to his people (6: 9): 'Hear indeed, but understand not; and see indeed, but perceive not.' When he speaks to his disciples, Jesus reiterates Isaiah's words: 'Unto you it is given to know the mystery of the kingdom of God: but unto them that are without, all these things are done in parables: That seeing they may see, and not perceive; and hearing they may hear, and not understand' (Mark 4: 11–12). Both Israel and the Gentiles can remain among 'them that are without'. Menuchim is within the narrative but 'without' its dominating culture, and silent on the religion which obsesses all the others.

Scripture and re-Scripture can be heard without being recognized, as in Menuchim's case. They can be read, and understood, as in Mendel Singer's case when, at the end, he feels he is reliving the experience of Job. *Job* is—exactly—a parable and a prophecy. One thing, however, it would seem to imply, unites the two readings: the waiting within hope. When Mendel tells Menuchim that there is no medicine that can help Miriam, his son replies, as we saw above, 'We will go to her. Wasn't I healed, father?' And Mendel's response is 'Yes, Menuchim [is] right. Man is never content . . . No sooner does he experience a miracle than he already wants another. *Warten, warten, Mendel Singer!* Wait, wait, Mendel Singer!'

Bibliography

THE following bibliography, organized according to chapter sequence, is for those who would like to do further reading in the subjects treated in this book. It also presents the secondary references which, in the absence of footnotes, might be essential to its reading. It is by no means exhaustive, but indicative and highly selective.

1. From J to M: Recognizing and Rewriting God

The text of the Hebrew Bible is the *Biblia Hebraica Stuttgartensia* (Stuttgart, 1990). The translations of Genesis are basically Robert Alter's in his *Genesis*, published by Norton in 1996. At times I also quote the King James Bible. Other Bible translations follow *The Jerusalem Bible*, *The Holy Scriptures*, the English text revised and edited by Harold Fisch (Jerusalem, 1992). I have also used the translation of, and commentary to, *Genesis* by E. A. Speiser in the Anchor Bible, the *Genèse* (LXX) edited by M. Harl for the Editions du Cerf, *Genesis* by Gerhard von Rad (Engl. trans., London, rev. edn., 1972); the two volumes (Engl. trans. by I. Abrahams) of U. Cassuto, *A Commentary on the Book of Genesis* (Jerusalem, 1961–4), and the three volumes (Engl. trans. by J. J. Scullion) by Claus Westermann, *Genesis: A Commentary* (London, 1984–7). *Bereshis: A New Translation with a Commentary Anthologized from Talmudic, Midrashic and Rabbinic Sources* (New York, 1980) is very useful. *Midrash Rabbah* (Genesis I-II) is available in English (London, 1939). U. Cassuto, *Le questioni della Genesi* (Florence, 1933), is still indispensable. For the *Glossa ordinaria*, see J. P. Migne (ed.), *Patrologia Latina*, 113. The *Glossa ordinaria* and the commentary of Nicholas of Lyra are printed in the six-volume *Biblia* (Lyons, 1545); the commentary by Hugh of St Cher in the *Opera Omnia in universum vetus et novum testamentum*, 8 vols. (Cologne, 1621). By Mario Brelich, it might be opportune to consult *Il sacro amplesso* (Milan, 1972). For Milton's *Paradise Lost* I use the text edited by A. Fowler (London, 1968). For Mann's *Joseph und seine Brüder* the

Fischer text (Frankfurt, 1982) and the English translation by H. T. Lowe-Porter published by Penguin (Harmondsworth, 1978). I also quote Mann's *Adel des Geistes* (Stockholm, 1945), and the English translation by H. T. Lowe-Porter, *Essays of Three Decades* (London, n. d.).

Critical material on Genesis and the Bible in general is of course endless. I have used above all the authors who treat the Book from a literary point of view: D. Norton, *A History of the Bible as Literature*, 2 vols. (Cambridge, 1993); E. Auerbach, *Mimesis* (Engl. trans. by W. R. Trask, Princeton, 1953); H. Fisch, *A Remembered Future* (Bloomington, Ind., 1984); H. Fisch, *Poetry with a Purpose: Biblical Poetics and Interpretation* (Bloomington, Ind., 1990); H. Fisch, *New Stories for Old: Biblical Patterns in the Novel* (London, 1998); H. Fisch, *The Biblical Presence in Shakespeare, Milton and Blake* (Oxford, 1999); R. Alter, *The Art of Biblical Narrative* (London, 1981); R. Alter, *The World of Biblical Literature* (New York, 1991); G. Josipovici, *The Book of God: A Response to the Bible* (New Haven and London, 1988); H. Bloom, *Ruin the Sacred Truths* (Cambridge, Mass., and London, 1989); M. Sternberg, *The Poetics of Biblical Narrative* (Bloomington, Ind., 1985); J. P. Fokkelman, *Narrative Art in Genesis* (Sheffield, 1991); H. C. White, *Narration and Discourse in the Book of Genesis* (Cambridge, 1991); M. Wadsworth (ed.), *Ways of Reading the Bible* (Brighton, 1991); R. Alter and F. Kermode (eds.), *The Literary Guide to the Bible* (Cambridge, Mass., 1987); N. Frye, *The Great Code: The Bible and Literature* (New York and London, 1982), and *Words with Power* (San Diego, New York, and London, 1992); E. Leach, *Genesis as Myth and Other Essays* (London, 1969); J. Licht, *Storytelling in the Bible* (Jerusalem, 1978); S. J. Brams, *Biblical Games: A Strategic Analysis of Stories in the Old Testament* (Cambridge, Mass., 1980); E. Leach and D. A. Aycock, *Structuralist Interpretation of Biblical Myth* (Cambridge, 1984); K. R. R. Gros Louis (ed.), *Literary Interpretations of Biblical Narratives*, ii (Nashville, Tenn., 1982); F. McConnell (ed.), *The Bible and the Narrative Tradition* (Oxford, 1986); S. Prickett, *Words and the Word: Language, Poetics and Biblical Interpretation* (Cambridge, 1986); S. Prickett, *Origins of Narrative: The Romantic Appropriation of the Bible* (Cambridge, 1996); *Exégèse et herméneutique* (Paris, 1971); P. Gibert, *Bible, mythe et récits de commencement* (Paris, 1986); H. N. Schneidau, *Sacred Discontent: The Bible and Western Tradition* (Baton Rouge, La.,

1976); M. Fishbane, *Biblical Interpretation in Ancient Israel* (Oxford, 1985); G. V. Savran, *Telling and Retelling: Quotation in Biblical Narrative* (Bloomington, Ind., 1988); F. Kermode, 'New Ways with Bible Stories', in his *Poetry, Narrative, History* (Oxford, 1990), 29–48. On Abraham, J. Magonet, 'Abraham and God', *Judaism*, 33 (1984), 160–70, and R. I. Letellier, *Day in Mamre Night in Sodom: Abraham and Lot in Genesis 18 and 19* (Leiden, New York, and Cologne, 1995) are illuminating. Amongst others, the following are important on the Joseph story: E. J. Lowenthal, *The Joseph Narrative in Genesis* (New York, 1973); E. McGuire, 'The Joseph Story: A Tale of Son and Father', in B. Long (ed.), *Images of Man and God: Old Testament Stories in Literary Focus* (Sheffield, 1981); J. S. Ackerman, 'Joseph, Judah, and Jacob', in Gros Louis (ed.), *Literary Interpretations of Biblical Narratives*, 85–113. Two works by James Kugel should be recommended: *In Potiphar's House* (Cambridge, Mass., 2nd edn., 1994), and *The Bible As It Was* (Cambridge, Mass., and London, 1997). The title of my chapter is obviously modelled on that of Harold Bloom's famous essay, 'From J to K, or the Uncanniness of the Yahwist', contained in the book edited by F. McConnell quoted above. Equally clearly, I do not agree with the theories expounded by Bloom in his *The Book of J* (New York, 1990). The book edited by D. H. Hirsch and N. Aschkenasy, *Biblical Patterns in Modern Literature* (Chico, Ca., 1984) has done pioneering work in the exploration of some types of Re-Scriptures.

For the sources of Mann's *Joseph*, see *Thomas Mann, Teil II: 1919–1943*, ed. H. Wysling and M. Fischer in the series 'Dichter über ihre Dichtungen', 14/11 (Munich, 1979), 82–353. For critical material, one would start with Mann's own Foreword to the English translation of *Joseph*, and then proceed to L. Secci, 'L'entelechia mitica di Thomas Mann', in her *Il mito greco nel teatro espressionista* (Rome, 1969); E. Heller, *Thomas Mann: The Ironic German* (Cambridge, 1981); K. Hamburger, *Thomas Manns biblisches Werk* (Frankfurt, 1984); W. R. Berger, *Die mythologischen Motive in Thomas Manns Roman 'Joseph und seine Brüder'* (Cologne and Vienna, 1971); M. Dierks, *Studien zu Mythos und Psychologie bei Thomas Mann* (Berne and Munich, 1972); S. Mannesmann, *Thomas Manns Romantetralogie 'Joseph und seine Brüder'* (Göppingen, 1971); G. Rohn, *Joseph: Bilder und Gedanken* (Hamburg, 1975); D. Mieth, *Epik und Etik. Eine theologisch-etische Interpretation*

BIBLIOGRAPHY   209

der Josephsromane Thomas Manns (Tübingen, 1976); E. Murdaugh, *Salvation in the Secular* (Berne, Frankfurt, and Munich, 1976); C. Jäger, *Humanisierung des Mythos—Vergegenwärtigung der Tradition* (Frankfurt, 1992); A. J. Swensen, *Gods, Angels, and Narrators: A Metaphysics of Narrative in Thomas Mann's 'Joseph und seine Brüder'* (New York, Berne, and Frankfurt, 1994). Eckhard Heftrich's massive work, *Geträumte Taten. 'Joseph und seine Brüder'* (Frankfurt, 1993), with a chapter on the problem of *Erkennen* to which I am particularly indebted, is fundamental.

2. Susanna in Excelsis

All quotations from the Susanna episode are from the Greek version of Theodotion (which was used by Hippolytus), published with the *Septuaginta*, ed. A. Rahlfs (Stuttgart, 1935), at the beginning of the Book of Daniel. The translation is mine: for it, I have also availed myself of the English *Daniel, Esther and Jeremiah: The Additions*, ed. C. A. Moore, Anchor Bible 44 (Garden City, NJ, 1977), and of the *Oxford Annotated Bible with the Apocrypha*, ed. H. G. May and B. M. Metzger (New York, 1965).

All references to, and quotations from, Hippolytus' *Commentary to Daniel* are based on *Commentaire sur Daniel*, ed. M. Lefèvre, (Paris, 1947). I have checked the passages surviving in the Greek original in *Hippolytus Werke*, i. *Exegetische und homiletische Schriften*, ed. G. N. Bonwetsch and H. Achelis (Leipzig, 1897), and in Migne, *Patrologia Graeca*, x. 261–962. For the exchange between Origen and Africanus, see Migne, *Patrologia Graeca*, xi. 4 ff.

Of the *Acta Sanctorum*, cur. J. B. Sollerio, J. Plinio, G. Cupero, P. Boschio, ed. nov. cur. J. Carnandet, one should read 'Augusti Tomus Secundus' (Paris and Rome, 1867), 'Die Undecima Augusti', 624–32, and consult V. I. Kennedy, *The Saints of the Canon of the Mass* (London, 1963), and H. Delehaye, *The Legends of the Saints* (London, 1962).

The text of Chaucer that I use is *The Riverside Chaucer*, gen. ed. L. D. Benson (Boston, 1987; Oxford, 1988). The text of Wallace Stevens's 'Peter Quince at the Clavier' is from his *Collected Poems* (New York, 1982).

On the Susanna theme, see this essential bibliography: W. Baumgartner, *Zum Alten Testament und seiner Umwelt* (Leiden,

1959), 42–67; E. Kirschbaum (ed.), *Lexicon der christlichen Ikono-graphie* (Rome, Freiburg, Basel, and Vienna), s.v. 'Susanna'; A. Miskimin, *Susannah: An Alliterative Poem of the Fourteenth Century* (New Haven and London, 1969), 189–99; J. Pépin, *Mythe et Allegorie* (Paris, 1976), 262–4; S. C. Walker, *Seven Ways of Looking at Susanna* (Provo, Utah, 1984); H. Engel, *Die Susanna Erzählung* (Freiburg, 1985); E. Spolsky (ed.), *The Judgment of Susanna: Authority and Witness* (Atlanta, 1996).

For the Susanna story in the Christian milieu the following should be consulted: H. Leclercq, 'Suzanne' and 'Défunts' in F. Cabrole and H. Leclercq, *Dictionnaire d'archéologie chrétienne et de liturgie* (Paris, 1953); J. Wilpert, *Le pitture delle catacombe romane* (Rome, 1903); L. Hertling and F. Kirschbaum, *The Roman Cata-combs and their Martyrs* (London, 1960). Besides those mentioned in this chapter, other representations of the Susanna stories are to be found in the catacombs of Domitilla (in the area of the Appian Way), of the Saints Marcellinus and Peter (Via Casilina), and in the 'Coemeterium Maius' (Via Nomentana), all going back to the fourth century. The fragment of a mosaic representing Susanna in the church of Santa Costanza in Rome (fourth century), next to the church and catacombs of St Agnes on the Via Nomentana, is now lost, but older copies of it survive: see F. Michel, *Die Mosai-ken von S. Costanza in Rom* (Leipzig, 1912).

The four Roman sarcophagi mentioned in this chapter are in the Museum of the Campo Santo Teutonico in the Vatican (six scenes), in the Museo Nazionale Romano; and two in the Lateran Museum (now part of the Vatican Museum). On these, see J. Wilpert, *I sarcofagi cristiani antichi* (Rome, 1929). Episodes of the Susanna stories have been found on sarcophagi at Arles (Musée d'art chrétien), at Narbonne (Musée Lamourguier), and at Gerona (church of San Felice). These go back to the late third, and the following century. Other early representations of Susanna are found on crystal cups: at Homblières (fourth century), Podgoritza (ninth century, now in St Petersburg), in the British Museum (the ninth-century cup of Lothar II). Finally, an ivory box with three Susanna scenes (presumably going back to the fourth century) survives in Brescia.

On liturgy I would recommend J. H. Srawley, *The Early History of the Liturgy* (London, 2nd edn., 1947); J. A. Jungmann, *The Early Liturgy to the Time of Gregory the Great* (London, 1961).

The best reconstruction of this historical period and of Callistus's story is by Santo Mazzarino in his *L'impero romano*, ii (Rome and Bari, 1973), 451–90. See also H. Chadwick, *The Early Church* (Harmondsworth, 1967), 84–113. On the history of the church of St Susanna in Rome, I refer the reader to R. Krautheimer, *Corpus basilicarum christianarum Romae* (Vatican City, 1937); A. M. Affanni, 'Inquadramento urbanistico e Santa Susanna', in *Santa Susanna e San Bernardo alle Terme* (Rome, 1993), 13–26. On the interior decoration, see R. Vodret, 'La decorazione interna', in *Santa Susanna e San Bernardo*, 28–48; B. Apollonj Ghetti, *Le chiese di Roma illustrate. S. Susanna* (Rome, 1965).

3. *In the Beginning Was a Cock: Animal Farms and the Plain Sense of Things*

The primary texts for this chapter are the following: Thomas Aquinas, *Summa Theologiae*, i, q. 1 (Madrid, 1965); Pierre Bersuire (Petrus Berchorius), *Ovidius Moralizatus* (Utrecht, 1962); Giovanni Boccaccio, *Genealogie Deorum Gentilium*, ed. V. Zaccaria (Milan, 1998); *Boccaccio on Poetry*, ed. C. G. Osgood (Princeton, 1930); *Caxton's Aesop*, ed. R. T. Lenaghan (Cambridge, Mass., 1967); *The Riverside Chaucer*, gen. ed. L. D. Benson (Boston, 1987; Oxford, 1988); John Dryden, *Poems and Fables*, ed. J. Kinsley (London, 1970); R. Henryson, *Poems*, ed. C. Elliott (Oxford, 1974); Isidore of Seville, *Etymologiarum Libri XX*, ed. W. M. Lindsay (Oxford, 1911); Jean de la Fontaine, *Fables* (Paris, 1966); A. J. Minnis and A. B. Scott (eds.), *Medieval Literary Theory and Criticism c. 1100–c. 1375: The Commentary Tradition*, (Oxford, 1988; for Conrad of Hirsau); Wallace Stevens, 'The Plain Sense of Things', in *Collected Poems*; Franz Kafka, 'The New Attorney', in *Parables and Paradoxes* (New York, 1961), 97–9; George Orwell, *Animal Farm* (Harmondsworth, 1964).

As for theoretical and historical material, I would recommend R. Alter, *The Pleasures of Reading in an Ideological Age* (New York, 1989); E. Auerbach, 'Figura', in his *Scenes from the Drama of European Literature* (Manchester, 1984); G. Beer, *Darwin's Plots* (London, 1983); P. C. Bori, *L'interpretazione infinita* (Bologna, 1987); B. Chatwin, *Anatomy of Restlessness* (London, 1996); H. De

Lubac, *Exégèse médiévale* (Paris, 1959–64); U. Eco, *I limiti dell'interpretazione* (Milan, 1990); A. C. Henderson, 'Medieval Beasts and Modern Cages: The Making of Meaning in Fables and Bestiaries', *PMLA*, 97 (1982), 40–9; F. Kermode, *The Genesis of Secrecy* (Cambridge, Mass., and London, 1979); F. Kermode, *An Appetite for Poetry* (Cambridge, Mass., 1989, for 'The Plain Sense of Things'); A. O. Lovejoy and G. Boas, *Primitivism and Other Related Ideas in Antiquity* (New York, 1965); C. Mésionat, *Poetica Theologia* (Rome, 1984); A. J. Minnis, *Medieval Theory of Authorship* (Aldershot, 1988); E. Schauber and F. Polsky, 'Stalking a Generative Poetics', *New Literary History*, 12 (1981), 397–413; B. Smalley, *The Study of the Bible in the Middle Ages* (Oxford, 1952).

Specific critical material on Chaucer's *Nun's Priest's Tale* includes: J. B. Allen, 'The Ironic Fruyt: Chauntecleer as Figura', *Speculum*, 66 (1969), 25–35; M. W. Bloomfield, 'The Wisdom of the *Nun's Priest's Tale*', in E. Vasta and Z. P. Thundy (eds.), *Chaucerian Problems and Perspectives: Essays Presented to Paul F. Beichner* (Notre Dame, Ind., 1979), 70–82; S. N. Brody, 'Truth and Fiction in the *Nun's Priest's Tale*', *Chaucer Review*, 14 (1979), 33–47; S. D'Agata D'Ottavi, 'Specularità e Parodia: La Mise en Abyme in *The Nun's Priest's Tale*', in D. Izzo (ed.), *Il Racconto allo Specchio* (Rome, 1990), 37–66; J. M. Donovan, 'The moralitee of the Nun's Priest's Sermon', *Journal of English and Germanic Philology*, 52 (1953), 493–508; P. Grimaldi Pizzorno, 'Chauntecleer's Bad Latin', *Exemplaria*, 4 (1992), 387–409; J. Mann, 'The *Speculum Stultorum* and the *Nun's Priest's Tale*', *Chaucer Review*, 9 (1975), 262–82; S. Manning, 'The Nun's Priest's Morality and the Medieval Attitude Toward Fables', *Journal of English and Germanic Philology*, 59 (1960), 403–16; M. E. McAlpine, 'The Triumph of Fiction in the *Nun's Priest's Tale*', in R. E. Edwards (ed.), *Art and Context in Late Medieval English Narrative* (Cambridge, 1994), 79–92; A. Schallers, 'The *Nun's Priest's Tale*: An Ironic Exemplum', *English Literary History*, 42 (1975), 319–37; S. Trigg, 'Singing Clearly: Chaucer, Dryden, and a Rooster's Discourse', *Exemplaria*, 5 (1993), 365–86; K. P. Wentersdorf, 'Symbol and Meaning in Chaucer's *Nun's Priest's Tale*', *Nottingham Medieval Studies*, 26 (1982), 29–46; E. Wheatley, 'Commentary Displacing Text: The *Nun's Priest's Tale* and the Scholastic Tale Tradition', *Studies in the Age of Chaucer*, 18 (1996), 119–41.

4. *Why Should Moses Go Down?*

The text of *Go Down, Moses* used in this chapter is the Penguin edition (Harmondsworth, 1970). The text of the Epistle to Cangrande is quoted from Dante Alighieri, *Opere Minori*, ii (Milan and Naples, 1979). The translation is Anita Weston's. On Faulkner, the following works should be consulted: A. Bleikasten, *The Ink of Melancholy: Faulkner's Novels* (Bloomington, Ind., 1990); J. L. Blotner, *Faulkner: A Biography* (New York, 1984); T. M. Davis, *Faulkner's 'Negro': Art and the Southern Context* (Baton Rouge, La., 1983); D. Fowler and A. J. Abadie (eds.), *Faulkner: International Perspectives,* 1982 (Jackson, Miss., 1990); D. Fowler and A. J. Abadie (eds.), *Faulkner and Popular Culture,* 1988 (Jackson, Miss., 1990); M. Gresset and N. Polk (eds.), *Intertextuality in Faulkner* (Jackson, Miss., 1985); M. Grimwood, *Heart in Conflict: Faulkner's Struggles with Vocation* (Athens, Ga., 1987); I. Howe, *William Faulkner* (New York, 1962); M. Jehlen, *Class and Character in Faulkner's South* (New York, 1976); D. Fowler and A. J. Abadie (eds.), *Faulkner and the Southern Renaissance* (Jackson, Miss., 1982); A. Lombardo (ed.), *The Artist and his Masks: William Faulkner's Metafiction* (Rome, 1991); M. Materassi, *I romanzi di Faulkner* (Rome, 1968); J. T. Matthews, *The Play of Faulkner's Language* (Ithaca, NY, 1982); F. J. Hoffman and O. W. Vickery (eds.), *William Faulkner: Three Decades of Criticism* (East Lansing, Mich., 1960); E. Harrington and A. J. Abadie (eds.), *Faulkner and the Short Story* (Jackson, Miss., 1992); R. C. Moreland, *Faulkner and Modernism: Rereading and Rewriting* (Madison, Wis., 1990); W. Morris and B. A. Morris, *Reading Faulkner* (Madison, Wis., 1989); W. R. Moses, 'Where History Crosses Myth: Another Reading of "The Bear"', *Accent*, 13 (1953), 21–33; L. Jenkins, *Faulkner and Black–White Relations: A Psychoanalytic Approach* (New York, 1981), 221–60; E. J. Sundquist, *Faulkner: The House Divided* (Baltimore, 1983); F. L. Utley, L. Z. Bloom, A. F. Kinney (eds.), *Bear, Man, and God: Seven Approaches to William Faulkner's 'The Bear'* (New York, 1964); W. Wadington, *Reading Faulknerian Tragedy* (Ithaca, NY, 1987); P. M. Weinstein, *Faulkner's Subject: A Cosmos No One Owns* (Cambridge, 1992); P. M. Weinstein (ed.), *The Cambridge Companion to William Faulkner* (Cambridge, 1995). The fundamental works on typology are: E. Auerbach, 'Figura'; L. Goppelt, *Typos* (Engl. trans., Grand Rapids, Mich., 1982);

J. Daniélou, *Sacramentum futuri. Etudes sur les origines de la typologie biblique* (Paris, 1950); A. C. Charity, *Events and their Afterlife* (Cambridge, 1966); S. Bercovitch (ed.), *Typology and Early American Literature* (New York, 1972; it includes T. M. Davis's 'The Tradition of Puritan Typology'); E. Miner (ed.), *Literary Uses of Typology from the Middle Ages to the Present* (Princeton, 1977; it includes K. Keller's 'Alephs, Zahirs and the Triumph of Ambiguity: Typology in Nineteenth-Century American Literature'); S. Bercovitch, *The American Jeremiad* (Madison, Wis., 1978); V. Bohn (ed.), *Typologie* (Frankfurt, 1988); F. Link (ed.), *Paradeigmata. Literarische Typologie des Alten Testaments* (Berlin, 1989); F. Ohly, *Tipologia: Forma di pensiero della storia* (Messina, 1994, the only volume to include all of Ohly's work on typology).

The edition of Michel Tournier's *Éléazar, ou La Source et Le Buisson* which I use is that published by Gallimard (Paris, 1996). The translation is mine. Other works of Tournier's referred to in this chapter are *Vendredi, ou les limbes du Pacifique* (Paris, rev. edn., 1972), *Le Coq de bruyère* (Paris, 1978), *Gaspard, Melchior & Balthazar* (Paris, 1980), *Le vent Paraclet* (Paris, 1977). I refer to Italo Calvino's *Six Memos for the Next Millennium* (Cambridge, Mass., 1988). André Chouraqui's remarkable *Moïse: voyage aux confins d'un mystère révélé et d'une utopie réalisable* (Paris, 1995) has inspired, according to the author, the construction and meaning of Tournier's novel. On Tournier, the following critical works should be consulted: J.-R. Austin de Drouillard, *Tournier, ou, Le retour au sens dans le roman moderne* (Berne, 1992); C. Baroche (ed.), *Michel Tournier*, special issue of *Sud*, 61 (Marseille, 1986); D. G. Bevan, *Michel Tournier* (Amsterdam, 1986); A. Boulomie, *Michel Tournier: le roman mythologique* (Paris, 1988); W. J. Cloonan, *Michel Tournier* (Boston, 1985); C. Davis, *Michel Tournier: Philosophy and Fiction* (Oxford, 1988); I. Degn, *L'Encre du savant et le sang des martyrs: mythes et fantasmes dans les romans de Michel Tournier* (Odense, 1995); G. Deleuze, *Logique du sens* (Paris, 1969); D. Gascoigne, *Michel Tournier* (Oxford, 1996); N. Guichard, *Michel Tournier: autrui et la quête du double* (Paris, 1989); *Images et signes de Michel Tournier: actes du colloque du Centre culturel international de Cerisy-la-Salle 1990*, ed. A. Bonomie and M. de Gandillac (Paris, 1991); M. Koopman-Thurlings, *Vers un autre fantastique: étude de l'affabulation dans l'oeuvre de Michel Tournier* (Amsterdam, 1995); S. Koster, *Michel Tournier* (Paris, 1995); J. M. Magnan, *Michel Tournier, ou La redemption paradoxale* (Paris, 1996); F. Merllie, *Michel Tournier* (Paris, 1988); S. Petit, *Michel Tournier's Metaphysical Fiction* (Amsterdam and Philadelphia, 1991); W. D. Redfern, *Michel Tournier: Le coq de bruyère* (Madison, Wis., and London, 1996); M. Roberts, *Michel Tournier: Bricolage and Cultural Mythology* (Saratoga, Calif., 1994); R. Rottgers, *Der Raum in den Romanen Michel Tourniers, oder, Reise an den Rand des Möglichen* (Cologne, 1993); L. Salkin Sbiroli, *Michel Tournier: la seduction du jeu* (Geneva, 1987); B. Scheiner, *Romantische Themen und Mythen im Frühwerk Michel Tourniers* (Frankfurt, 1990); J.-B. Vray, *Michel Tournier et l'écriture seconde* (Lyons, 1997).

5. *To Recognize Is a God: Helen, Mary Magdelene, Marina—Menuchim*

The text of Euripides' *Helen* is R. Kannicht's *Helene*, 2 vols. (Heidelberg, 1969), with extensive commentary; the translation (often changed for greater fidelity to the original) P. Vellacott's in the Penguin edition (Harmondsworth, 1984 edn.). A useful commentary by A. M. Dale is available in Euripides, *Helen* (Oxford, 1967). I have consulted Gorgias' *Encomio di Elena*, ed. F. Donadi (Rome, 1982). Secondary material would have to include W. Stanford, *Greek Tragedy and the Emotion* (London, 1983), and C. Segal, *Interpreting Greek Tragedy: Myth, Poetry, Text* (Ithaca, NY, and London, 1986) as general introductions. The following have been essential in shaping my thoughts on these problems: C. Diano, *Forma ed evento* (Venice, 1993); C. Diano, *Saggezza e poetiche degli antichi* (Vicenza, 1968); C. Diano, *Studi e saggi di filosofia antica* (Padua, 1973); E. R. Dodds, *The Greeks and The Irrational* (Berkeley, 1951); T. Gould, *The Ancient Quarrel Between Poetry and Philosophy* (Princeton, 1990); W. F. Otto, *Theophania* (Frankfurt, 1975); J. Pépin, *Idées grecques sur l'homme et sur Dieu* (Paris, 1971). On Euripides I recommend S. A. Barlow, *The Imagery of Euripides* (London, 1971); A. P. Burnett, *Catastrophe Survived: Euripides' Plays of Mixed Reversal* (Oxford, 1971); J. De Romilly, *L'Évolution du pathetique d'Eschile à Euripide* (Paris, 1961); V. Di Benedetto, *Euripide: teatro e società* (Turin, 1971); M. McDonald, *Terms for Happiness in Euripides* (Göttingen, 1978); G. Paduano, *La formazione del mondo ideologico e poetico di Euripide*

216 BIBLIOGRAPHY

(Pisa, 1968); G. Paduano, *Il nostro Euripide l'umano* (Florence, 1986); C. Segal, *Dionysiac Poetics and Euripides' 'Bacchae'* (Princeton, 1982); P. Vellacott, *Ironic Drama: A Study of Euripides' Method and Meaning* (Cambridge, 1975); R. P. Winnington-Ingram, *Euripides and Dionysus: An Interpretation of the Bacchae* (Amsterdam, 1969). A general survey on Helen is to be found in J. L. Backès, *Le Mythe d'Hélène* (Paris, 1984). On Euripides' *Helen*, I have found particularly useful the following: U. Albini, 'Miracolo e avventura nell'"Elena"', in his *Interpretazioni teatrali: da Eschilo ad Aristofane* (Florence, 1972–81); K. Alt, 'Zur Anagnorisis in der "Helena"', *Hermes*, 90 (1962), 6–24; F. Bertini, 'L'eidolon di Elena', in *Mythos. Scripta in honorem M. Untersteiner* (Genoa, 1970), 81–96; A. P. Burnett, 'Euripides' "Helen": A Comedy of Ideas', *Classical Philology*, 55 (1960), 151–63; G. Cerri, 'La Madre degli dèi nell'"Elena" di Euripide: tragedia e rituale', *Quaderni di storia*, 18 (1983), 155–96; F. Jesi, 'L'Egitto infero nell'"Elena" di Euripide', *Aegyptus*, 45 (1965), 56–69; K. Matthiessen, *Elektra, Taurische Iphigenie und Helena* (Göttingen, 1964); K. Matthiessen, 'Zur Theonoeszene der euripideischen "Helena"', *Hermes*, 96 (1968), 685–704; C. Segal, 'The Two Worlds of Euripides' "Helen"', *Transactions and Proceedings of the American Philological Association*, 102 (1971), 553–614; W. Verrall, *Essays on Four Plays of Euripides* (Cambridge, 1910); C. W. Willink, 'The Reunion Duo in Euripides' "Helen"', *Classical Quarterly*, 39 (1989), 45–69; G. Zuntz, 'On Euripides' "Helena": Theology and Irony', in J. C. Kamerbeek *et al.*, *Euripide. Sept exposès* (Entretiens sur l'antiquité classique, 6), 199–227.

For the text of John, and of the New Testament in general, I have used E. and E. Nestle and B. and K. Aland, *Novum Testamentum Graece et Latine* (Stuttgart, 3rd edn., 1994). The translations are from the Authorized Version and from R. Brown's volumes cited below. R. Bultmann's commentary (Engl. trans. by G. R. Beasley-Murray), *The Gospel of John: A Commentary* (Oxford, 1971) is a classic. The two massive volumes (29 and 29a) of the Anchor Bible devoted to the Gospel of John by Raymond Brown (Garden City, NY, 1982), present an indispensable translation, guide, and commentary. To them should now be added vol. ix of the *New Interpreter's Bible* (Nashville, Tenn., 1995). I owe much to Frank Kermode's essay, 'John', in the *Literary Guide to the Bible* edited by him and R. Alter (Cambridge, Mass., 1987), and to George Steiner's essays, 'Two Cocks' and 'Two Suppers' (in particular to the latter), in his *No Passion Spent* (London and Boston, 1996). S. Haskins, *Mary Magdalene: Myth and Metaphor* (New York and London, 1994) is also full of suggestions. Exegetical and critical material on John is as endless as that on Genesis. I list here only the works that have been essential for me: P. Benoit, *The Passion and Resurrection of Jesus Christ* (New York, 1969); O. Cullmann, *Salvation in History* (New York, 1967); J. D. M. Derrett, 'Miriam and the Resurrection (John 20, 16)', *Downside Review*, 111 (1993), 174–86; M. Dibelius, 'Die alttestamentliche Motive in der Leidensgeschichte des Petrus- und des Johannes-Evangeliums', in *Botschaft und Geschichte* (Tübingen, 1953), i. 221–47; C. H. Dodd, *The Interpretation of the Fourth Gospel* (Cambridge, 1953); C. H. Dodd, *Historical Tradition in the Fourth Gospel* (Cambridge, 1963); C. H. Dodd, 'The Appearances of the Risen Christ: An Essay in Form-Criticism', in *Studies in the Gospel* (Oxford, 1957), 9–35; R. H. Fuller, *The Formation of the Resurrection Narratives* (London, 1980); A. Guilding, *The Fourth Gospel and Jewish Worship* (Oxford, 1960); C. Lavergne, 'Le Sudarium et la position des linges après la résurrection', *Sindon*, 3 (1961), 1–58; J. Marsh, *The Gospel of St. John* (Harmondsworth, 1968); D. Mollat, *Introductio in exegesim scriptorum sancti Joannis* (Rome, 1961); B. Schwank, 'Die Ostererscheinungen des Johannesevangelium und die Post-mortem Erscheinungen der Parapsychologie', *Erbe und Auftrag*, 44 (1968), 36–53; R. Brown, *The Death of the Messiah* (New York and London, 1994).

I use here the text of Shakespeare's *Pericles* as edited by E. D. Hoeniger for the Arden edition (London and New York, 1969), but I have constantly consulted also *Shakespeare: i drammi romanzeschi*, edited by G. Melchiori (Milan, 1981), and the Penguin edition of *Pericles* by P. Edwards (Harmondsworth, 1976). A. Serpieri's introduction and commentary to *Pericle* (Milan, 1991) and F. Marenco's 'Pericle: teatro come felicità', the Introduction to *Pericle* translated by A. Giuliani for the Teatro di Genova (Genoa, 1982), are very good. On romance in general, see N. Frye, *The Secular Scripture* (Cambridge, Mass., and London, 1976); on the Apollonius theme, E. Archibald, *Apollonius of Tyre: Medieval and Renaissance Themes and Variations* (Cambridge, 1991). A bibliography on *Pericles* is available in N. C. Michael, *Pericles: An Annotated Bibliography* (New York, 1987). The criticism which has most counted for my reading includes C. L. Barber, '*Thou that beget'st him that did thee beget*: Transformations in *Pericles* and *The Winter's Tale*', *Shakespeare Survey*, 22 (1969), 59–67; A. Barton, '"Enter Mariners wet"': Realism in Shakespeare's Last Plays', in her *Essays, Mainly Shakespearean* (Cambridge, 1994), 182–203; M. C. Bradbrook, *The Living Monument: Shakespeare and the Theatre of His Time* (Cambridge, 1976); J. P. Brockbank, '"Pericles" and the Dream of Immortality', *Shakespeare Survey*, 24 (1971), 105–16; L. Caretti, 'La fuga di Pericle', in A. Lombardo (ed.), *La Tempesta e l'ultimo Shakespeare* (Rome, 1980–1); I.-S. Ewbank, '"My name is Marina"': The Language of Recognition', in P. Edwards, I.-S. Ewbank, and G. K. Hunter (eds.), *Shakespeare's Styles: Essays in Honour of Kenneth Muir* (Cambridge, 1980), 111–30; N. Frye, *A Natural Perspective* (New York, 1965); F. Kermode, *W. Shakespeare: The Final Plays* (London, 1963); G. W. Knight, *The Crown of Life: Essays in Interpretation of Shakespeare's Final Plays* (London, 1947); F. Marenco, 'From Romance to Ritual: Memory and the Community in Shakespeare's Last Plays', in K. Elam (ed.), *Shakespeare Today* (Florence, 1984); F. Yates, *Shakespeare's Last Plays: A New Approach* (London, 1975); F. W. Brownlow, *Two Shakespearian Sequences: Henry VIII to Richard II and Pericles to Timon of Athens* (London, 1977); C. Czach, *Die Logik der Phantasie: Shakespeares Spätstücke* (Frankfurt, 1986); H. W. Fawkner, *Shakespeare's Miracle Plays: Pericles, Cymbeline, and The Winter's Tale* (Rutherford, NJ, and London, 1992).

The text of T. S. Eliot's 'Marina' is from his *Collected Poems 1909–1962* (London, 1963). On Eliot, see R. Bush, *T. S. Eliot: A Study in Character and Style* (Oxford, 1984); A. Charity, 'The Dantean Recognitions', in A. D. Moody (ed.), *'The Waste Land' in Different Voices* (London, 1974); J. Chiari, *T. S. Eliot, Poet and Dramatist* (New York, 1979); H. Gardner, *The Art of T. S. Eliot* (London, 1968); L. Gordon, *Eliot's New Life* (Oxford, 1988); M. Grant (ed.), *T. S. Eliot: The Critical Heritage* (London, 1982); H. Kenner, *The Invisible Poet: T. S. Eliot* (London, 1960); J. D. T. Margolis, *T. S. Eliot's Intellectual Development: 1922–1939* (Chicago, 1972); A. D. Moody, *T. S. Eliot: Poet* (Cambridge, 1994); A. D. Moody (ed.), *The Cambridge Companion to T. S. Eliot* (Cambridge, 1994); J. Olney (ed.), *T. S. Eliot* (Oxford, 1988); W. Riehle, *T. S. Eliot* (Darmstadt, 1979); R. Sencourt, *T. S. Eliot: A Memoir* (London, 1971); M. Scofield, *T. S. Eliot: The Poems* (Cambridge,

1988); W. Skaff, *The Philosophy of T. S. Eliot* (Philadelphia, 1986); K. Smidt, *Poetry and Belief in the Work of T. S. Eliot* (London, 1967); K. Smidt, *The Importance of Recognition* (Tromso, 1973); S. Spender, *T. S. Eliot* (New York, 1975); J. H. Timmerman, *T. S. Eliot's Ariel Poems: The Poetics of Recovery* (Lewisburg, Pa., London, and Toronto, 1994); L. Unger, *Eliot's Compound Ghost: Influence and Confluence* (University Park, Pa., 1981).

For the text of the Book of Job, see the *Biblia Hebraica Stuttgartensia* (Stuttgart, 1990). I have used here Harold Fisch's translation, but also constantly employed the Italian translation, the splendid commentary, and the Appendix by G. Ravasi, *Giobbe* (Rome, 1984), and consulted Jean Lévèque, *Job et son Dieu* (Paris, 1970) and N. C. Habel, *The Book of Job* (London, 1985), but I cannot forget that my passion for the Book of Job was decidedly increased by Guido Ceronetti's Italian translation, and by the marvellously furious essay with which he accompanied it (Milan, 1972). Likewise crucial was the booklet edited by M. Ciampa, *Domande a Giobbe* (Rome, 1989), with a very good Introduction and many essential pieces by Kierkegaard, Barth, Weil, Von Balthasar, Wiesel, etc. Among the infinite literature on this Book, I would recall here only C. G. Jung, *Antwort auf Hiob* (Zurich, 1952); G. Mura, *Angoscia ed esistenza* (Rome, 1982); R. Girard, *Job the Victim of his People* (Engl. trans. by Y. Freccero, London, 1987); R. Alter, *The Art of Biblical Poetry* (New York, 1985); H. Fisch, 'Job: Tragedy is Not Enough', in his *Poetry with a Purpose*; M. Greenberg, 'Job', in R. Alter and F. Kermode (eds.), *The Literary Guide to the Bible*; J. Gerald Janzen, *Job* (Atlanta, Ca., 1985); J. Kahn, *Job's Illness: Loss, Grief and Integration* (Oxford, 1975); M. Weiss, *The Story of Job's Beginning* (Jerusalem, 1983); J. W. Whedbee, 'The Comedy of Job', *Semeia*, 7 (1977), 1–39; R. B. Seawall, *The Vision of Tragedy* (New Haven, 1956). Gregory the Great's *Moralia in Job* (Migne, *Patrologia Latina*, 75–6) constitutes the basis of all subsequent Christian exegesis and is still thought-provoking. L. L. Besserman, *The Legend of Job in the Middle Ages* (Cambridge, 1979), offers important hints for the 'Job tradition' in the Middle Ages and opens up new vistas on modern literature.

For Joseph Roth's *Hiob* I have used the Rowohlt edition (Reinbeck bei Hamburg, 1976). The English translation is by D. Thompson (London, 1983 edn.), at times corrected on the basis of the original. To understand Roth, C. Magris, *Lontano da dove* (Turin, 1971) and 'L'Ulisse ebraico-orientale'. Joseph Roth fra l'impero e l'esilio', *Studi Germanici*, 8 (1970), 179–223, are indispensable. On *Job*, I have used S. Rosenfeld, 'Joseph Roths Hiob: Glaube und Heimat im Bild des Raumes', *Journal of English and Germanic Philology*, 66 (1967), 489–500; R. Frey, *Kein Weg ins Freie*. *Joseph Roths Amerikabild* (Frankfurt and Berne, 1983); L. Mathew, *Ambivalence and Irony in the Works of Joseph Roth* (Frankfurt, 1984); W. Müller-Funk, *Joseph Roth* (Munich, 1989); B. M. Kraske (ed.), *Joseph Roth: Werk und Wirkung* (Bonn, 1988); H. L. Arnold, *Joseph Roth* (Munich, 1982); A. Pfabigan, *Geistesgegenwart: Essays zu Joseph Roth* (Vienna, 1991); G. Shaked, *The Shadows Within* (Philadelphia, 1987); E. Göggel, *Joseph Roth, Hiob* (Stuttgart and Dresden, 1993); H.-J. Blanke, *Joseph Roth. Hiob* (Munich, 1993); and above all H. Fisch's beautiful 'Being Possessed by Job', now in his *New Stories for Old*, 100–15.

On the problem of recognition (for the present and the first chapter) I refer the reader to F. Kermode, 'Recognition and Deception', in his *The Art of Telling* (Cambridge, Mass., 1983), 92–113; to G. Wunberg, *Wiedererkennen* (Tübingen, 1983); to D. Culbertson, *The Poetics of Revelation: Recognition and the Narrative Tradition* (Macon, Ga., 1989); to my 'Anagnorisis and Reasoning: Electra and Hamlet', *REAL* 7 (1990), 99–136; to the two chapters on the theme in my *The Tragic and the Sublime in Medieval Literature* (Cambridge, 1989), where I examined amongst other things some rewritings of the Thomas scene; and above all to T. Cave, *Recognitions: A Study in Poetics* (Oxford, 1988).

Index